INSIGHT CITY GUIDE

WASHINGTON D.C.

Discovery CHANNEL

APA PUBLICATIONS L

Part of the Langenscheidt Publishing Group

※ INSIGHT GUIDE
WaSHINGTON D.C.

Editor
Brian Bell
Updating Editor
Rosanne Scott
Principal Photographer
Richard T. Nowitz
Art Director
Klaus Geisler
Picture Editor
Hilary Genin
Cartography Editor
Zoë Goodwin

Distribution

UK & Ireland
GeoCenter International Ltd
The Viables Centre, Harrow Way
Basingstoke, Hants RG22 4BJ
Fax: (44) 1256-817988

United States
Langenscheidt Publishers, Inc.
36–36 33rd Street 4th Floor
Long Island City, New York 11106
Fax: (1) 718 784-0640

Canada
Thomas Allen & Son Ltd
390 Steelcase Road East
Markham, Ontario L3R 1G2
Fax: (1) 905 475 6747

Australia
Universal Publishers
1 Waterloo Road
Macquarie Park, NSW 2113
Fax: (61) 2 9888 9074

New Zealand
Hema Maps New Zealand Ltd (HNZ)
Unit D, 24 Ra ORA Drive
East Tamaki, Auckland
Fax: (64) 9 273 6479

Worldwide
**Apa Publications GmbH & Co.
Verlag KG (Singapore branch)**
38 Joo Koon Road, Singapore 628990
Tel: (65) 6865-1600. Fax: (65) 6861-6438

Printing

Insight Print Services (Pte) Ltd
38 Joo Koon Road, Singapore 628990
Tel: (65) 6865-1600. Fax: (65) 6861-6438

©2005 Apa Publications GmbH & Co.
Verlag KG (Singapore branch)
All Rights Reserved

First Edition 1992
Fourth Edition 2005

ABOUT THIS BOOK

This guidebook combines the interests and enthusiasms of two of the world's best-known information providers: Insight Guides, whose titles have set the standard for visual travel guides since 1970, and Discovery Channel, the world's premier source of nonfiction television programming.

The editors of Insight Guides provide both practical advice and general understanding about a destination. Discovery Channel and its Web site, www.discovery.com, help millions of viewers explore their world from the comfort of their own home.

How to use this book

The book is carefully structured to convey an understanding of the city:

◆ To understand Washington today, you need to know something of its past. The first section covers the city's history and culture in lively essays written by specialists.

◆ The main Places section provides a full run-down of all the attractions worth seeing. The main places of interest are coordinated by number with full-colour maps.

◆ Photographic features show readers around major attractions such as the National Gallery and the National Museum of American History, and identify the highlights.

◆ Photographs are chosen not only to illustrate geography and buildings but also to convey the moods of the city and the life of its people.

◆ The Travel Tips listings section provides a point of reference for information on travel, hotels, shops and festivals. Information may be located quickly by using the index printed on the back cover flap – and the flaps are designed to serve as bookmarks.

LEFT a Viking exhibit at the National Museum of Natural History.

from the best-selling first edition edited by **Martha Ellen Zenfell**. The chapters detailing the city's tumultuous history were written by **John Gattuso**, who has edited more than 20 books for Insight Guides and is based in New Jersey. Many of the features were written by **Martin Walker**, a former DC bureau chief for a British national newspaper, and his wife **Julia Watson**, a journalist and novelist. The "How the Federal Government Works" essay was written by **B. Claiborne Edmunds**.

Two writers produced the bulk of the Places chapters. **Maria Mudd** has also written for *National Geographic Traveler* magazine, *Islands* and the *Washington Post*. **Alison Kahn** is a former *National Geographic* magazine staffer whose research skills were honed at the Smithsonian. The short piece on the C&O Canal was written by **Elaine Koerner**.

Among the most important aspects of an Insight Guide are the pictures, and two photographers whose work has graced many Insight Guides and many issues of National Geographic feature prominently here. **Richard T. Nowitz**, whose recent assignments for Insight have ranged from Beijing to Utah, is based in Rockville, Maryland. **Catherine Karnow**, who recently brought Las Vegas vividly to life for a companion book in this series, switched between the family home in Potomac and an apartment in lively Adams Morgan while photographing the book.

The contributors

This new edition was edited by **Brian Bell**, Insight Guides' editorial director, and its text was thoroughly updated and expanded by **Rosanne Scott** to paint an involving portrait of life in the city today.

Scott arrived in Washington with a political science degree "not long after Jimmy Carter moved into the White House – that would be the mid-1970s; we tend to think in terms of administrations rather than calendar dates – and, in a city whose population turns over with every shift in the political wind, I've been here long enough now to claim status as a native." She has worked in the federal government and in the graphic arts, and has written for Time-Life Books and for the *Washington Times*.

Much material has been retained

CONTACTING THE EDITORS

We would appreciate it if readers would alert us to errors or outdated information by writing to:

Insight Guides, P.O. Box 7910, London SE1 1WE, England. Fax: (44) 20 7403-0290. insight@apaguide.co.uk

NO part of this book may be reproduced, stored in a retrieval system or transmitted in any form or means electronic, mechanical, photocopying, recording or otherwise, without prior written permission of *Apa Publications*. Brief text quotations with use of photographs are exempted for book review purposes only. Information has been obtained from sources believed to be reliable, but its accuracy and completeness, and the opinions based thereon, are not guaranteed.

www.insightguides.com

Contents

Maps

Travel Tips

THE BEST OF WASHINGTON, DC

**Setting priorities, saving money, unique attractions...
here, at a glance, are our recommendations, plus tips
and tricks even Washingtonians won't always know**

WASHINGTON FOR FAMILIES

These attractions are popular with children,
though not all will suit every age group.

- **National Aquarium**
Great fun for younger
kids. *See page 125.*
- **National Air and
Space Museum** Every
sort of flying machine.
See page 76.
- **National Museum of
Natural History**
Dinosaurs, bugs,
rocks. *See page 81.*

ABOVE: street performer.

- **National Museum of
American History**
Lincoln's hat, First
Ladies, Dorothy's red
slippers. *See page 30.*
- **Bureau of Engraving
and Printing** How
money's made. *See
page 88.*

- **Washington Monu-
ment** The essential
DC monument. *See
page 87.*
- **Lincoln Memorial**
An example of great-
ness. *See page 92.*
- **Ford's Theatre**
Where Lincoln was
shot; see the theater
box, visit the museum.
See page 121.
- **National Museum of
the American Indian.**
Native life yesterday
and today. *See page 77.*
- **National Zoo** Pandas,
tigers and more! Oh,
my! *See page 164.*
- **National Geo-
graphic's Explorer's
Hall** Amazing objects
from around the
world. *See page 119.*
- **The Capital Chil-
dren's Museum**
Climb a pyramid,
learn animation.
Hands-on fun for all.
See page 111.
- **National Postal Mu-
seum** All about
stamps, stationery and
the mail. *See page 111.*
- **George Washington's
Mt. Vernon** The
founding father's
sprawling Virginia
estate. *See page 185.*

The Washington
Monument as
viewed from
Room 1212 of
the Willard Hotel.

BEST VIEWS OF THE CITY

- **National Cathedral**
Ride the elevator to
the top of the Obser-
vation Gallery and
enjoy the wide vista
from the city's highest
spot. *See page 161.*
- **Washington Monu-
ment** From 555 ft
(169 meters) up, you
can see all of DC and
more. *See page 87.*
- **Old Post Office
Pavilion** Only 270 ft

(82 meters) up, but a
good Plan B if you
can't manage to lay
hands on one of the
timed tickets you
need to see the Wash-
ington Monument.
See page 124.
- **The Potomac River**
Take a sightseeing
cruise and see the
gleaming monuments
from the water. *See
page 217.*

BELOW the view from the top of Washington Cathedral.

BEST MEMORIALS AND MONUMENTS

- **Washington Monument, Jefferson Memorial, Lincoln Memorial** These are the three must-sees, a principal reason for visiting DC. *See pages 87, 90, 92.*
- **FDR Memorial** Celebrates the 12-year presidency of the 20th-century statesman *(below)* in four outdoor park-like galleries. *See page 92.*
- **Vietnam War Memorial** Names of the dead on a wall. Sounds humble, but it's the experience of seeing them, all 58,229 of them, that's most humbling. An argument against unjustifiable war if there ever was one. *See page 94.*
- **Grant's Statue** When you're on Capitol Hill, take a minute to see the world's second largest equestrian statue. Troubled though his post –Civil War presidency was, Grant, militarily speaking, saved the Union. *See page 105.*
- **Neptune Fountain** Bronze and gushing water outside the Library of Congress on Capitol Hill and one of the city's treasures. *See page 107.*
- **Iwo Jima** In Arlington, Virginia, and marks a valiant moment in the WW2 Pacific theater when, on 23 February 1945, US Marines raised the American flag on this Japanese-held island in a pivotal battle. *See page 182.*

ABOVE: a representational statue of three soldiers is part of the Vietnam Veterans Memorial on the Mall.

FREE D.C.

- **Museums** Most everything worth seeing, namely the Smithsonian museums and the National Gallery of Art, is free.
- **Monuments and Memorials** The National Park Service takes care of all the major must-sees.
- **Seat of Power** Tour all the major Capitol Hill sites – the US Capitol, the Supreme Court, the Library of Congress – free of charge.
- **Art galleries** Many galleries offer "first Friday" openings where you can browse, nosh on a bit of cheese, buy something if you like it.
- **Music** There's always a military band concert, church organ recital, jazz group, street band or string quartet playing somewhere for free. The Sylvan Theater near the Washington Monument is a venue of free concerts, and the National Symphony plays on the Capitol grounds during holiday celebrations. The Kennedy Center also has free concerts and performances on its Millennium Stage. The *Post's* "Weekend" section has listings.

BEST FESTIVALS AND EVENTS

- **Cherry Blossom Festival** Celebrate spring in Washington when the cherry trees are in perfect pink bloom. First weekend in April. *See page 90.*
- **Smithsonian Folklife Festival** Huge celebration of ethnic foods and traditions from around the world. On the Mall. Last week of June through 4th of July. *See page 70.*
- **4th of July** Annual bash on the Mall with day-long free entertainment followed by fireworks, of course. *See page 70.*
- **Presidential Inaugural Parade** On January 20 every four years the president-elect parades down Pennsylvania Avenue, accompanied by marching bands, floats, and of course a large Secret Service force. *See page 44.*

BELOW: free music by the Reflecting Pool.

8

ABOVE: taking a stroll by the C&O Canal.

BEST MUSEUMS

SMITHSONIAN MUSEUMS ON THE MALL

- **National Museum of American History** "America's attic" is stuffed with Americana from flags to First Ladies' inaugural gowns. *Pages 30, 82.*
- **National Museum of the American Indian** The Mall's newest and a center for the preservation of the artifacts of the Western Hemisphere's native peoples. *See page 77.*
- **Sackler Gallery and National Museum of African Art** Ancient ritual and traditional objects from Asia and Africa. *See page 73.*

- **National Museum of Natural History** The Hope Diamond's here, plus zillion-year-old fossils, dinosaurs, and the creepy but fabulous Insect Zoo. *See page 81.*

- **National Air and Space Museum** Reputed to be the world's most visited museum with early flight to space-age specimens, a planetarium and IMAX theater. *See page 76.*
- **Freer Gallery of Art** Asian artifacts including scrolls, ceramics, statuary, plus the opulent Peacock Room. *See page 71.*
- **Hirshhorn Museum and Sculpture Garden** Art in the round includes sculptures, works on paper and more from modern art's trailblazers. *See page 75.*

OTHER MUSEUMS

- **National Gallery of Art** West Building loaded with Old Masters; East Building packed with Modern Masters. On the Mall; stay here all day. *See pages 78, 84.*
- **Phillips Collection** Original home of arts patron turned into the nation's first museum of modern art. Small enough to do in an afternoon. *See page 152.*
- **Corcoran Gallery of Art** The city's first museum, opened in 1874, with a grand staircase, lots of 19th and 20th century gems. *See page 133.*
- **International Spy Museum** All spy paraphernalia, practical to the wacky, and hugely popular. *See page 121.*

GARDENS, PARKS AND GREEN PLACES

- **US Botanic Garden** Lush greenery adjacent to cooling Bartholdi Fountain. *See page 106.*
- **National Arboretum** Acres of plantings, miles of pathways. *See page 171.*
- **Enid A. Haupt Garden** Small, well groomed, between Sackler and African Art museums on the Mall. *See page 72.*
- **Rock Creek Park** A cool green urban patch with hiking trails and picnic areas. *See page 159.*
- **C & O Canal** Towpath parallels the Potomac from DC to the Maryland mountains. Boat rides, biking, walking. *See pages 141, 165.*
- **Bishop's Garden** Herbs and roses in a peaceful setting at the National Cathedral. *See page 161.*
- **Kenilworth Aquatic Gardens** Acres of water plants beside the Anacostia River. *See page 176.*
- **Great Falls** The Potomac rushes over dramatic outcroppings and challenges even experienced kayakers. *See page 188.*

ABOVE: Great Falls.

BEST INFO

"Weekend" is the *Washington Post*'s supplement of cultural events published on Fridays. It has the latest on gallery and museum openings and closings, plays, movie listings, restaurant reviews and more.
Washingtonian A monthly magazine that bills itself as the one that Washingtonians live by, which probably overstates the case though the magazine is a useful resource of current cultural happenings. Available on newsstands, or at www.washingtonian.com

BEST HISTORIC HOUSES

- **Decatur House** One of the city's oldest, on Lafayette Square and home of the country's first real naval hero. *See page 116.*
- **Hillwood** Mansion full of French and imperial Russian objects attached to luscious gardens. *See page 163.*
- **Dumbarton Oaks** Byzantine and pre-Columbian art in a former ambassador's home and where talks that resulted in the formation of the United Nations were held. *See page 143.*
- **Old Stone House** 18th-century home and perhaps the city's oldest. *See page 141.*
- **Tudor Place** Home of George Washington relation; quirkily decorated, but with stories. *See page 142.*

BEST HOT SPOTS

- **Citronelle** Classy Georgetown restaurant and liable to be the city's best for a while. *See page 145.*
- **Café Milano** Georgetown's swankiest and where the in crowd, including politicos and Hollywood celebs breezing through town, gathers to be seen. *See page 145.*
- **Monocle** Though not exactly swingin' it's a favorite with deal-making Capitol Hill big wigs, a few of whom you'll likely run into. *See page 113.*
- **Madam's Organ** Long time and way past cool Adams Morgan nightspot. *See page 229.*
- **Blues Alley** One of the country's best jazz venues; in Georgetown. *See page 144.*

ABOVE: the National Shrine of Immaculate Conception.

A LITTLE PEACE AND QUIET

- **Franciscan Monastery** Founded to educate Franciscan missionaries bound for the Holy Land, this retreat with garden and St. Francis statue is guaranteed to refresh sightseers. *See page 170.*
- **National Shrine of Immaculate Conception** Classically cruciform Roman Catholic shrine also has 60 chapels and oratories where you're sure to find a quiet spot for private recollection. *See page 169.*
- **Washington National Cathedral** Grandly Gothic and home to the Episcopal Diocese of Washington with lovely garden. *See page 161.*

MONEY-SAVERS

Half-price Tickets You can buy a half price ticket for any show in town on the day of the performance if you go to Ticket Place, 407 7th Street, NW, between D and E streets, or Tel: 202-842-5387. They're open Tuesday through Saturday, 11am to 6pm. There's a 12 per cent surcharge, depending on the price of the ticket.

Metro Pass Buy the all-day Metro pass for $6 and get on and off the subway as many times as you like. It's cheaper this way, and more convenient since you'll avoid the lines at the machines where you pay your fare.

ONLY IN WASHINGTON, DC...

- **The White House** You can't go inside, but the nearby Visitors Center offers the next best thing. *See pages 59–67.*
- **Library of Congress** Crammed full of world treasures, many often on exhibit in the great Jefferson building. *See page 106.*
- **US Capitol** Where Democrats and Republicans try to work it out. Impressive architecture, good stories, great art surrounds the government's legislative branch. *See pages 101–6.*
- **Supreme Court** Where the judiciary system tries to make sense of what the legislative branch has done. *See page 109.*
- **Arlington Cemetery** 240,000-plus graves of heroes and patriots including JFK; very moving. *See page 181.*

ABOVE: Blues Alley is DC's most renowned jazz club.

A CAPITAL IDEA

John F. Kennedy's jibe that Washington mixes
Southern efficiency with Northern charm may no
longer be true, but this surprisingly small place
– a town more than a city – is one of the most
contradictory capitals in the developed world

"**W**ashington has only politics; after that, the second biggest thing is white marble," said an East Coast notable some years ago. It's certainly true that politics is much in evidence, and that the white marble monuments are striking signature images. But there's more to it than that.

Washington is neither Southern nor Northern. It retains characteristics of both but remains aloof from each. The city has more black residents than white and more lawyers than probably anywhere else on the planet. Compared to other American cities there's little "old money" around, just new administrations every four years. It's a town of meetings and agendas, of ethnic groups and power struggles, both in the boardrooms and on the streets. Its boulevards are broad and among the nation's most beautiful. Even some of the ghettos are attractive, their buildings of architectural significance. Yet Washington has one of the highest murder rates in America.

The "public face" of DC can slip in a matter of minutes. Taxis, for instance, are allowed to pick up more than one passenger at a time. On a sweltering summer's day, squashed in a cab with an Ethiopian driver, four stony-faced, perspiring strangers and a broken-down air-conditioning system, the cool corridors of Washington can feel like a Third-World *barrio*.

The capital is not known primarily for its restaurants, yet the variety is excellent and expanding. As for culture, there are small museums and galleries with a continuing schedule of first-rate activities, to say nothing of the grand Smithsonian museums and the National Gallery on the Mall.

The city has a hot, sticky climate, but cool bathing beaches are only an hour's drive away. You can go hiking in the mountains, sailing in the bay, swimming in the ocean, or boating on the canal. This, in a town more noted for its indoor accomplishments than its outdoor pursuits.

Politics does propel Washington and, on moonlit nights, when strolling along the Mall with the Lincoln Memorial to the left, the Capitol to the right and the Washington Monument soaring high above, it does seem as if the city were composed of white marble. But to dismiss the nation's capital in such a narrow way is like calling the president of the United States a public official. It's true – but it's not the whole story. ❑

PRECEDING PAGES: the Jefferson Memorial; the reading room of the Library of Congress.
LEFT: Washington is a city of classical statues.

THE MAKING OF A CAPITAL

A regional compromise determined the site of the nation's capital on the banks of the Potomac, a marshland until Pierre L'Enfant envisioned a grand metropolis. But along with monumental buildings came colossal social problems

Washington, DC was hacked out of the wilderness with one purpose in mind: to serve as the nation's capital. Appropriately, the whole thing started with a political deal. Its architects were Thomas Jefferson and Alexander Hamilton, the nation's first Secretary of State and Secretary of Treasury and two of the young republic's savviest political operators. The year was 1790, about one year after George Washington's presidential inauguration; the place was Philadelphia, temporary headquarters of the fledgling government.

Northern delegates to Congress wanted to keep the capital in the North. Southern delegates wanted to move it to the South. The eventual deal was simple. In exchange for the necessary Southern votes in favor of Hamilton's financial plan, the Northerners agreed to vote for a federal capital farther south than they previously wished for – that is, on the banks of the Potomac River.

Within a year, the 10-mile-square District of Columbia was ceded to the federal government by the states of Maryland and Virginia. The president, a no-nonsense businessman, went to Suter's Tavern in Georgetown to negotiate personally with the landowners. He offered them $66.66 an acre, a modest amount even then, but Washington was nothing if not persuasive. It was their land, after all, on which the "seat of empire" would be built.

LEFT: the new city was to strive for the highest ideals, embodied in the Supreme Court's architecture.
RIGHT: the Declaration of Independence having been signed in 1776, the hunt began for a new capital.

Tidewater colony

More than 180 years earlier, in 1608, Captain John Smith, a founding member of Jamestown, Virginia, the first permanent English colony in North America, became the first European to chart the inland waterways of the tidewater region. He hoped to find gold along the Potomac or, failing that, a shortcut to the South Seas. What he found instead were several Indian villages, many willing to trade for much-needed provisions. The villages were members of a loose Indian confederacy led by Chief Wahunsonacoock, known to the English as King Powhatan. Several months earlier, Smith had met Powhatan after he and a few of his men were captured by an Indian hunting party. According to legend – and most of it is probably true – Powhatan's daughter, Pocahontas, successfully begged the old chief to spare Smith's life.

Despite the Indians' help, life in the early years of the colony was a constant struggle for survival. The arrival of several hundred new colonists in 1610 put the wretched little settlement back on its feet and, thanks to the tyrannical leadership of the new governor, Sir Thomas Dale, who employed whipping, burning at the stake and exile to motivate slackers, Jamestown finally sunk roots into the tidewater's marshy soil. The introduction of a

strain of West Indian tobacco underpinned Virginia's economy, as the "precious herb" was much in demand in England at the time.

L'Enfant's city

The American Revolution had little military impact on the Potomac, although the British blockade of Chesapeake Bay virtually shut down the tobacco trade out of Georgetown and Alexandria. After the British defeat at Yorktown, General George Washington had hoped to retire to his Mount Vernon estate near the Potomac, but in 1789, he accepted his election to the new office of president.

Washington saw the Potomac as a gateway

to the resources and markets of the Ohio and Mississippi valleys, and had helped create the Potomac Company to make the upper river navigable. Thomas Jefferson, a fellow Virginian, shared Washington's enthusiasm for the region, and when the search began for a permanent federal capital it seemed only natural to them that the Potomac be placed at the top of the list. To design the new Federal City (the self-effacing Washington didn't like to refer to it as the City of Washington), the president selected Major Pierre Charles L'Enfant.

Several years earlier, at the age of 22, L'Enfant had left the French court of Versailles and arrived in America to serve as a private in the Continental Army. After the Revolutionary War, he supervised an extensive renovation of Federal Hall in New York City, site of Washington's first inauguration and temporary seat of the infant US government.

L'Enfant was hired to lay plans for the capital in 1791. With memories of Versailles lingering in his mind, L'Enfant conceived a city of broad boulevards, sweeping vistas, and stately public buildings on the monumental scale of classical Greece or Rome. The plan also incorporated civic open spaces, markets, fountains, monuments, and squares.

On Jenkins Hill, the city's highest prominence, L'Enfant placed the Capitol, seat of the Congress, the very embodiment of the young nation's democratic principles. On the banks of the Potomac, commanding a view of Alexandria, he placed the Executive Mansion, known later as the White House.

Unfortunately, what L'Enfant possessed in architectural skill he lacked in social grace. Arrogant, impetuous, and incapable of subordinating himself to authority, the Frenchman immediately ran afoul of his superiors, a commission of prominent landowners. Less than 12 months after he started, L'Enfant was discharged. He became a common sight in the capital, his shabbily dressed figure pacing the avenues of a city that, only years before, existed solely in his imagination. He died in 1825 and is buried in Arlington Cemetery.

Building a nation

By 1809, Thomas Jefferson's last year as president, Washington was still a frontier town, criss-crossed with rutted trails, littered with debris and surrounded by wilderness. Work had proceeded at a snail's pace over the intervening years and neither the White House nor the Capitol building were complete. The nation's 106 delegates huddled in the House of Representatives – known derisively as "the oven" because of its poor design – while construction continued on the remainder of the building.

When in 1812 President James Madison led the country into a second war against the British, whose Royal Navy had been harrassing American shipping, the British attacked the city, torching many public buildings, including the Capitol and the White House. With the city in shambles and the government in disarray, some feared that the republic itself might crumble.

But with American forces rallying against the British outside Baltimore and later at New Orleans, anxiety over the capital's and the country's future began to fade. With news of Yankee victories arriving daily in Washington, Congress reconvened in the cramped quarters of the Post Office, the only public building left undamaged, and voted to stay in Washington.

The original architect, James Hoban, was called in to supervise the reconstruction of the White House. At the other end of Pennsylvania Avenue, Benjamin Latrobe worked to restore the Capitol.

Up from the ashes

Washington was expanding in other areas, too. The short-lived Chesapeake & Ohio Canal, thought to be the key to Washington's commercial success, opened for business in 1830, but was quickly superseded by the Baltimore & Ohio Railroad. Georgetown University, founded in 1789, was joined by Columbian College (later George Washington University) in 1822. A grant bequeathed by an eccentric British scientist, James Smithson *(see page 74)*, in 1829 was finally discharged for the use of the Smithsonian Institution, housed in a medieval-style "castle" on the Mall. And in 1859, W. W. Corcoran began building the handsome Corcoran Gallery to house his coveted art collection.

Unfortunately, the city's problems were

growing as fast as its buildings. Washington's notorious alleys were already filled with shacks and shanties and crowded with an ever increasing population of poor people. Vacant lots, many of them squeezed between the city's finest buildings, were heaped with trash and overgrown with weeds. Sanitation, never very sophisticated, was woefully inadequate, and crime was becoming a major concern.

The slave trade

Many visitors were disturbed by the presence of slavery, which they felt ill-suited in the capital of a nation dedicated to life, liberty and the pursuit of happiness. Around 3,000 slaves

lived in the District of Columbia, prominent slave traders advertised in local newspapers, public slave auctions were regularly held, and slaves could be seen on the streets marching in chains or being held for sale in slave pens across from the Smithsonian Institution.

In 1849 a little-known Illinois representative, Abraham Lincoln, introduced legislation outlawing slavery in the District of Columbia, but the bill was quickly defeated. Instead, Congress adopted Henry Clay's Compromise of 1850, which, among other measures, abolished the slave trade in the District of Columbia but did not outlaw slave ownership.

LEFT: architect Pierre L'Enfant (1754–1825).
RIGHT: British troops burn the city in 1814.

George Washington

There could have been no more reluctant person to serve as the country's first president than George Washington. "I greatly fear that my countrymen will expect too much from me," he wrote soon after his inauguration in New York in April 1789. By then he had already been elevated to the status of a minor god. Lavishly praised by his countrymen, he was known as "our Savior," "our Redeemer," and "our star in the east."

More a monument than a man, Wash-

ington, with little in his early life to prepare him for future greatness, labored under the burden of his own celebrity to lead the new nation when there was no precedent for such leadership. Born in 1732 to a Virginia tobacco farmer and his second wife, Washington grew up near Fredericksburg, Virginia. After his mother died when he was 11, his older half-brother Lawrence encouraged frequent visits to his own estate, Mount Vernon, near present-day Washington. From a wealthy neighbor, Washington learned surveying and signed on to explore what was then the colonial western frontier. For 12 years he was an active-duty sol-

dier, much of that time served unsuccessfully. In 1754 he ambushed a French patrol on the frontier, an event that triggered the French and Indian War. During the Revolutionary War, he fought nine battles, losing or fighting to a draw six of them.

Lacking military genius, he also did nothing to distinguish himself intellectually. He had no appreciation for music or literature and, though he could hold his own in a social setting, he wasn't particularly gregarious. Even Jefferson, his close friend, could not avoid remarking on Washington's shortcomings. His talents, as Jefferson put it, "were not above mediocrity."

What Washington was, however, was scrupulously decent, his real source of power concentrated in the nobility of his character. Perhaps his most virtuous act was his resignation in December 1783 as commander-in-chief of the American forces when he was at the height of his powers and could easily have declared himself king. But Washington wished only to retire to his beloved Mount Vernon, a modern Cincinnatus, the Roman who returned to his farm after saving his country.

Washington's strength, as first president, lay in his embodiment of people's aspirations and fears, and his ability to hold together a collection of former colonies that had no love for one another. Any impression that the colonies collectively united against the British is pure myth. As Boston lawyer James Otis put it in 1765: "Were these colonies left to themselves tomorrow, America would be a shambles of blood and confusion."

The Revolutionary War lasted 8½ years and, when it ended in 1783, America, though a name on a map, was hardly a country. It was into the ensuing fractiousness and chaos as America struggled to define itself and establish a constitution that Washington, coming out of retirement, stepped in to lead for two full terms as president. Whatever native abilities he may have lacked, Washington, to his lasting credit, understood that the American experiment could not be allowed to fail. ❑

LEFT: Washington bust, National Gallery of Art.

"A house divided"

On November 8, 1860, Abraham Lincoln was elected president without a single Southern electoral vote and on a minority of the popular vote. South Carolina immediately seceded, and six other states followed.

On March 4, 1861, Lincoln was inaugurated under the watchful eyes of sharpshooters patroling nearby rooftops. In his inaugural address he appealed to the newly formed Confederacy to reject civil war. But, on April 12, Confederate cannons fired at Fort Sumter. Virginia seceded two weeks later, following Arkansas, North Carolina and Tennessee.

Washington was in a perilous situation. It iation of the Union defeat, and the panicked retreat of soldiers and civilians back into the capital, convinced even the most cocksure that this was to be a long and bloody fight. Soldiers flooded the city, swelling the population from 61,000 to more than 1 million in a single year. Some 50,000 wounded men filled makeshift hospitals in churches and public buildings.

In April 1862, President Lincoln freed slaves in the District of Columbia and then, in January of the following year, issued the Emancipation Proclamation, abolishing slavery in the Confederate states. In September 1864, Union general William Tecumseh Sherman delivered the *coup de grâce* at Atlanta.

was a Northern capital in a Southern city, nearly half of its population hailing from, or sympathetic to, the Confederate states. As Southern soldiers resigned their posts and joined the Confederate Army, Lincoln called for 75,000 volunteers to come to the Union's defense. Thousands of troops poured into a capital that was little prepared to receive them.

When a showdown between Union and Confederate troops developed at Bull Run, Virginia, Washington's society people turned out in their finest carriages, fully expecting a glorious Union victory. The horror and humil-

ABOVE: Georgetown as it looked in 1864.

Richmond fell several months later, isolating the bulk of the Confederate Army. Surrounded by Union forces, General Robert E. Lee surrendered to General Ulysses S. Grant at Appomattox Courthouse on April 9, 1865.

Lincoln's assassination

Five days later, Lincoln reluctantly agreed to attend a play, *Our American Cousin*, at Ford's Theater on 10th Street. While Lincoln sat in the balcony, John Wilkes Booth, a well-known actor and Confederate conspirator, crept behind the President, shot him, and then leapt to the stage below, crying "*Sic semper tyrannis!* The South is avenged!", breaking his leg in the fall. Lincoln, fatally wounded, was rushed to a nearby boarding house and died the next morning.

Malaria and monuments

The Civil War left Washington a less provincial, less Southern and, all things considered, a less agreeable place to live. But, by winning the war, the city was for the first time seen as the place where the destiny of the nation would be determined. The bureaucracy exploded, and Americans thronged to the city to take up federal jobs and to be at the center of power. In the decade following the Civil War, the population doubled to 175,000, overtaxing city services,

such as they were, to the point that the nation's capital was turning into, as the *Washington Post* put it, "a malarial joke."

The first effort to rebuild the city began in the early 1870s with the appointment of Alexander "Boss" Shepherd to the newly constituted Board of Public Works. A single-minded, energetic bull of a man, Shepherd ran herd over the local blue bloods and the District government in his efforts to make the "Federal City worthy of being in fact, as well as in name, the Capital of the nation." A second wave of civic improvements was launched at the turn of the century by Michigan Senator James McMillan, who set out to sweep away the run-down buildings, roads and railways that had cluttered the Mall for years, to build a bridge connecting the Mall to Arlington National Cemetery, and to erect monuments to Lincoln and Jefferson.

With the industrial revolution in full bloom, a new breed of "social Darwinists" gravitated toward the capital, housing their families in extravagant Victorian mansions in the West End, particularly on Massachusetts Avenue (now "Embassy Row"). Electric lights made an illuminating debut in the 1880s, and by the late 1910s motor cars were chugging through the streets and terrorizing pedestrians.

Most of all, though, it was America's entry into World War I in 1917 that transformed Washington. Military advisers, scientists, intellectuals, industrialists and clerks poured into the city; the federal government expanded dramatically; government housing was hastily erected; and boxy "tempos" were thrown up

FRANCIS SCOTT KEY'S NATIONAL ANTHEM

Francis Scott Key, born in Frederick County, Maryland, in 1779, was a lawyer and sometime poet who lived and practiced in a small house along the Potomac in Georgetown. He happened to be in Baltimore the night the British invaded on September 13, 1814, trying to save a friend from being impressed onto a British warship. In the course of the negotiations, Key, too, was detained, and along with his friend, watched as the British bombarded Fort McHenry that night, firing as many as 1,800 shells.

At dawn, when the American flag was still flying, though much the worse for wear, Key hurriedly penned the words that would become the National Anthem. Soon

the poem was being sung across America to the tune of "To Anacreon in Heaven," a British drinking song:

Oh, say can you see by the dawn's early light
What so proudly we hail'd at the twilight's last gleaming...

Key, who died in 1843, did not live to see his poem immortalized. By presidential proclamation, Key's poem finally became the nation's song in 1931 when, in the grip of the Great Depression, Americans turned to the words for strength and inspiration.

In 1948, Key's home was torn down to make way for the Whitehurst Freeway and for the bridge that is named in his honor and links Arlington, Virginia, to Georgetown.

along the Mall to use as office space. Once a "sleepy country town," Washington suddenly became a major player in global politics.

Good times, bad times

The hardships of the Great Depression that began in 1929 were slow to reach Washington, but when they hit, they hit hard. City-wide income was slashed by nearly half; unemployment soared to 25 percent, 50 percent among blacks.

The New Deal offered by President Franklin D. Roosevelt, who came to power in 1932, brought some relief by creating hundreds of federal jobs. Workmen were hired to scrub the

girls" arrived in the capital to take up posts as secretaries and clerks. The newly built Pentagon (completed in 1943), the largest office building in the world, quickly filled with military personnel.

The obsession with Communism

When the war ended in 1945, the Truman administration turned its attention to the "containment" of Communism, spawning a new generation of think tanks, consulting firms, political-interest groups and bureaucrats dedicated to the pursuit (and some would say the perpetuation) of the Cold War. Senator Joseph McCarthy targeted the State Department and

Washington Monument and to manicure parks; artists were commissioned to decorate public buildings; librarians and archivists were given work tending government documents. But the Depression's grip on Washington didn't truly ease until the US entry into World War II at the end of 1941.

Faced with the enormous task of building and coordinating a 7-million-man military, the federal government grew faster and larger than ever before. Hundreds of "government

other branches of the government in his hunt for "Communist sympathizers." Blacklists, red-baiting and loyalty oaths became the order of the day in Washington.

The election of John F. Kennedy in 1960 brought a welcome change of atmosphere to the city. Although an ardent supporter of the Cold War, the young charismatic president forged an idealistic national agenda stressing individual activism ("ask not what your country can do for you, but what you can do for your country") and promising a "new frontier" of social reforms. He became increasingly preoccupied with the explosive issue of desegregation, and with the growing urgency of the

LEFT: Lincoln's memorial nears completion.
ABOVE: Franklin D. Roosevelt, president 1933–45.
RIGHT: ice-skating on the Reflecting Pool in the 1930s.

civil rights movement and its most prominent leader, Dr Martin Luther King, Jr.

In the early 1960s, Washington itself was still very much a segregated city. District schools had been openly segregated until the Supreme Court's 1954 Brown vs Board of Education of Topeka decision. Not long before, black congressmen were barred from whites-only bathrooms on Capitol Hill.

While Kennedy was trying to push a civil rights bill through Congress in early 1963, plans were already being drawn up by Martin Luther King and other civil rights leaders for a massive March on Washington. On August 28, some 250,000 people converged on the capital

ernment's commitment to civil rights. He pressured Congress to pass the civil rights bill in 1964, and developed comprehensive social programs, including a massive "war on poverty." But it was a long way from Capitol Hill to the poorest neighborhoods, however, and racial conflict was approaching flashpoint in cities throughout the country. In the spring of 1968, Martin Luther King organized a second March on Washington to drive home the need for economic equality as well as equal rights.

But King never made it to Washington. On April 4, 1968, while members of King's Poor People's Campaign awaited his arrival at Resurrection City – a small shantytown located on

to voice their support for civil rights legislation. As the nation watched, whites and blacks locked arms and marched to the Lincoln Memorial, chanting slogans, carrying placards and singing "We Shall Overcome."

For many, it was the high point of the civil rights movement. Yet three months later Kennedy's bill was still stalled in the House of Representatives when, on November 22, 1963, the news reached Capitol Hill of the president's assassination in Dallas.

Crisis of confidence

If anything, Kennedy's successor, Lyndon Baines Johnson, deepened the federal gov-

the Mall – he was assassinated in Memphis, Tennessee. As the news of King's death spread, an angry crowd began gathering at the corner of 14th and U streets in Washington, while groups of youths went to neighborhood shops demanding they close in deference to King's passing. By the following day, the crowds had turned into unruly mobs, and the scattered outbreaks of arson and looting had blossomed into a full-scale riot.

The situation continued to spin out of control, and police were unable to slow it down, much less stop it. Entire city blocks were engulfed in flame, belching thick black smoke over Capitol Hill and the White House; shops and supermarkets were gutted by looters and set on fire; clashes between the police and rioters grew increasingly brutal. In 36 hours of rioting, the city sustained 12 deaths, 1,000 injuries and $27 million in property damage.

Sit-ins, tent-ins and think-ins

Protestors had always come to Washington to air their grievances, but starting in the mid-1960s they seemed to come in ever-increasing numbers and with a burning sense of urgency. To oppose the Vietnam War, they staged sit-ins, tent-ins, think-ins and peace-ins.

Disenchantment with the "establishment" crystallized further in 1973 as President Richard Nixon and key members of his staff were being investigated for their part in the cover-up of a break-in at the Watergate building, which housed the Democratic Party's headquarters. Nixon denied any knowledge of the attempted burglary and wiretapping, but as evidence of White House involvement piled up, he was forced to announce his resignation on August 8, 1974.

Democratic president Jimmy Carter, who took office in 1976 promising to move beyond the malaise and disaffection of the Vietnam and Watergate years, was politically paralyzed by a major recession, a Mideast oil crisis, a revolution and seizure of Western hostages in Iran and a botched rescue attempt. When Ronald Reagan took office in 1980 after a landslide victory for the Republicans, Washington's conservative political establishment was on the eve of a major resurgence, but Washington itself – the city beyond the marble monuments – was a city split increasingly apart by an ever widening economic divide.

Washington today

The 1980s brought mixed fortunes. A real-estate investor with money in a plush downtown property, or a young professional riding the crest of Reaganism, probably did very well indeed. The '80s catch-phrase "greed is good!" was as valid in the capital as on Wall Street.

For Washington's lower classes, however, things didn't go well. People on the lower rungs of the economic ladder slipped through the cracks and the fall-out was painfully obvious. Today there are an estimated 6,000 to 10,000 homeless people in the city, many camped out on ventilator grates, in doorways, overcrowded shelters and welfare hotels.

Despite the metropolitan area's considerable wealth (an average annual income of close to $50,000 per household, well above other cities), one in five of Washington's residents, according to the latest census report, live below the US poverty line, and most of them are black. The average income of black households is half that of whites. Infant mortality is nearly double the national average.

Public school drop-out rates are among the worst in the country. And signs of improvement are on the distant horizon.

By the late 1980s, Washington was also suffering from a drug problem of epidemic proportions. And with drugs came violence. Between 1985 – the year crack cocaine was introduced – and 1988, the number of yearly homicides in Washington jumped from 148 to 372, giving Washington the highest per capita murder rate in the country (60 per 100,000) and an undisputed claim to being the murder capital of the nation. In 1990, the number leapt again, to far more than one murder every day.

Three-term mayor Marion Barry, an out-

LEFT: Martin Luther King delivers his historic "I have a dream" speech in Washington in 1963.
RIGHT: Marion Barry, a controversial mayor.

spoken veteran of the civil rights movement, blamed much of the capital's crisis on the lack of federal dollars. But the charges of corruption that plagued 12 city officials in his administration and the drug charge that finally landed him in jail did nothing to loosen Congress's grip on the purse strings. Nor has it had the effect of permanently removing him from public life. In 2004, Barry won a seat on the City Council with an unheard-of 91 percent of the vote. He serves under the most recent mayor, Anthony Williams, whose soft-spoken, bow-tied style is refreshingly polished. While Williams has had his own political troubles, these are only temporary distractions from the

main issue which remains the struggle to win statehood status from a Congress that persists in its patriarchal attitude.

Home rule

The District of Columbia is not only the capital of the US, it is purported to be the capital of the free world. So why is it that DC has no representatives in the US Senate and only one non-voting delegate in the US House of Representatives?

The answer is simple: because the District of Columbia is not a state. It has enough people to be a state (the District's population is higher than that of Vermont's, Alaska's or Wyoming's), and its residents certainly pay enough federal taxes. But as supporters of statehood often point out, a new state of Columbia would be entitled to two seats in the Senate and one voting seat in the House of Representatives. And considering the District's demography, those seats would most likely be filled by black Democrats.

As Senator Edward Kennedy, a longtime supporter of DC statehood, put it, Washington suffers from the "four toos": "The District of Columbia and its residents are too urban, too liberal, too Democratic and too black."

The big challenge

What the future holds for Washington is anybody's guess, but the city's social problems are undeniably daunting. The District's substantial black middle class, frightened by urban violence, has fled to the suburbs, taking their substantial tax dollars with them. The city itself is almost bankrupt. Putting Washington back on an even keel, and managing the historic tug of war between City Hall and Capitol Hill, is a serious political challenge for this most political of cities.

However, few cities can draw on the pool of talent and resources available to the national capital. Optimists say that Washington has already got a hold of its bootstraps and that it's only a matter of time before it pulls itself up: one indication was the opening of a Metro station in Anacostia; another the revitalization of downtown and of Southwest. ❑

THE HOMELESS

Out of mind, perhaps, but seldom out of sight, Washington's homeless are a persistent presence in many parts of the city. Some actually have jobs but can't afford the high cost of housing. If you want to help but aren't sure how wise it is to give money directly to someone who may be a drug addict, or possibly even a con artist, here are two responsible organizations to which you can send a check.

So Others Might Eat: 70 O Street, NW, Washington, DC 20001; tel: 202-797-8806
Catholic Charities: 924 G Street, NW, Washington, DC 20001; tel: 202-772-4300

LEFT: dedicated fans render the national anthem at a Redskins football game.

The Terrorist Threat

Since the terrorist attacks of September 11, 2001, Washingtonians have become noticeably more security-conscious. Unlike many foreign capitals, where bomb scares, searches, and other inconveniences were a regular way of life, Washington, since the Civil War, had little experience of violence directed at it from an outside source.

With barely a check of identification by the guards, public buildings were largely accessible to most. And until the attacks, delivery trucks bringing printed matter and other supplies necessary for the business of Congress drove unimpeded to the open loading docks of the buildings on Capitol Hill. Free and open to the public, Washington seemed to operate on faith that the long-established democratic principles that guide the nation would somehow keep it from harm.

Though inexperienced with this sort of wholesale and spectacular violence, Washingtonians nevertheless rose to the occasion. On the morning of the attacks, workers left their offices and, without panicking, calmly headed home to their families. On that blue-sky and crisp autumn day, streams of people walked quietly across the city, northward into Maryland, and across the bridges into Virginia. They waited patiently for trains at the Metro stations. They were aware of what had happened, but not yet sure why, and the atmosphere all over the city was eerily silent.

But by the next morning, everyone had returned to work, and the business of government went on as usual, though in the following months federal workers went about their jobs with an increased sense of mission. In the weeks after the attacks, air patrols flew day and night over the city.

Many of the attractions that draw tourists were closed until security could be increased. Reagan National Airport was closed and was the last airport in the nation to re-open. With the tourists staying away, there were suddenly no lines at the museums, and suddenly locals had a choice of tables at the city's best restaurants. Most of the sites have re-opened and the crowds are back, though the everyday routine has been affected.

Security has been tightened all over the city, with checks conducted at every tourist site and government building. Activities that seem even remotely suspicious are no longer ignored, but reported to the police. Some streets, especially those around Capitol Hill, are blocked to vehicular traffic, as the White House has been since before the attack. The White House has suspended tours, the Pentagon has no plans to allow anyone inside who isn't there on official busi-

ness, and there is ongoing talk of installing more surveillance cameras across the city, much to the annoyance of those who still believe that Washington, if no longer entirely safe from foreign threat, must itself remain free and open.

Life has changed in Washington, and daily life, as a result of the attacks, has undeniably become less convenient. Washingtonians, though, are an intrepid breed, and many of those who have made the city their home are driven by the sense of duty that led them into public service in the first place. No matter what happens next, one thing is certain: Washington won't shut down. ❑

RIGHT: the Pentagon after terrorists crashed a hijacked plane into it on September 11, 2001.

Decisive Dates

The Early Years

1608 Captain John Smith sails up the Potomac.
1662 The first land patent in the area is granted.
1749 Nearby Alexandria, Virginia, is established.
1751 Georgetown is established.
1775 The American Revolution begins.
1776 Members of the Continental Congress sign the Declaration of Independence.
1783 The Revolution ends with the surrender of General Charles Cornwallis at Yorktown, Virginia.
1789 The US Constitution is ratified.
1790 With land ceded by Maryland, the site that

will be the nation's capital is chosen.
1791 Alexandria, Virginia, is added to the territory that makes up the Federal City; Major Pierre L'Enfant lays out a plan for the city.
1792 The cornerstone for the White House, the city's first public building, is laid.
1793 The cornerstone for the Capitol is laid.
1800 President John Adams is the first president to occupy the White House; the population of Washington is 14,000.
1802 The city of Washington is chartered.
1802 Eastern Market, the city's oldest surviving marketplace, is opened.
1812 The War of 1812 follows years of serious maritime trade disputes with the British.
1814 The British set fire to the White House, the Capitol and other public buildings.

Washington Comes into its Own

1815 President James Madison signs the Treaty of Ghent ending the War of 1812. The City Canal opens, along what is now Constitution Avenue.
1820 District's population exceeds 33,000.
1829 Wealthy British scientist James Smithson dies and leaves his fortune to the US for the establishment of an institution in his name.
1832 A severe cholera epidemic strikes the city.
1835 Baltimore and Ohio Railroad reaches DC.
1846 The Smithsonian Institution is established.
1848 Work begins on Washington Monument.
1849 The first gas works is built and the White House now lit with gas. The District's population surpasses 51,000.
1850 The Chesapeake and Ohio canal is completed. Congress abolishes the slave trade in the District, although owning slaves is still legal.
1855 The Castle, the Smithsonian's first building, is opened on the Mall.
1861 The Civil War begins and a series of forts is erected around the District to protect it.
1863 President Lincoln signs proclamation abolishing slavery. Capitol is completed.
1865 The Civil War ends. Lincoln is shot dead.
1867 Howard University, the prestigious black institution, is set up.

The New Era

1871 Congress votes $20 million for civic improvements such as sewers and paving streets. Georgetown is incorporated into Washington.
1874 The Corcoran Gallery, the city's first art museum, opens.
1874 After a brief experiment at self-government, control of the city reverts to Congress.
1877 The *Washington Post* begins publication. Black leader Frederick Douglass is appointed Marshal of the District and Recorder of Deeds.
1879 There are 400 telephones in operation in the city, and one operator.
1880 After the Civil War, citizens flock to the capital of the preserved nation and the population swells to more than 175,000.
1884 Washington Monument is completed.
1889 National Zoo is founded.
1897 The Library of Congress building opens.
1899 Congress limits the height of buildings in downtown, so precluding skyscrapers.

1890 Rock Creek Park, a 4-mile (6-km) stretch of woodland, is established.

Modern Times

1902 Much needed restoration work begins on the White House; the West Wing, which includes the Oval Office, is added.

1908 The railroad station on the Mall is moved to Capitol Hill, becoming Union Station.

1912 Griffith Stadium opens and President William Howard Taft throws out the first baseball of the season, beginning an annual tradition.

1913 Last farm animal in the White House, a cow named Pauline, leaves with outgoing President Taft.

1914 The Lincoln Memorial is begun.

1918 War War I ends. The District's population exceeds 400,000.

1922 Lincoln Memorial is dedicated.

1924 Baseball's Washington Senators beat the New York Giants to win their first and only World Series at Griffith Stadium in the city.

1935 The Supreme Court takes up residence in its new building on Capitol Hill.

1939 Denied permission to perform at DAR Constitution Hall because she is black, famed operatic singer Marian Anderson performs for a crowd of 75,000 before the Lincoln Memorial.

1941 The US enters World War II. The first plane lands at National Airport. The National Gallery of Art opens on the Mall.

1943 The Pentagon is completed.

1945 World War II ends.

1949 The Whitehurst Freeway is completed along the Georgetown waterfront.

1952 President Truman moves back into the White House after extensive restoration work.

1961 John F. Kennedy is inaugurated as the 35th President. Congress gives District residents the right to vote in presidential elections.

1963 Martin Luther King, Jr. addresses a crowd of 200,000 in front of the Lincoln Memorial and gives his famous "I Have a Dream" speech.

1967 Congress establishes a new political structure for the District and appoints a mayor.

1968 Rioting erupts following the assassination of Dr. King, costing 12 lives.

1971 The Kennedy Center opens.

LEFT: Abraham Lincoln photographed in 1861.
RIGHT: a woman is arrested in front of the White House after a 1963 anti-racism demonstration.

1972 Burglars break into Democratic Party HQ at the Watergate, beginning the saga that leads to President Richard Nixon's 1974 resignation.

1975 The first elected mayor, Walter Washington, and a city council take office.

1976 Metrorail opens its first subway route.

1982 The Vietnam War Memorial is dedicated.

1983 The renovated Willard Hotel and the Old Post Office building open.

1990 The Washington National Cathedral, begun in 1907, is completed.

1993 The Vietnam Women's War Memorial is dedicated. The US Holocaust Museum opens.

1995 The Korean War Memorial is dedicated; Washington hosts the Million Man March.

1997 Memorial to Franklin D. Roosevelt opens.

1999 President Bill Clinton impeached by House of Representatives, but acquitted by Senate.

2001 On September 11, Islamic terrorists crash a hijacked plane into the Pentagon, killing 189.

2002 Memorial to founding father George Mason, responsible for the Bill of Rights, is dedicated. Two snipers terrorise the city and the surrounding area for three weeks, killing 10 in random attacks.

2003 The White House and the Pentagon are nerve centers for the war against Iraq.

2004 World War II Memorial is dedicated. Smithsonian American Indian Museum opens. George W. Bush wins second term in White House. ❑

THE NATIONAL MUSEUM OF AMERICAN HISTORY

If it has anything to do with American history or culture, it's here – from lightbulbs to locomotives, from red slippers to ceremonial swords

If Uncle Sam had a garage, here's some of what he would have crammed into it: George Washington's ceremonial sword, an 1880 incandescent lightbulb of Thomas Edison's, Jackie Kennedy's 1961 inaugural gown, a 90-ft steam locomotive weighing 260 tons, Roberto Clemente's Pittsburgh Pirate's baseball uniform, assorted Tupperware, a cast of Lincoln's hands, a Woodstock poster from 1969, Thomas Jefferson's laptop desk on which he wrote the Declaration of Independence, Dorothy's red slippers from the 1939 classic *The Wizard of Oz* and the stock car driven by Richard Petty in Daytona Beach in 1984.

All this and much more is spread out over three capacious floors totaling 750,000 sq. ft in the National Museum of American History, part of the Smithsonian Institution on the Mall. It all started with the pack rats at the US Patent Office who apparently saved most of the inventions Americans submitted to them for copyright, then put everything on display in Philadelphia in 1876 to celebrate the nation's 100th birthday. When the Centennial Exposition was over, the collection was moved to what is now the Arts and Industries building. Naturally enough, the collection swelled past the building's capacity to hold it until finally, in 1964, the American History building opened. Since then it has become the official repository of all objects uniquely emblematic of the American experience.

● *Location, contact details and opening times: page 82.*

ABOVE: centerpiece of the "America on the Move" exhibit, this 90-ft (27-meter) steam locomotive was hauled through a window opening before the museum was completed.

ABOVE: the display of First Ladies' inauguration gowns, on the second floor, is the museum's most popular exhibit.

LEFT: humorist Edgar Bergen's wooden wisecracker Charlie McCarthy, a popular star of the radio era.

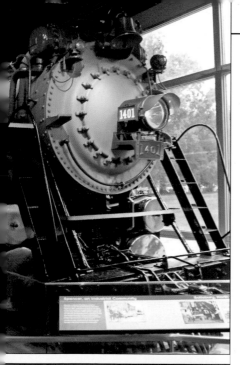

THE MAIN HIGHLIGHTS

First Ladies. Personal artifacts and photos, including a display of inauguration gowns, give clues about life under the political spotlight for America's most notable women.

Lincoln's artifacts. You can see the top hat he wore the night he was assassinated, plus other personal objects in The American Presidency exhibit.

Woolworth's Lunch Counter. The place where four African-Americans dared to change history in 1960 is preserved and serves to remind that freedom in America can be selective.

Dorothy's red slippers. Judy Garland wore them in *The Wizard of Oz*. They're here with other iconic items from Hollywood in the Popular Culture exhibit.

Star-Spangled Banner. The original that inspired the National Anthem flew in Baltimore harbor during the War of 1812. Worse for wear, but still grand.

America on the Move. From trolley cars to stock cars in this exhibit of more than 300 objects.

The Price of Freedom. Artifacts and images of America's wars and how they changed society.

Hall of Musical Instruments. As well as a collection of old instruments, there are regular concerts by the Smithsonian Chamber Music Society and the Smithsonian Jazz Masterworks Orchestra.

ABOVE: Julia Child's Cambridge, Massachusetts, kitchen has been reassembled here complete with 1,200 gadgets and utensils and her collection of cookbooks.

RIGHT: this 1840 marble statue of George Washington weighs in at 12 tons and was modeled on the Greek god Zeus. It was intended to top the Washington Monument.

ABOVE: an item in the "On Time" exhibit, which covers times zones and tells how World War I soldiers made wristwatches popular.

LIFE IN WASHINGTON

As the permanent population swells, the city is becoming more distinctive and dynamic, influenced by factors other than the changing fortunes of politics

Washington is an almost laughably small place, a diamond-shaped area of modest residential streets, more a town than a city – and a pretty provincial one at that. It appears devoted to official buildings, official business and people who visit. It seems detached from the nation it governs. But to its inhabitants it is very much an established city – in fact, it is really four cities.

The four faces

There is the Washington that is most generally conjured up by the name – the administrative city that governs a vast military and bureaucratic machine. This is the city defined by the White House, the Pentagon and the Capitol, and the legions of local inhabitants who make the machine work.

Then there is social Washington, hovering not so discreetly behind the closed doors (to anyone who does not clutch an engraved invitation) of the exclusive salons of Georgetown, Kalorama and Embassy Row. Its purpose is to woo, soothe, encourage, coerce and promote useful relationships among the politically influential. For this is not a city like New York or San Francisco that has grown up around the more usual physical and cultural needs of a socially integrated community. Its crème de la crème are not drawn together by vibrant local theater, innovative restaurants, imaginative grocery stores, fashionable, witty or daring style. The thing that counts most is power. It is in its exclusive Georgetown salons that potential leaders are subtly appraised.

The third Washington is the city that is

three-quarters black and known as a drug and murder capital. But there is a fourth Washington, and it is this Washington that is finally forcing the capital into becoming a coherent, normal place to live, functioning beyond the shadow of the Capitol. It is the Washington that lies outside the District of Columbia line.

In Chevy Chase, Bethesda, Arlington and the nearby environs of Maryland's Prince George's County plus the wealthier counties of Montgomery in Maryland and Fairfax in

PRECEDING PAGES: a concierge to count on.
ABOVE: on parade for the Fourth of July.
RIGHT: taking tea at the Willard Hotel.

Virginia – are the suburbs where these days you will find burgeoning business and residential Washington. While demolition teams scrape away downtown DC to erase the old ghettos still clinging to the skirts of Capitol Hill, out beyond the DC line a vibrant new Washington has been growing.

The face of the future

DC, kept deliberately unattached to either of its neighboring states in order not to show favoritism, is probably the last American city under renovation and construction in the classical quasi-European style. Yet while old columned buildings receive facelifts and once-

problem areas become gentrified, what is now recognized as the standard modern American city mushrooms on the other side of the District line. Pushing outwards beyond the Beltway (the 8-lane traffic nightmare of a highway that girdles the city) are the high-rise office buildings, the shopping malls, the freeway strips that signify the city of the future anywhere in America.

This new Washington is the city that has grown out of President Lyndon Johnson's grandiose Great Society program in the 1960s, which increased staff levels at government departments. Unable to adequately accommodate these new bureaucrats in the old federal

LAWYERS AND SHRINKS

The growth in government, banking, and institutions has drawn to the city a positive plethora of lawyers, to the point where they have become the butt of caustic jokes.

There are over 55,000 of them working in practices large and small, but over 100,000 people in Washington actually have law qualifications. This is more than the number of doctors in the city, despite the fact that in the Maryland suburb of Bethesda sits the vast compound of the National Institute of Health, the prestigious research center set up by President Nixon's government to find a cure for cancer. But government needs lawyers to construct and implement the law and to protect itself, and

businesses need lawyers to confront the government. Now litigation appears to have become a way of life among the residents, too.

Washington has also become a major employer of specialists in emotional problems, with more therapists, counselors and psychiatrists per capita than any other American city. Perhaps the pressures of power are just too great for some. Despite this growth, however, Washington is still a comparatively slow-paced, provincial city, although its polish increases daily. While its New York neighbors may find it, as the actress Barbra Streisand did, "a stuffy city," it is no longer the backwoods hick town.

buildings and state departments in town, some offices made the move into the suburbs. Major international banking and communications institutions followed, spreading outwards in Virginia in the direction of Dulles International Airport and making the suburb of Reston a burgeoning city. The effect is almost a reversing of the power process, with the activity of the arteries in the suburbs helping the central body function. Increasingly, what takes place on the outskirts of town supports, justifies and shores up the activities and continued existence of the business of the center.

What pushed, with explosive suddenness, the process of transforming Washington from

a sleepy Southern town into a forceful power city were the race riots of 1968 that followed the assassination of Dr Martin Luther King. What these fires began, the demolition teams continued, and the political process took over. In 1970 the redevelopment of Washington began, including the idea of pulling it down and rebuilding it afresh.

Marion Barry, who took office as mayor in 1978, used his powers to push the construction program forward with even greater fervor. Whole areas were razed while others were restored. To see the contrast between old and new, stand on Dupont Circle, where Massachusetts Avenue crosses Connecticut Avenue. The Connecticut Avenue to your south is new and high-rise. The block of Connecticut to your north is jumbled, low-rise and on a more human scale.

Permanent residents

With this transformation, Washington began to attract people with firm commitments to putting down roots. This was unlike the intentions of the original founding fathers, who sited the capital in an uncongenial spot because they hoped this would discourage politicians from spending too much time here gathering power. While the backbone of government bureaucracy is necessarily run by a permanent staff, people in high political office have traditionally committed themselves to Washington only for the duration of the President who appointed them. But these days politicians who once would have returned home after the end of their term of office now choose, in

THE SPORTING CITY

Regardless of the huge social and economic gaps that fragment Washingtonians, the city is brought together by the Washington Redskins. Home games are played at the new FedEx Field in nearby Laurel, Maryland, which seats more than 86,000. The team's owner, Dan Snyder, an ambitious advertising mogul, paid a record $800 million for the Redskins. Ticket prices soared and, as for a ticket to a single game, forget it – no such thing exists.

Baseball offered more hope when Washington finally acquired a team in time for the 2005 season at Robert F. Kennedy Stadium. Basketball fans are luckier: both men's and women's professional teams play downtown at the

MCI Center, along with Georgetown University's Hoyas. The men's professional team, the Washington Wizards haven't had a good season in decades. The Washington Mystics, the women's professional team, draws big crowds. And the city's golden boys are the Georgetown Hoyas.

From October through April, the MCI Center is home to the Washington Capitals, the city's National Hockey League team which may just win a Stanley Cup yet.

Because of its cultural diversity, the DC area is as soccer-friendly as you can get in the US. The RFK Stadium is home to the DC United, which is made up of both top US players and foreign stars.

increasing numbers, to stay on to become PR executives, lobbyists or consultants in the mushrooming think-tanks, trade associations, and law firms. You can understand their desire to stay put. Washington is an attractive and lucrative city in which to play power games.

Culture central

There are more than 5,000 restaurants in the city, where Washingtonians can dine on the national cuisine of practically any country in the world. There are good theater companies, much relished by indigenous Washingtonians, including the world-class Shakespeare Theatre, plus the Kennedy Center, home to the

yuppie community, there is no glitzy night life for the power people. This is part cultural: Washingtonians have to get up far too early to party all night long and political Washington closes down early.

Civilized and violent

To anyone familiar with other American cities, Washington is perhaps the most handsome. Yet, despite appearances, and incongruously for a city so taken by surprise by 2001's terrorist attacks, it also has one of the world's highest murder rates. Nearly all these crimes occur in the Northeast and Southeast, predominantly African American and Hispanic areas.

National Symphony Orchestra, the National Theater, which hosts many of the Broadway companies on tour, and several outstanding repertory theaters. There are also concerts, lectures, classes, and art exhibits of every type throughout the city in small galleries and halls, and of course at the Smithsonian, whose prestige attracts the finest performers, artists, writers, and historians as instructors and lecturers for its wide offering of classes.

While there is a constant carousel of nightclubs and music cellars for students and the

American apartheid may legally have ended in 1964, but Washington is an apartheid city, with middle-class whites living west of the 16th Street line that divides the city from the north down to the White House. Unemployment and violence are part of the daily lives of those who live in the east.

But this focus on one part of Washington should not obscure the others. This is, after all, four cities. Desperate, magnificent, stylish and provincial, Washington is also a town which possesses a rare, distinctive quality. It's a place where, in the words of Ralph Waldo Emerson, "an insignificant individual may trespass on a nation's time."   ❏

LEFT: the Washington Redskins attract loyal fans,
ABOVE: fast food at Adams Morgan's street festival.

THE ETHNIC MIX

The city's new communities are diverse and vibrant, adding culture and culinary variety. But there is tension between the new immigrants and young males from Washington's extensive black neighborhoods

For years, Washington's black neighborhoods were known collectively as the "secret city," the city behind the marble edifices and the pomp and politics of official Washington, the city segregated from white Washington. Within these cloistered avenues existed a vital and thriving social and economic culture whose citizens overcame the barriers of discrimination, realizing their full potential and in the bargain enriching American life. Like other American cities, DC continues to undergo the changes that result in gentrification, shifting demographics, and the flight to the suburbs. But, block by block, Washington is reclaiming itself, tearing down the old and putting up the new, and with each passing year black Washingtonians are finding a viable place for themselves, contributing to the resurgence of the city.

High-ranking supremos

Black Washington is more than just the figure of Marion Barry, whose behavior when mayor garnered him many national headlines. There have been a number of high-ranking supremos, including Sharon Pratt Kelly, the city's first black woman mayor, General Colin Powell, former Secretary of State, Eleanor Holmes Norton, District delegate to the House of Representatives, and Condoleezza Rice, George W. Bush's former national security advisor turned Secretary of State.

But within a few blocks of the Capitol, in and around Mt. Pleasant, and along the Anacostia waterfront, real life asserts itself in the form of drugs, poverty, and increasing discontent between long-time African-American residents and newly arrived Latinos. Gang wars and bloodshed define life in these neighborhoods, unshakable despair displacing hope.

Yet Washington is also the home of a prominent black middle class. The city's Dunbar High, on the corner of 1st and N streets NW, was the first black high school in the country, and produced generations of black leaders. The relatively new University of DC and the long-established Howard University, often called "the black Harvard" with its 18 schools, 12,000 students, 8,000 employees and $500 million annual budget, have created a strong intellectual foundation. While the city's public school system has one of the country's highest drop-out rates, DC still has the highest percentage of black college grads of any major American city.

Along Upper 16th Street, known locally as the Gold Coast, is a suburb of expensive homes for the city's black elite. On Sunday mornings, the streets around the fashionable black churches of the Gold Coast and Shepherd Park are thronged with luxury cars and well-dressed families. But this prosperous and growing middle class tends increasingly to behave like its white counterparts, and flee the problems of the inner city. Head north-east of the DC boundary and you reach Prince

ital was born in the curious contradiction between slavery and black genius.

When the city's architect Pierre L'Enfant was dismissed by George Washington for insubordination, his initial sketches were reconstructed and made into a viable design plan by a free black surveyor, Benjamin Banneker. Son of a former slave and an English indentured servant girl, Banneker was born in 1731 and raised on a farm near Baltimore. The wife of the farmer taught him to read, but Banneker taught himself astronomy and mathematics. When Major Andrew Ellicott, L'Enfant's replacement and a neighbor of Banneker's, needed a surveyor the much admired black

George's County, which in 1990 became the first suburban county in the country to have a black majority population.

Deep roots

The roots of Washington's black community go back to the founding of the city in the established white South. Located south of the Mason-Dixon line, the old boundary between the slave and the free states, the nation's cap-

LEFT: a mural on U Street celebrates Duke Ellington, who led the city's leading society band in the 1930s.
ABOVE: black power – Condoleezza Rice succeeded Colin Powell as Secretary of State in 2005.

intellectual was immediately recruited.

Banneker, however, was the exception. Fully 80 per cent of the black population living in the city that he was surveying was enslaved and after the British destroyed the city in 1814, much of the physical effort of rebuilding fell to those slaves. As early as 1808 a $5 fine was imposed on any black person found on the street after 10pm; two years later, a jail term was added. On the eve of the US Civil War in 1860, there were 11,000 free blacks in the city, and more than 3,000 slaves.

Beginning in 1866, all adult men were given the vote, regardless of race, and by 1870 blacks were legally permitted service in restaurants and other public places, though these laws were not widely enforced.

Early in the 20th century, blacks held few jobs in the government of the city or in the federal government. In 1922, when the Lincoln Memorial was dedicated to the Great Emancipator, a separate stand was erected for black dignitaries, a symbol of the segregation that still governed the city's schools, restaurants and theaters. Only the trolleys, the buses and the stands of Griffith Stadium, the field where the famed Washington Senators baseball team played, were integrated, but not the field itself.

The problem of Washington's brand of racism was pointedly demonstrated in 1939

when the famed black contralto Marian Anderson was denied permission to sing at Constitution Hall, the concert venue owned and operated by those denizens of white American respectability, the Daughters of the American Revolution. Eleanor Roosevelt, the outraged wife of the president, stepped in and arranged for the singer to perform in front of the Lincoln Memorial. Anderson's outdoor concert drew tens of thousands but did nothing to change the Daughters' stance.

The black character of modern Washington was shaped by two crucial events. The first was the Supreme Court's order to desegregate the public school systems in 1954, which dramatically accelerated the white flight to the suburbs. And, 14 years later, the assassination of Martin Luther King sparked off the racial riots and the looting and burning which reached within four blocks of the White House. The white flight was followed by the steady drift of shops and service industries and jobs to the suburbs, and created the social condition which became known as the inner city. The 1968 riots and the fires created the conditions for a rebirth.

The riots reinforced the case for giving the national capital enough democracy to elect its own form of civic government. After a century as a fief of Congress, the city was able to vote for its own school board in 1968, and for its own (non-voting) delegate to Congress in 1971. In 1974, the city finally won the right to elect its own mayor and largely black city council. This helped spur the growth of the black middle class, as they appointed sympa-

COUNTRY COOKING

"Washington is not a nice place to live in. The rents are high, the food is bad… and the morals are deplorable," wrote Horace Greeley in the *New York Tribune* in 1865. Well, at least the food's improved. Indeed, one popular reinterpretation of the CIA's initials is "the Culinary Institute of America." This is a dig at the extraordinary coincidence of the surge in new ethnic restaurants that comes with the ebb and flow of political events around the globe. Democratic American voters – and Republicans, too – may object to some of the meddling in the internal affairs of small and distant countries, but they can always look forward to something new to eat at the end of the revolution.

After the fall of Saigon, Washington was suddenly introduced to the delights of Vietnamese cooking. And not just with one single restaurant. The whole extended family fled too; uncles, aunts, cousins, in-laws established Vietnamese eating places all over town. Wilson Boulevard in Arlington, Virginia, on the other side of the Potomac, is fondly know as Little Saigon. In the early 1980s, Ethiopian cooking, influenced by the Italians who occupied the African country in the 1930s, became popular. And, with the Soviet invasion of Kabul, an assortment of Afghani restaurants sprang up. More recently, Latin American cooking became all the rage.

thetic police chiefs and blacks rose in the civic bureaucracy. In the District Courts on Indiana Avenue, for all the depressing parade of black defendants in the dock, mostly charged with drug-related offenses, the black lawyers and black judges and black reporters on the press benches suggest a more hopeful society emerging, however slowly.

The melting pot

The original "melting pot" that America held itself to be was based on a mix of European races. These days, as America's political influence stretches throughout the entire world, immigrants come from every nation. Once

thriving. Members of the ethnic groups confined to "the stans" easily settled in after the Soviet collapse, along with new arrivals from Pakistan and India. Africans have brought their customs to the streets of Adams Morgan which they share with a Latino population growing so fast that Spanish is the most common foreign language you're likely to hear.

By and large, each community of new Americans gets on fine with each other because most are equally balanced and relatively small. Besides, they recognize that they are still the newcomers. They are committed to making a success of their new status that will benefit their children for generations to come. There are ten-

here, the new Americans tend to gravitate towards the areas of the city in which their fellow countrymen are already established and to the jobs their fellow countrymen already hold. A large number of Washington's cab drivers are Iranian and Ethiopian. Filipino women become housekeepers and cleaners, while the Chinese congregate in Chinatown on H Street NW and join the catering trade.

Russians are represented here, too, and in numbers sufficient to keep two Orthodox churches and several synagogues active and

sions, but, apart from the disturbing suspicion and rivalry which has grown worse between the growing Hispanic community and the African-American community, the dividing line in Washington is less between the individual ethnic communities, than between white Americans and everyone else.

Of all the murders that take place regularly in the capital, almost all occur in the non-white sections of Washington, particularly the east. But Washington's ethnic mix has made for a city that has lost its provincial edges by embracing a multitude of cultures. Any day of the week you can hear on the streets of downtown four or five different languages. ❏

LEFT: there's a strong Asian element to the ethnic mix.
ABOVE: art for sale in the Eastern Market.

THE POWER BEHIND THE POLITICS

Plenty of good food, political contributions, and a steady stream of lobbyists keep Washington's power players energized and at the top of their political game

Washington is the most political of cities, designed and built to be the capital of what has become the world's sole superpower. But while the stone and marble structures which house and embody government power are plain to see, the reality of power remains elusive. An American president may find it easy to despatch aircraft carriers and troops around the globe, but he can have trouble getting his budget, or his nominee to run a major department, through Congress. Congress may pass a law, only to find the White House defies it, or the Supreme Court redefines it.

The power and the story

For the visitor, therefore, the power structure of Washington which is on show in Congress and the White House can be deeply misleading; it is part of the reality of power, but only a part. The rest is private, secret and composed of a series of subtle and personal links through which power is wielded and enjoyed.

One axis of power runs along Pennsylvania Avenue, from the White House to the US Capitol and the Supreme Court just behind. To the south of this great artery is the Federal Triangle, housing the great departments of government from Justice to Agriculture to the National Archives, and the Federal Trade Commission and the Internal Revenue Service. Another axis runs to the Pentagon, across the river. A third heads out to the Virginia suburbs in McLean, where the CIA has its vast headquarters.

Each of these power centers has its own suburb. The Pentagon has spawned its own bureaucratic military-industrial complex. And the US Congress has become a veritable city in its own right, with its own subway system to ferry the senators and representatives and their staffs around the complex of office buildings which surrounds the Capitol.

To the north are the Dirksen and Hart and Russell buildings, each named after a powerful senator, and each containing the vast and formal committee rooms where so many public hearings and so much history has taken place. Joe McCarthy's Communist witch-hunts, the Fulbright hearings into the Vietnam War, Sam Ervin's Watergate probes, Anita Hill's testimony against Justice Clarence Thomas,

Condoleezza Rice's obstreperousness before the 9/11 Commission – these marble halls witnessed all these dramas and more.

Less well-known are the grandiose office suites where each of the 100 senators have more than 30 staff members whose salaries are paid by the taxpayer. Much of their time is taken up processing the 25 million letters a year Congress receives from the voters.

House of Representatives

To the south of the Capitol stand the Cannon, the Longworth, the Rayburn and Ford buildings where the 435 members of the House of Representatives reside in slightly more mod-

It is by no means a conspicuously luxurious place. The swimming pool is a modest 60 ft (18 meters) long, and it contains a basketball and paddle ball court, weights, stationary bicycles, two treadmills and a stairmaster. The Helene Curtis company provides free soap, and there are constant complaints that the towels are too small.

Because of the cramped locker room, it is a single-sex gym. A smaller women's gym has been opened upstairs. But the House gym is getting too crowded for serious workouts; when a noted Speaker of the House decided to lose 100 pounds, he went to the gym of the University Club on 16th Street instead.

est splendor. House members average about 14 staff members, but their committee rooms defer not at all to the Senate's self-importance. The basement of the Rayburn building contains the House gym, one of the few places where the legislators can get away from voters, journalists and lobbyists and hang around with each other. Celebrities can be squeezed in, but only to be useful, like the way Arnold Schwarzenegger was recruited to give advanced tuition in weight-lifting.

LEFT: keeping in touch on Capitol Hill.
ABOVE: these days the president watches his inaugural parade from behind bullet-proof glass.

Executive suburb

One of the fastest-growing suburbs is the White House itself. The Treasury huddles close alongside to the east, but beyond the western wing, which Richard Nixon transformed from a swimming pool into a press room, stands the evidence of the growth industry of the presidency: a large 19th-century building of gray stone and pillars, the Executive Office Building. It used to be sufficient to house the entire civil service, the Navy and Commerce and the State Department. These days, it cannot even house the White House staff, whose more than 2,300 members have spilled over into a red-brick New Executive Office Building on the far side of Pennsylvania Avenue. It is more luxurious than it looks – $350,000 was spent just to redecorate the gym – and has the best 24-hour vending machines and automats in town.

The serious political sessions, when the fund-raisers confer with the Congressmen, take place in private dining rooms in the big hotels, or in the corporate suites and the think-tanks. Powerful people have to eat, and on any given day, they will be breakfasting, lunching and drinking in a series of discreet places. The hosts may often be lobbyists (the term derives from the 19th-century influence peddlers who congregated in the lobbies of public buildings, most especially the Willard Hotel near the White House). Today there are an estimated 23,000 special interests groups in Washington with as many as 90,000 people engaged in promoting a huge variety of interests. The pharmaceutical industry has 623 lobbyists alone on Capitol Hill, a striking imbalance considering there are only 535 Congressmen.

Inauguration Day

There is only one event which needs so many limos that reinforcements have to be driven down interstate 95 from New York City. This takes place every four years in January, on the president's inauguration day. The evening's inaugural balls take place all across the city, in the vast and echoing Building Museum, in the marbled hall of Union Station, and at the big hotel ballrooms, bringing together political power brokers from all 50 states, plus fund-raisers and campaign donors.

Sex scandals

The real pleasure of Washington is not in the lavish and sleek way this city entertains itself, but in the erotic grip of power. Henry Kissinger was never a handsome man, but his power was aphrodisiac enough for his escorts to be some of the most beautiful women in the country. But sex is dangerous in Washington, as Bill Clinton discovered. The writer Gore Vidal observed that the city had become the modern Rome, and it was therefore to be expected that it would develop its own scandals to rival those of the Caesars. ❑

LEFT: lobbyists in the lobby of the Willard Hotel.

POLITICAL PARTIES

Except for the occasional third political party, such as the Know-Nothings of the 1850s, the Mugwumps of the 1880s, or Texan Ross Perot's United We Stand of the 1990s, America's political system is comprised of two parties. The Democratic Party is the oldest continuous political party in the world. It was founded in the 1780s in opposition to the Federalists, who believed that the country's interests ought to be put before those of the states. Thomas Jefferson was the first president under the Democratic-Republican Party, as it was known then. Over time the party's principles have shifted to embrace social reform, the redistribution of wealth through taxation, and the protection of the "common man." The Republican Party, on the other hand, is typically less interested in the disenfranchised, although it drew its initial strength from the anti-slavery movement. It was founded in 1854 and its first president was Abraham Lincoln. Since then, its objectives have become more closely aligned with big business and the wealthy.

The symbols of the parties were created by 19th-century cartoonist Thomas Nast. His Democratic donkey was seen as representing stubbornness in protecting the rights of the working class, and his Republican elephant signified that party's ponderous resistance to change. Nast himself was a Republican.

Foreign Affairs

Washington's 175 embassies are for the most part wonderfully pompous or exotic edifices, with columns, turrets, gargoyles, stucco and fluting and – considering their central situations – set in astonishingly large gardens. Most of the embassies line Massachusetts Avenue and 16th Street.

When you set foot in one of Washington's 175 embassies, you are literally standing on a piece of foreign territory. The impressions you take away from that experience help form a sense of that country's character, a character that many diplomats are hoping reaches beyond the stereotypical. The Romanians, for instance, would like to be known for more than Dracula, the Swedes for more than Volvos. To that end, almost every embassy offers a program of cultural activities open to the public *(see page 150)*. Where else, as one *Washington Post* reporter observed, can you experience an Indonesian jazz violinist decked out in Tibetan headdress, singing scat?

Diplomatic life appears from the outside a pleasant, if repetitious, affair. There are the stylish parties, the useful luncheons, the important dinners, the drinks parties, the cultural events and National Day celebrations. At the British Embassy, a traditional brick manor house designed by the Edwardian architect Sir Edwin Lutyens, dinner guests raise their glasses to the Queen.

For the diplomatic wives who don't work there are charities and fund-raising committees to join, art gallery lectures to attend, instructive courses to take and amateur theatricals to give one's all to. The Adventure Theater at Glen Echo for children is a popular repository of diplomatic talent, with embassy wives throwing themselves into dramatizations of fairytales.

These wives' spouses may arrange small informal lunches to lobby mid-level Capitol Hill bureaucrats, or an off-the-record meeting ("but read my lips") with local journalists and foreign correspondents, while

their ambassadors tackle the serious negotiations with Congressional heavyweights and State Department officials.

Taking note of all this in the hope of making sense of it for the readers back home are the foreign correspondents. There are over 1,000 of them, including film cameramen, filing constantly for newspapers, journals, radio and TV stations. The foreign community also includes vast numbers of employees of foreign businesses, large and small. As political decisions back home may be taken on the basis of a reporter's editorial or an embassy's briefing, the profits of many conglomerates

depend on the Washington office analysis of what is taking place on the Hill, in the Pentagon budget, at the World Bank or the International Monetary Fund.

A posting to Washington may be glamorous, but the focus on American and world affairs takes up so much time and energy that some members of the foreign community have been known to leave the capital without ever having bothered to know any Americans who didn't have a desk on the Hill. That attitude is changing, however, as cultural attachés realize the need to sell their own cultures more forcefully to the world's only superpower. ❑

RIGHT: lunchtime at the official French residence.

How the Federal Government Works

The American experiment in democratic self-government entered its third century in 1991 with the bi-centennial of the Bill of Rights. These rights are now codified in 10 amendments to the Constitution and were drafted shortly after the Constitution itself to settle lingering anxieties about the limits of state powers over the lives of individuals.

Educated in the social theories of such European Enlightenment thinkers as John Locke, Thomas Hobbes, and Jean-Jacques Rousseau, the founders shared a deep mistrust of any concentration of power, having recently overthrown the rule of a despotic English king. The system of Thomas Jefferson, James Madison and Alexander Hamilton was designed to ensure that no institution or faction could seize control of the apparatus of government.

The system is a federal one, so the national government's powers are limited. Most criminal law, for example, is written by state legislatures. When Americans refer to the Federal government they mean Washington, DC. The government has three branches, each able to limit the powers of the other two. This is known as the separation of powers and the system of checks and balances. The three branches are organized by function: the legislative, executive, and judicial branches.

The legislative power is vested in Congress, which consists of two bodies, the House of Representatives and the Senate. Both are elected directly by the people and act according to majority vote. They are organized into committees, which consider, amend and send to the entire membership bills which win a majority of committee members. Bills which fail in committee can be resurrected by a majority of the entire membership of the House or Senate.

The House of Representatives

Membership in the House of Representatives is apportioned according to population. The total number of Representatives is fixed at 435, and they are allocated to each state's proportion of the total national population. Each decade a census determines the official population and congressional seats are

adjusted accordingly. Bills can be introduced in either body of Congress, but only the House can initiate appropriations of funds, the real business of policies.

The Senate is considered the senior body. Senators represent larger constituencies and are elected to six-year terms. They are meant to operate on a broader scale than House members, thinking more of the nation as a whole. Each State has two Senators, so a large state such as Texas has no more Senators than a tiny one like Rhode Island. This was another means of balancing things out. The original small colonies feared dominance by the large ones.

The Senate

The Senate is nominally run by the Vice President of the US. But his (or her) power in the Senate is limited to voting only when there is a 50–50 tie. The majority and minority leaders, elected by their memberships, exert the real power, as do the committees which conduct the detailed analysis and the behind-the- scenes politicking.

When a bill passes majorities of both bodies, it is sent to the President for signature and can then become law. Frequently a bill has been amended by each body in different ways, so it is then referred to a "conference" committee in which Representatives and Senators hammer out the differences and reintroduce the bill.

The Presidency

The Executive power resides in the Presidency. Presidential and Vice Presidential candidates always run as a team, so there is no practical way they could be of different parties. They are the only officials elected by all the people, and are thus presumed to have a mandate to govern along the lines of their campaign programs. While the people vote for a presidential candidate by name, they are in fact voting for a slate of electors pledged to that candidate.

Each state has electoral votes equal to the sum of its two Senators and all its Representatives. This is called the electoral college. The electors vote not in proportion to the popular vote

in their states, but all vote for the candidate receiving a majority. Consequently, Presidential elections focus on closely contested states, especially on the large states. Presidents and Vice-Presidents are limited to four-year terms, and each can be re-elected once for a total of eight years in office.

The President proposes a program of legislation and expects Congress to act upon it favorably. When the same party controls both branches, this can go smoothly.

The President's best-known role is in the for-

ABOVE: the president delivers his annual State of the Union message directly to Congress.

eign policy area, negotiating treaties, and in moments of international tension, as the Commander-in-Chief of the Armed Forces. The Congress, however, must ratify the treaties and has the power to declare war.

The Executive is charged with enforcing laws and implementing legislation. The President appoints members of the Cabinet. They are the leaders of the executive departments such as the Departments of State (the foreign office), Justice, Treasury, Agriculture, Labor, Commerce, and so on.

When Congress passes legislation to the President for enactment, it can be signed into law or vetoed. A veto stands unless the Congress can then muster a two-thirds vote in each house to override it.

The Judiciary

This is the third branch. Members of the Supreme Court, the Appeals Courts, and lower-level federal courts are appointed for life by the President but must be confirmed by the Senate. The courts interpret the Constitution and laws passed by Congress and the President.

A by-product of the split between the parties has been that much legislation emerges from revision and compromise with ambiguous meaning and ends up being adjudicated by the Supreme Court. Since the Constitution and most of its amendments were written and ratified a long time ago, there is always a debate on their proper application in the very different economic, technological, and cultural environment of today.

The Court can invalidate a law by determining that it violates the Constitution. But Congress and the President can usually enact the main parts of such laws by amending them to delete the parts deemed unconstitutional.

There is another *de facto* branch consisting of semi-autonomous regulatory groups, charged with watching over securities markets, foods and drugs, interstate commerce, telecommunications, and other fields. These groups are established by Congressional acts and their leaders are presidential appointees requiring Congressional confirmation.

The American system is complicated and not as efficient as a more authoritarian one might be. It requires much balancing and compromise, and can be frustrating to the citizenry. ❏

ARTS AND ENTERTAINMENT

The choice is wide, embracing a world-class symphony and opera company, clubs, theaters, and, of course, the Smithsonian, whose vast holdings are the city's chief draw

Compared to many of Europe's capitals, Washington was often regarded as a hardship post among diplomats not only because of the insufferable summer heat but also because, until well into the 20th century, it was a cultural backwater. Washington, still mostly mud and malaria until after the Civil War, was a place so lacking of a sense of itself in the broader cultural world that so-called March King John Philip Sousa remained its chief claim to fame long after the US Marine Band conductor died. Unlike some lesser ranked countries, the US has no minister of cultural affairs, no single keeper of the nation's cultural spirit, and such government funds as are available to promote and encourage its cultural identity are usually given grudgingly.

The most notable exception to the unwritten rule that government has little or no place in the arts is the Kennedy Center, that big concrete slab of a building that overhangs Rock Creek Parkway. It may not look like much from the outside but, thanks to President Eisenhower's prodding Congress in the 1950s to establish a national cultural center, it's now a fulcrum of Washington cultural life. Named for the succeeding and fallen president, the Kennedy Center's performance spaces include the Concert Hall, venue for the National Symphony Orchestra, and the Opera House, recently upgraded and an acoustical gem.

Established in 1931, the National Symphony Orchestra was at first disregarded by audiences and critics in favor of the then better known Philadelphia Orchestra whose followers willingly made the three-hour car trip

to hear real music. Since then, the National Symphony Orchestra has risen to world-class status and, under the direction of Leonard Slatkin, its musicianship is now a matter of national pride and draws loyal subscribers.

As for Washington Opera, it too had meager beginnings when it was founded in 1956, but since then, under the direction of no less a talent than famed tenor Placido Domingo, it wins raves for its vibrant stagings of such masterpieces as Verdi's *Il Trovatore* and its willingness to undertake new and inventive work, such as playwright and librettist Romulus Linney's new *Democracy: An American Comedy*, a poke at the political tomfoolery that plagued the post-Civil War Grant administration.

For whatever else it may be, Washington is no longer a wasteland but a cultural rival with a ceaseless schedule of top-notch concert performances, many of them free of charge. Two of the best "freebies" include the Library of Congress's series of vocalists and chamber orchestras that perform in the small but exquisite Coolidge Auditorium, and the National Gallery Orchestra's Sunday evening concerts held in the marbled court of the National Gallery of Art. And don't overlook the armed forces bands, who perform for free on summer evenings at the Capitol, at the Syl-

van Theater near the Washington Monument, and in winter in DAR Constitution Hall, once the city's largest concert space and still, acoustically, one of the best anywhere.

One of the loveliest concert sites is the Wolf Trap Farm Park's Filene Center in Vienna, Virginia, near Dulles Airport. Easiest to access by car, though you can hop Metro and then catch a shuttle bus, this open-air auditorium is set among sweeping lawns. You can picnic while enjoying ballet, musical comedy and jazz and pop performances under the stars.

LEFT: Placido Domingo, the big noise in local opera.
ABOVE: hitting the right notes in Blues Alley.

Jazz, blues and rock 'n' roll

When it comes to jazz and blues, the legendary Blues Alley, just off M Street in Georgetown, is not only the city's best but the nation's oldest jazz supper club. It opened in 1965 in an 18th-century brick warehouse and since then audiences, who number no more than 125 on a packed night, have enjoyed name performers such as Dizzy Gillespie ("Now this is a jazz club," he declared), Charley Bird, Quincy Jones, Wynton Marsalis and Eva Cassidy. Other popular spots include the 9:30 Club on V Street and the Black Cat in Adams Morgan for music that's innovative and, if nothing else, loud. The State Theater in Falls Church, Virginia, accessible by Metro, hosts touring vintage '60s rock and blues bands, and the Birchmere, in Alexandria, Virginia has everything from bluegrass to Judy Collins.

Museums

The Smithsonian is the world's largest museum complex. Besides paintings, sculptures and other cultural artifacts for free viewing, it also offers an on-going reasonably priced series of popular lectures, concerts, performances, classes, and excursions around and beyond the city through its Resident Associates Program which, even if you're only in town for a few days, you can take advantage of by contacting the Smithsonian (tel: 202-356-3030; www.ResidentAssociates.org). Other, smaller museums, such as Dumbarton Oaks, the Phillips Collection, and the Corcoran, one of the oldest museums in the US, boast excellent permanent collections and regularly rotating new exhibits, plus a schedule of musical performances, lectures and demonstrations.

Theaters

It may not be New York, but Washington, with no fewer than two dozen companies, is not lacking for theater. The best include Arena Stage, the Folger, the Studio Theatre, Wooly Mammoth and the Shakespeare Theatre on Seventh Street and the city's newest, offering the bard's works and other classics and drawing name featured performers. You can catch performances of national touring companies, including musicals, comedy acts and one-person shows at the Warner and National theaters, two of the city's old-line venues. ❏

PLACES

A detailed guide to the city and its surroundings, with the principal sites clearly cross-referenced by number to the maps

Driving around Washington, it seems like everybody knows where they're going but me," observed a resident of eight months' standing. In fact, even long-term Washingtonians with a fixed destination often find themselves navigating the city's traffic circles more often than they would like. Frustration is intense because, on a map, getting around the District appears manageable.

Architect Pierre L'Enfant's 1791 design was a masterpiece of city planning. Based on a diamond-shaped grid, with the Capitol as its central point, the city is divided into four quadrants: Northeast, Northwest, Southeast and Southwest. North and South Capitol streets form the border between east and west, while the Mall and East Capitol Street serve as the division between north and south. The quadrants are mirror images of each other: numbered streets run north and south, lettered streets run east and west. Once the alphabet has been used up, east/west streets have two-syllable names: Adams, Bryant, Channing, etc. When these run out, three-syllable names begin: Albemarle, Brandywine, Chesapeake, etc.

Unfortunately, this elegant system is then invaded by rogue elements, like diagonal avenues – named for American states – and other streets, which criss-cross in a disorganized fashion. Contemporary planners have added to the confusion by implementing one-way systems and changes of lanes during rush hours. A simple way around all this is to walk, rather than drive. "Monument Washington" is perfect for pedestrians, although bear in mind that the historic appellation "The City of Magnificent Distances" still applies – things are further away than they look. Fortunately, Washington has more open spaces than almost any other town in America, so finding a place to rest footsore feet, either around the Mall or in areas like Georgetown or Dupont Circle, is rarely a problem.

Neither is finding a Metro stop, even outside the city in nearby Arlington or Falls Church. Beyond the suburbs are western Maryland's green rolling hills. To the east lies the sparkling Chesapeake Bay, good for sailing, and the cities of Baltimore and Annapolis. Virginia has the cool, smoky Blue Ridge Mountains, perfect for hiking and camping, and more Civil War battlefield sites than any other state. ❑

PRECEDING PAGES: the architecture is classical; "the city of white marble."
LEFT: statue of Jefferson in the rotunda of the Jefferson Hotel.

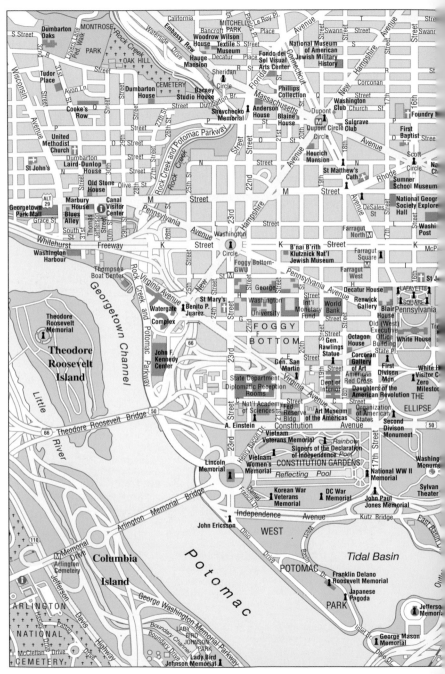

THE WHITE HOUSE

As official residences of world leaders go, this 132-room building is among the less remarkable, and in a city full of gracious mansions it is by no means the most magnificent. It is, however, the most important.

Presidents come and go, but the White House **❶** endures, physical evidence of the founding fathers' intention that the president is first a citizen in service to his country, here temporarily and beyond the need of princely trappings. Oddly enough, the president who foresaw the need for an official residence and who was responsible for seeing to its construction, George Washington, was the only president who did not live here. He died before the house was completed.

Through its history, presidents have chronically complained of its inadequacies and undertaken to improve it, often with mixed results, and while it is stately, it is not an imposing fixture on the landscape. Nor is it so sacred. Once it was burned nearly to the ground, and twice structural engineers have pronounced it beyond the bother of saving and recommended that it be pulled down altogether.

It has even been vandalized. At populist president Andrew Jackson's 1828 inaugural, rowdy celebrants , convinced that the participatory democracy he espoused made the White House quite literally their own, destroyed what furnishings they didn't carry off as souvenirs.

Over the years the "people's house," as it is sometimes viewed,

has become increasingly off limits to the very people to whom it stands as a symbol, owing chiefly to security concerns. East and West Executive avenues, which flank the White House, have been closed for decades. Pennsylvania Avenue in front of the White House, however, is open again after a long closure. It has been spruced up with granite pavers good for strolling, though the house remains off limits. Of course, American democracy is not about a house. It's about an idea, and that

Map on page 61

LEFT: the White House in 1850.
BELOW: George and Laura Bush in the Oval Office.

Until World War II, you could walk right into the White House and shake hands with the president. During his term, Herbert Hoover (1929–33) complained of "wasting a whole hour every day, shaking hands with 1,000 to 1,200 people." Now even a tour is all but impossible.

idea has been the singular force that has shaped the White House into the unique residence that it is for the American presidency.

A sense of history

Because of anti-terrorism precautions, the White House has permitted only limited tours with advance reservations; these are generally available only to American citizens who can arrange them through their congressional representative. While you may not be able to tour it, you can still get an excellent sense of the house and its history if you stop by the **Visitor Center** ❷ at 15th and E Streets, NW in the Department of Commerce building (daily 7.30am–4pm; closed January 1, Thanksgiving Day, December 25; tel: 202-208-1631, or www.whitehouse.gov, or for information regarding special events tel: 202-456-7041). The National Park Service rangers who staff the center are helpful, and in lieu of a tour there are several exhibits, a 30-minute film entitled *Within These Walls*, and a gift shop.

Lines to tour the White House

were traditionally long, much longer than the free 20-minute self-guided tour itself. There were no docents on duty to offer commentary or answer questions – a strange arrangement, considering the history and the stories associated with the house and everything in it.

Fits and starts and fire

The White House, the oldest public building in Washington, was designed by the architect James Hoban, who drew on the Georgian-style manor houses of his native Ireland for inspiration. His plan, for which he was awarded the $500 prize in an open competition, called for an elegant three-story stone structure with a columned portico and an eagle carved into the pediment. Construction began in October 1792, but a lack of funds and skilled stonemasons stalled the project. A year later, at George Washington's request, Hoban redrew his plan, omitting the third floor and reducing the overall dimension as a cost-saving measure. Work began, but at a snail's pace. When the US govern-

BELOW:
19th-century elegance.

ment officially moved from Philadelphia to Washington in November 1800, the house still wasn't finished.

John Adams, the second president, and his wife Abigail were first to take possession of the still incomplete house, grumbling all the while about the slow pace of Southern workmen and the lack of convenience. Thomas Jefferson, who described the presidency as a "splendid misery," followed the grumbling Adamses, expressing displeasure with what he regarded as the mansion's excess. It was, as he wrote, "big enough for two emperors, one Pope, and a grand Lama." Always the architect, Jefferson designed low-terraced pavilions for either side of the house to add much needed utility and to give it a more graceful appearance. During his eight-year tenure he indulged in his other favorite hobby, landscaping, by planting formal gardens and installing a circular carriage drive to service the north entrance.

In August 1814, the house was torched by the British but spared total destruction when a violent thunderstorm suddenly erupted, dousing the flames. James and Dolley Madison, then in residence, moved to the nearby Octogan House, owned by the prominent Tayloe family, and called in Hoban to oversee the restoration. The walls of the White House still stood, but the stone had cracked in the intense heat of the fire followed by the sudden cooling of the rain.

In the two weeks that followed, 32 stonemasons set to work restoring the walls, which Hoban had ordered painted white to cover the charring from the fire and which unofficially gave the house its name. It took another two years to replace the roof. Although most of the rooms were uninhabitable, President James Monroe, who followed Madison, was determined to move in and hold the traditional open house on New Year's Day in 1818, wet paint,

Dolley Madison, (1768–1849), a Quaker, was a 26-year-old widow when she married James Madison, 17 years older. She was known for her social graces and political skills.

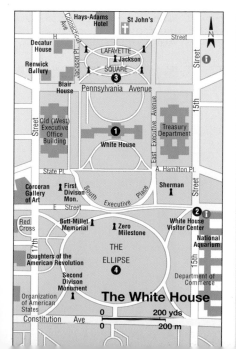

The White House

Modern Conveniences

The original White House had no plumbing, and water for John and Abigail Adams, the first occupants, had to be hauled from half a mile away. Thomas Jefferson erected a cistern in the attic and installed an ingenious system of wooden pipes, which were connected to two water closets. In the 1830s, Andrew Jackson was able to enjoy the White House's first real plumbing system, which offered both hot and cold water delivered in iron pipes. At 340 pounds, William Howard Taft, who arrived at the White House in 1908, presented an entirely different sort of bathroom problem, solved by an a team of ingenious plumbers who fashioned a custom bathtub to fit the hefty president and which was big enough to hold four ordinary sized men.

In the 1840s, James Polk replaced the candles and kerosene lamps with gas. In 1865, Andrew Johnson had a telegraph installed, and in 1870 Rutherford Hayes brought in a telephone and the typewriter. Electricity came with Benjamin Harrison in the 1890s. Harry Truman had the first White House TV set, and Jimmy Carter the first computer.

THE PRESIDENTS WHO LIVED IN THE WHITE HOUSE

(The first president, George Washington, 1789–97, died before it was completed)

John Adams (F)	1797–1801
Thomas Jefferson (D-R)	1801–09
James Madison (D-R)	1809–17
James Monroe (D-R)	1817–25
John Quincy Adams (D-R)	1825–29
Andrew Jackson (D)	1829–37
Martin Van Buren (D)	1837–41
William Henry Harrison (W)	1841
John Tyler (W)	1841–45
James K. Polk (D)	1845–49
Zachary Taylor (W)	1849–50
Millard Fillmore (W)	1850–53
Franklin Pierce (D)	1853–57
James Buchanan (D)	1857–61
Abraham Lincoln (R)	1861–65
Andrew Johnson (R)	1865–69
Ulysses S. Grant (R)	1869–77
Rutherford B. Hayes (R)	1877–81
James A. Garfield (R)	1881
Chester A. Arthur (R)	1881–85
Grover Cleveland (D)	1885–89
Benjamin Harrison (R)	1889–93
Grover Cleveland (D)	1893–97
William McKinley (R)	1897–1901
Theodore Roosevelt (R)	1901–09
William H. Taft (R)	1909–13
Woodrow Wilson (D)	1913–21
Warren G. Harding (R)	1921–23
Calvin Coolidge (R)	1923–29
Herbert C. Hoover (R)	1929–33
Franklin D. Roosevelt (D)	1933–45
Harry S. Truman (D)	1945–53
Dwight D. Eisenhower (R)	1953–61
John F. Kennedy (D)	1961–63
Lyndon B. Johnson (D)	1963–69
Richard M. Nixon (R)	1969–74
Gerald Ford (R)	1974–77
Jimmy Carter (D)	1977–81
Ronald Reagan (R)	1981–89
George Bush (R)	1989–1993
Bill Clinton (D)	1993–2001
George W. Bush (R)	2001–

Parties: D = Democratic; D-R = Democratic-Republican; F = Federalist; R = Republican; W = Whig

wet plaster, and all. That day, 3,000 visitors showed up to admire the restored house which Hoban had rushed to complete, taking shortcuts by using timbers instead of brick in some of the bearing walls, which would cause trouble later.

Home renovations

In 1901, when Theodore Roosevelt and his wife Edith moved in with their six children, they were at once struck by the house's inadequacies. Besides the fact that there were only two bathrooms, the State Dining Room, where the president was expected to entertain guests, was so small that it could hold only six people. To prevent collapse during large receptions, the floors had to be propped up from the cellar. An elevator that had been installed for the president's convenience shot out sparks when it wasn't broken down entirely. A team from the Army Corp of Engineers examined the house and suggested that it be torn down, but Roosevelt insisted on restoration instead and hired the architectural firm of McKim, Meade, and White.

The architects fashioned a new public entrance on the east side, and most importantly, created the West Wing, a presidential working space with a Cabinet Room and the president's private Oval Office, though that wouldn't be completed until President Taft's time.

Besides the addition of the third floor, part of Hoban's original plan and finally installed during the Coolidge administration, little was done to maintain the house over the next 40 years. Investigations into its structural integrity during Harry Truman's presidency revealed that it was again on the verge of collapse. The point was rather dramatically brought home in 1948 when the leg of a piano in daughter Margaret Truman's room broke through two floorboards and knocked the plaster down in the family dining room below. The engineers reported that the exterior walls could be salvaged (though as Truman put it, they were "standing up purely from habit"), but the house itself had to be gutted.

The Trumans moved across the street into Blair House, while architect Lorenzo S. Winslow and his team set to work underpinning the original stone walls with concrete and erecting new steel framing at a cost of $6 million. They completely built out the walls, floors, and ceilings of each room, and added Truman's famous south portico balcony.

Later, the interior of the White House underwent substantial redecoration, starting with the efforts of Jacqueline Kennedy, who formed a Fine Arts Committee to restore the rooms to their original style and grandeur. The project institutionalized the idea of the White House as a place to reflect American history through furnishings, and renewed the sense of the White House as a house of history.

The grounds

Thanks to a permanent crew of arborists, landscape architects and gardeners, the White House grounds are a showcase of 500 trees, 4,000 flowering shrubs, and 12 acres of impeccably green lawn. In 1877, Rutherford B. Hayes began the still surviving tradition of each president

Map on page 61

Theodore Roosevelt, in 1902, was the first president to ride in a car, no doubt cruising DC's streets unimpeded. Not so today. Among its other distinctions, DC ranks second behind Los Angeles as having the nation's worst traffic.

LEFT: Ulysses S. Grant, president 1869–77.
BELOW: demonstration of the Wright Type B airplane in 1911.

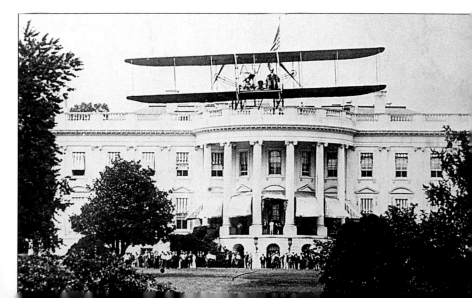

Although the Oval Office has starred in many movies, one of the most accurate depictions was in "The West Wing" TV series, filmed in Burbank, California. The producers even ordered fabric for the set's chairs from the firm that supplies the real White House. One inaccuracy was the absence of the bullet-proof glass shields that stand between the windows and the president's desk – they would be too reflective for the powerful TV lights.

RIGHT: view of the White House from Lafayette Park.

ceremonially planting a tree on the grounds.

The park in front of the White House, **Lafayette Square** ❸, where office workers enjoy their lunches in good weather and protestors routinely congregate for their marches, was originally part of the White House grounds until Pennsylvania Avenue was cut through in 1822. For much of the 19th century the **south grounds** were open to the public and served as a park for picnickers.

Flanking the White House, **East Executive Avenue** was added in 1866 and **West Executive Avenue** in 1871, though for security reasons both are now closed. As part of the city's public works project during the 1870s, the canal to the south, basically an open sewer, was covered over and the **Ellipse** ❹ was installed. It's here every year that the president presides over the lighting of the National Christmas Tree.

The famous **Rose Garden** adjacent to the Oval Office was originally planted on the White House grounds by Woodrow Wilson's wife Ellen in 1913 and was redesigned by

Jackie Kennedy. Later, Lady Bird Johnson installed a companion garden complete with reflecting pool and named it the **Jacqueline Kennedy Garden**.

Public spaces

Five public rooms are on show when tours are available: the **East Room**, the **Green Room**, the **Blue Room**, the **Red Room** and the **State Dining Room**, with the rest of the house comprised of private family rooms and offices which have always been off-limits. Tours enter through the **East Wing** and into the **Ground Floor Corridor** and past the **Library** where a **Gilbert Stuart** portrait of George Washington, painted about 1805, hangs over the fireplace.

Across the hall from the Library is the **Vermeil Room**, sometimes called the **Gold Room**, and used as a ladies' sitting room during formal occasions. The **China Room** and the **Diplomatic Reception Room**, where foreign dignitaries are officially received and where Franklin Roosevelt delivered his "fireside chats" to the nation during World

First Pets

Chickens, cows and pigs roamed the White House grounds well into the 20th century, the last barnyard animal being William Howard Taft's cow Pauline, who left when the president vacated the White House in 1913. Herbert Hoover's son Allan had a pair of alligators, which he tried but often failed to keep contained in a bathtub. Among Secret Service agents who guarded him, Franklin Roosevelt's faithful Scottie dog Fala was also known as The Informer. Whenever the president stumped the country by train, Fala, who had to be walked, was first off the train as soon as it stopped, thereby confirming to all that the president was on board. The Kennedy menagerie was probably the largest and included Pushinka, a pup of the Russian space dog Strelka given as a gift by Soviet leader Nikita Kruschchev, plus hamsters, canaries, lovebirds, ducks, a cat, a Welsh terrier, a police dog, and a pair of ponies known as Leprechaun and Macaroni. Perhaps the most unusual pets were a pair of tiny dogs whose breed was known as Sleeve that Commodore Matthew Perry brought back from the Orient and gave to President Franklin Pierce. The tiny dogs could fit comfortably in a coffee cup saucer.

War II, are also off this corridor which features several official portraits of recent First Ladies. A Sheraton-style breakfront made in Baltimore around 1800 holds several pieces of official White House china, including a plate George Washington used, and some pieces of the service used by Lincoln.

The East Room

The gleaming white and gold **East Room** reflects the kind of elegance you'd expect considering the caliber of "public" that gathers here – the monarchs, the heads of state, the celebrities and politicians. Designed originally as a Public Audience Room, it normally contains little furniture and is used for the entertainments that follow state dinners and formal receptions.

The room's centerpiece is the **Steinway grand piano** supported by gilded eagles. The full-length Gilbert Stuart portrait of Washington that hangs here, the only object original to the White House, was rescued by Dolley Madison when the British set fire to the mansion *(see page 61)*. In this all-purpose room, seven presidents have lain in state, including Lincoln and Kennedy; two presidential daughters, Alice Roosevelt and Lynda Bird Johnson, were married; and Richard Nixon delivered his resignation speech in 1974.

In the 1880s President Chester Arthur called on the famed New York designer Louis Tiffany to completely redecorate not only this room, which was soon covered in velvet swags and fringe and outfitted with an ornate tin ceiling, but all the others as well. The Victorian-era transformation was so heavy-handed that afterward the White House was rather snidely referred to as the "steamboat palace" until Teddy Roosevelt arrived. He swept away all the heavy adornments and, moving from the sublime to the ridiculous, turned this room into a sort of gymnasium. In the evenings, wrestling matches were held here for the president's entertainment, and during the day the Roosevelt children circled the perimeter in their roller skates.

During World War II, a secret bunker was constructed for the president beneath the White House. Bullet-proof glass and black-out curtains were installed in the Oval Office. The city's great monuments were left unlit. There was even a plan to paint the Capitol dome black in order to protect it from air attack.

BELOW:
the East Room.

In December 1941 Winston Churchill secretly arrived at the White House to confer with the then president, Franklin Roosevelt. He stayed 24 days, spending much of that time, to the distress of Mrs. Roosevelt and the staff, in the buff, sipping brandy and filling the house with cigar smoke. After that, presidential visitors were put up across the street at Blair House, which remains the official guest house.

RIGHT: the Blue Room

The Green Room

Although it too has served many purposes, the **Green Room** was originally designed as a dining room. Thomas Jefferson is thought to have been first to choose the color scheme, covering the floor with a then stylish green-painted cloth in lieu of carpeting. It's full of early 19th-century furniture, acquired during the Coolidge administration and fashioned by the New York Scottish-born cabinet maker Duncan Fyfe, including a pair of rare mahogany work tables ingeniously designed with hidden compartments. The present green silk wall coverings were chosen by Jacqueline Kennedy and installed by Pat Nixon.

The Blue Room

The **Blue Room** is a small, oval-shaped chamber where the President and First Lady often receive visitors. Its elliptical shape is owing to George Washington's preference for having his visitors standing in a semi-circle around him, although he never had the privilege of greeting them here

since the White House was not completed until after his death.

With the identically shaped Yellow Room above and the Diplomatic Reception Room below, it forms the most elegant feature of original architect James Hoban's plan. Decorated in the Empire style and in a strikingly blue-and-gold color scheme, this is where the First Family usually has a Christmas tree. An 1800 portrait by Rembrandt Peale of Thomas Jefferson hangs in this room along with John Trumbull's portrait of John Adams.

The Red Room

The **Red Room** has always been the province of the first ladies, who entertain their guests here. During Dolley Madison's day, the room was the site of her famous Wednesday night receptions and musicals, which featured exquisite French food, fine wines, and entertainment. No invitation was required and Dolley, a Quaker by upbringing but a gregarious socialite by nature, encouraged anyone in Washington with any sort of talent to attend.

The **State Dining Room**, whose 1902 wood paneling was painted a pale green under President Truman's incumbency, is now the antique ivory color selected by Jacqueline Kennedy to complement the gold curtains and gold chandeliers. The room originally could hold no more than six, but during the 1902 renovations during Teddy Roosevelt's administration it was expanded to allow for seating 140. TR's roughrider tastes dictated that the room be decorated with his big-game trophies, but it has since been elegantly transformed.

Private rooms

Out of bounds to the public are nine rooms on the second floor, the **Yellow Oval Room**, the **Treaty Room**, the **Queen's Bedroom**, the family bedrooms, the **President's Dining Room,** the family's **West Sitting Hall**, and the one that sparks the most interest, the **Lincoln Bedroom**. Between 1830 and 1902 this room served as either an office or a cabinet meeting room, but never as Lincoln's bedroom. Lincoln used it as an office, heaping his newspapers, mail and paperwork on the floor and tacking to the walls the maps detailing Civil War troop movements. This is where he signed the Emancipation Proclamation on New Year's Day 1863, which officially, if not practically, ended slavery.

When the second floor offices were moved to the West Wing during the Roosevelt renovation, this room became a private family room. In the Truman years, Lincoln's imposing rosewood bed, more than 8 ft long and 6 ft wide (2.4 by 1.8 meters) to accommodate the tall Lincoln, was moved here. Mrs Lincoln bought the bed in 1861, but Lincoln never slept in it.

The West Wing is also closed to the public. Here is where the President's **Oval Office** lies, his desk made of the timbers from *HMS Resolute*. Also here are the **Cabinet Room**, the **Appointments Lobby** and the **Roosevelt Room**, where staff conferences take place and which was known during Franklin Roosevelt's time as the Fish Room because of the aquarium it contained. ❑

Map on page 61

TIP

if you're in town in early December, it's worth catching the official lighting of the National Christmas Tree on the Ellipse, a public event hosted by the vice president's wife. You might then keep in the spirit by having dinner at 1789 (see page 145) in Georgetown, where the lavish decorations are a festive tradition.

BELOW:
the State Dining Room.

THE MALL EAST

City planner Pierre L'Enfant envisioned the Mall as a grand commerical and residential central boulevard. What the city ended up with was a great, grassy, pebble-pathed pedestrian strip lined on both sides with world-class museums.

Until ground was broken in 1848 for the Washington Monument, and then for the Smithsonian castle the following year, the Mall, which today stretches between 3rd and 14th streets, sat largely undeveloped. Then in 1850 landscape architect Andrew Jackson Downing was commissioned to transform L'Enfant's plan for a grand avenue into a "public museum of living trees and shrubs." But before he could execute his plans he died in a steamboat explosion, thus further delaying plans for the Mall. The next half century saw the great, grassy strip used as a cow pasture before it deteriorated into an unsightly collection of ramshackle houses and business establishments, a railroad station on the present site of the National Gallery of Art its most prominent feature.

The 1901 plan

The colossal green expanse you see today, which is flanked by two narrow drives named for presidents Madison and Jefferson, bears the mark of the McMillan Commission, established in 1901 to translate L'Enfant's ideas into a new city plan. The railroad was moved to the present site of Union Station, building restrictions went into effect, and land was set aside for the future Lin-

coln Memorial. The Mall had been cleared, but little else was done to improve it for another half-century, until after World War II when museum building began in earnest.

The Mall has many moods, determined by the light, by the time of day, and by the seasons. When empty it is a reflective space where you can appreciate the scale and the grandeur of the monuments, and the precision of the planner. Best known as the front yard of the Smithsonian museums and the National Gallery,

Map: pages 70–71

LEFT: early flying machine at the National Air and Space Museum.
BELOW: Indian puppeteer at the Smithsonian's Folk Art Festival.

TIP

Opening times: The Smithsonian museums and galleries are open every day except December 25, from 10am to 5.30pm. The Castle's hours are 9am–5.30pm.
Tel: 202-357-2700 or visit www.si.edu for information about special exhibits and tours.

BELOW: the Smithsonian's "Castle."

it also serves as a giant jogging track and a softball field for congressional leagues. Frequently the setting for concerts, festivals, gatherings, and all manner of happenings, it is also the traditional rallying point for protest marches and demonstrations, especially during the 1960s. Among the first protestors to gather here were women suffragists and Bonus marchers, veterans of World War I demanding payment of their bonuses.

Among the major events staged here is the annual Smithsonian Folklife Festival, held from late June through the July 4th holiday, which transforms the Mall into a sizzling circus of smells, tastes, sights and sounds from the US and cultures farther afield. If you don't mind picnicking blanket-to-blanket with the crowds, this is the place to be on the Fourth of July, where the gala celebration features a free concert by the National Symphony Orchestra and, of course, a fireworks extravaganza.

Museums on the Mall

Silhouetted in late afternoon light, the sleek obelisk of the Washington Monument contrasts dramatically with the Norman-style towers of the **Smithsonian Institution Building**, aptly nicknamed **the Castle ❶**. James Renwick, Jr, architect of the Renwick Gallery and New York's St Patrick's Cathedral, designed this red sandstone structure, which was completed in 1855 – the Smithsonian Institution's first building. Today it holds administrative offices and the Woodrow Wilson International Center for Scholars, as well as an **information center**.

To get your bearings, stop first at the Castle, which opens at 9am (an hour before the museums). It has maps, leaflets, interactive screens, a 20-minute orientation film, and sev-

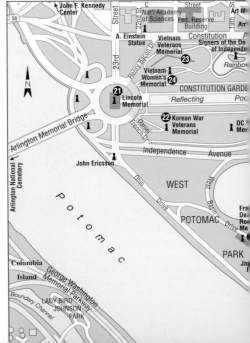

eral friendly docents to help you decide what to see. It also holds the crypt containing the body of Smithsonian founder James Smithson *(see page 74)*. All museums and attractions on the Mall are free, except for the IMAX features and the planetarium in the Air and Space Museum, and the IMAX and Immersion Theaters in the Natural History Museum.

The elegant Florentine Renaissance palace nearby – small-scale compared to the other Mall-side monoliths – is the **Freer Gallery of Art** ❷. The Smithsonian's first art museum, opened in 1923, is an intimate collection of mainly Asian art donated by a self-made Detroit industrialist and art connoisseur, Charles Lang Freer. Freer's gift included his collection of etchings, plus the only collaborative assemblage of works by his friend, the painter James McNeill Whistler. Freer retired from railroad-car man-

ufacturing when he was 45, having already made his fortune, and by his death in 1919 had bequeathed 9,000 works to the Smithsonian. Its Asian collection has grown to over 27,000 pieces and includes ornamental objects from the Ming and Quing dynasties, plus Chinese jades and lacquerware dating from 3500BC, Korean ceramics, and fine works of Japanese calligraphy.

The American collection contains several works by Whistler, including the impressive **Harmony in Blue and Gold: The Peacock Room**, the artist's only existing interior design which had been commissioned by an English shipping tycoon to show off his collection of Chinese porcelains. Intricate and luminescent paintings of peacocks embellish every surface, from walls to ceilings. In 1904, Freer bought the room and its contents from a London dealer and shipped it to his

Map below

The Freer gallery contains works by Charles L. Freer's friend James Abbott McNeill Whistler (1834–1903). A renowned wit, critic, dandy and eccentric as well as a painter, Whistler is best remembered today for the 1872 portrait of his mother which hangs in the Louvre in Paris. His etchings and lithography were acclaimed.

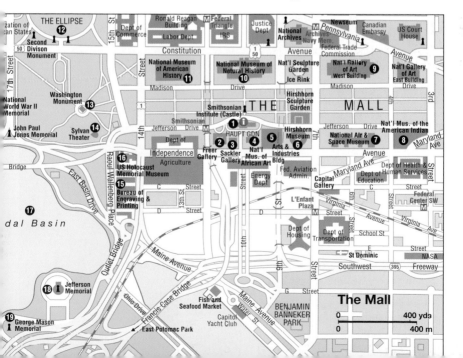

The Mall

0   400 yds

0   400 m

The Arthur M. Sackler Gallery of Asian Art.

RIGHT: Asian art in the Sackler Gallery of the Smithsonian.

home in Detroit before donating it to the Smithsonian. In 1988 the museum was renovated and includes an underground exhibit area that permits passage through to the Sackler Gallery.

Asian and African art

Between the Freer and the Castle, a copper-domed kiosk marks the entrance to the **S. Dillon Ripley Center**, part of the quadrangle complex on Independence Avenue opened in 1987, which also includes the **Arthur M. Sackler Gallery**, the **National Museum of African Art**, and the **Enid A. Haupt Garden**.

The garden itself (open daily at 7am, closing times determined by the season) is a magical mosaic of decorative sub-gardens, whose themes clearly reflect those of the surrounding museums. In fact, the whole complex is a marvelous harmony of form: the Sackler's diamond motif complements the spires of the Arts and Industries Building, while the African's circles relate to the Freer's arches.

The Ripley Center, which con-

tains classrooms and offices, is named for S. Dillon Ripley, secretary of the Smithsonian between 1964 and 1984. During that time New York psychiatrist and researcher Dr Arthur M. Sackler made a generous pledge of his Asian artifacts, but Ripley lacked a suitable space for them. Ripley was also struggling with the problem of what to do with the African collection. Begun privately in 1964, then given to the institution in 1979, the Smithsonian's collection of African art was rapidly outgrowing its space in a former home of abolitionist and educator Frederick Douglass on Captiol Hill. The solution to both problems turned out to be this innovative underground complex linking the two museums.

While the descent to the subterranean galleries of the Sackler and the African is akin to entering a mausoleum, the galleries are warm and the collections – each of which runs the gamut from ancient to contemporary – are often remarkable.

Aside from the art, you can admire the galleries' remarkable feat

Survival Tips for Museums

The Mall is more than a mile long and is lined with millions of square feet of museum space, so the essential advice is: wear comfortable shoes. There's too much to see in one visit, so set your preferences by checking in first at the Castle, Smithsonian's "information central", or by visiting the website at www.si.edu.

Driving to the Mall is not recommended. Parking is timed and extremely limited, and with two nearby Metro stops, there's no need for a car. The Smithsonian station is on the Orange and Blue lines and will let you off near the center of the Mall. The L'Enfant Plaza station, near Independence Avenue, is a major transfer point on the Green, Yellow, Orange, and Blue Lines. Anti-terrorist security has become much tighter. You can expect your bags to be searched at the entrance of every museum.

Try to visit in the fall and winter when there are fewer crowds. If you must come during the summer, be aware that Washington's summers are brutally hot and dress accordingly. As for restroom facilities, they're plentiful, easily accessible, and clean.

of engineering. Ninety-six percent of the quadrangle is below ground to a depth of 57 ft (17 meters), which required waterproofing the entire structure and designing a special roof to support the 4-acre (1.6-hectare) garden above – much of which is deliberately landscaped to conceal structural elements below. As if that weren't enough, the architect also had to figure out how to preserve a century-old linden tree.

Highlights from the **Sackler Gallery ❸** include ritual bronze and jade objects, more than 450 of them dating from about 3000BC. Also on display are ancient metalwork vessels and ornaments from Iran and Turkey. The **National Museum of African Art ❹** has more than 7,000 items, mostly of the traditional arts of the peoples of sub-Sahara. Many of the objects – masks used in rites of passage, fertility figures, medicinal objects and tools of divination, all of which are made of bone, fiber and other organic materials – are religious in nature. Standouts of the collection include objects from the kingdom of Benin.

The nation's attic

The Philadelphia Centennial of 1876, which celebrated the Industrial Revolution, lives on inside the **Arts and Industries Building ❺** – the cheerful Victorian structure flanking the quad's east side. When this 19th-century World's Fair closed, some 40 freight-car loads of leftover international exhibits were shipped to the Smithsonian, prompting the Institution to build the National Museum, as it was then called, to store all of the items – an episode which earned the Smithsonian its enduring reputation as "the nation's attic."

Finished in 1881, the exposition-style building was the most modern museum in the country. Every item displayed in its dizzyingly busy interior was either exhibited at the Expo or produced during that era, including furniture, jewelry, and even horse-drawn carriages. The museum shop is good for inexpensive Victorian-repro gifts and, in keeping with the mood, an old-fashioned carousel still turns and grinds on the Mall outside the museum's

Map: pages 70–71

What is now the Enid A. Haupt Garden was the site of the city's first zoo. Begun in 1887, it featured animals retrieved from the American West, including mule deer, prairie dogs and lynx.

BELOW: the Arts and Industries building – "the nation's attic."

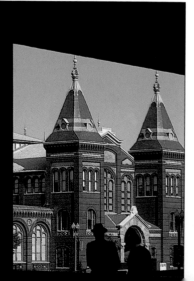

James Smithson

No one knows why, exactly, an independently wealthy Englishman, James Smithson, left his fortune to the US government, although resentment probably had something to do with it. Smithson, originally named James Lewis Macie, was born out of wedlock in 1765 to Elizabeth Keate Macie and Hugh Percy, the newly enobled Duke of Northumberland. As a student at Oxford, Smithson distinguished himself by publishing scholarly scientific papers and discovering a carbonate of the mineral zinc. In 1800, he inherited his mother's fortune, and in 1806 legally adopted his father's original surname of Smithson.

Illegitimacy precluded his rising through the ranks of English aristocracy. His plan was to leave his money to his nephew Henry James Hungerford, but only if Hungerford produced heirs. When Hungerford died childless, Smithson rewrote his will. He left his fortune of $500,000 to the United States, which he had never visited, "to found at Washington, under the name of the Smithsonian Institution, an establishment for the increase and diffusion of knowledge." Smithson, it seemed, was determined to make sure that, despite his beginnings, his name lived "in the memory of men, when the titles of the Northumberlands are extinct and forgotten." He died in 1829 and nine years later, after some legal wrangling during which his relations contested the will, 105 bags of gold coins were shipped across the Atlantic to the Philadelphia Mint.

For the next eight years, despite Smithson's clear stipulations, Congress argued over what to do with the money. Finally, in 1846, President James Polk signed the bill that established the Smithsonian Institution.

Congress mandated that the Smithsonian be governed by a board of regents and that the new institution be comprised of a library, a museum and an art gallery. As its first secretary, the board elected Joseph Henry, a physicist from Princeton.

Between 1846 and 1878 Henry devoted his energies to the "increase of knowledge," shaping the Smithsonian into a research institution. The second secretary, Spencer Fullerton Baird, changed course, moving away from research to supervise the new National Museum Building, now the Arts and Industries Building, and putting his efforts toward increasing the institution's collections.

As the new nation expanded westward, the Smithsonian proved to be an ideal repository for such items as American-Indian artifacts and recently discovered plants. A large donation came from the US Exploring Expedition of 1838–42. Led by Lt Charles Wilkes, the group sailed around the world under orders from the US government to map uncharted lands, and study and collect animals and plants. During their four-year voyage they covered 87,000 miles (140,000 km), mapping 1,500 miles (2,400 km) of uncharted Antarctic coastline. The thousands of rare items given to the Smithsonian included an armadillo from South America, a Hawaiian human-hair necklace, and collections of rare gems, rocks, minerals, and tropical plants.

The Smithsonian's "pack rat" mentality lives on. It is comprised of 16 museums, 9 of which are on the Mall, and has in its holdings some 140 million objects. ❑

LEFT: James Smithson, who never visited the US.

entrance just as it has since 1940. Children enjoy this museum, especially the Discovery Theater, which has live educational performances.

Modern art

The mood next door at the **Hirshhorn Museum and Sculpture Garden ❻** is quite different. This contemporary museum-in-the-round has been aptly described by E. J. Applewhite, author of the well-regarded *Washington Itself* (1981), as a concrete doughnut in a walled garden. In summer, there is an outdoor café among the bevy of enormous abstract sculptures.

It was the wish of Latvian immigrant and self-made millionaire Joseph Hirshhorn to donate his entire collection of 4,000 paintings and 2,000 sculptures – notable both for its size and its variety of late 19th- and 20th-century art – to the country that had served him so well. The bequest, twice as large as the collection amassed in 50 years by New York's Museum of Modern Art, made the Hirshhorn an instant treasure, long before it even had walls.

Several other countries tried to entice Hirshhorn to leave his collection to them, but in the mid-1960s Secretary Ripley with assistance from President Lyndon Johnson, who had a reputation for never taking no for an answer, convinced the Wall Street broker and uranium magnate that Washington, DC was the only place worth considering.

Paintings are arranged chronologically top to bottom beginning with the works of Edward Hopper, Georgia O'Keeffe, Mark Rothko, and Willem de Kooning among others. Late 20th-century artists such as Andy Warhol and Jasper Johns are featured on the bottom floor. The circular galleries along the circumference of the second and third floors display small sculptural works by such artists as Henri Matisse and Pablo Picasso.

Outside in the fountained plaza there are works by Alexander Calder and Claes Oldenburg. And it's worth visiting the landscaped, sunken sculpture garden (open 7.30am to dusk), which has on display Auguste Rodin's famous *Burghers of Calais*.

Map:
pages
70–71

TIP

The Hirshhorn runs occasional free film shows – often short films and documentaries on art and artists. Film makers and directors are often invited along to discuss their work. For details, tel: 202-357-2700 or visit the website www.hirshhorn.si.edu

BELOW: Juan Munoz's bronze *Conversation Piece* sculptures on the Hirshhorn's lawns.

Yesteryear's flight at the National Air and Space Museum.

BELOW AND RIGHT: milestones of flight at the Air and Space Museum.

Air and Space

The **National Air and Space Museum** ❼ (tel: 202-357-1400 to schedule a tour, or visit www.nasm.edu) next door is the world's most popular museum, drawing 10 million visitors a year. Although the experts who designed the three-block-long glass and marble building lacked museum experience, it only takes a glance around the main exhibit hall at the Mall entrance to realize that the concept, like the 90-ft (27-meter) tall hangar-like structure, not only works – it soars. Suspended from the ceiling are such air-age stars as the Wright brothers' *Flyer*, Lindbergh's *Spirit of St Louis*, and the *Apollo 11* space craft.

And that's just the beginning. There are 23 galleries here, a theater, a planetarium, a museum store (well stocked with puzzles, games, kites, and "space food" for children), and a research library which you can access by prior appointment. The information desk offers a detailed guide.

The Smithsonian has always had an interest in flight. In 1861, Joseph Henry, the institution's first secretary, was involved with balloon experiments that led Lincoln to use them for military purposes during the Civil War. The institution's third secretary, Samuel Pierpont Langley, a renowned astronomer and inventor, was deeply involved in the theory of flight when he joined in 1887. In 1946 Congress established a National Air Museum, and in 1976 the Air and Space museum opened in time for the bicentennial celebrations.

Perhaps the most popular stop is the **Lockheed Martin IMAX Theater** (tel: 202-357-1686; admission fee), to see the special film presentations, especially the perennial favorite "To Fly." The screen is 70 ft wide and 50 ft high (21 by 15 meters) and the sensation is close to reality as you soar above the treetops and look out across the earth's landscape from the gondola of a hot air balloon.

The Albert Einstein Planetarium (tel: 202-357-1686; admission fee) is equipped with a Zeiss VI projector to create a regular schedule of starry shows beamed on an over-

head dome. In the **Golden Age of Flight** gallery you'll see the history of aviation between the two world wars. In the **World War II Aviation** gallery you can see a Messerschmitt Bf 109, a Supermarine Spitfire, and a North American P-51D Mustang, among others.

Space Hall has the infamous V-2 rocket, a model of the Columbia Space Shuttle, and a replica of the Hubble Space Telescope. **The Pioneers of Flight** gallery features several planes that made historic flights, including the Wright EX Vin Fiz (so named for the sponsor's grape drink). Galbraith Perry Rodgers made the first coast-to-coast flight in this plane between September 17 and November 5, 1911, covering 4,300 miles (6,900 km) at an average speed of 52 mph (84 km/h).

Take the shuttle bus ($7 per person, round trip) from the museum's Mall entrance to the new **Steven F. Udvar-Hazy Center** near Dulles Airport in Virginia *(see page 187)*. Named after the benefactor who donated $66 million to help build it, the collection, laid wingtip-to-wingtip inside an enormous airplane hanger, includes the thin, sleek Blackbird, the world's fastest jet; the *Enola Gay*, whose bomb bay released the atomic bomb that helped end World War II; the tiny aerobatic stunt plane known as the Little Stinker; plus more than 300 other airplanes, helicopters, space craft and assorted flying machines too big to fit in the main Air and Space Museum.

American Indian Museum

Although Air and Space claims to be the world's most visited museum, it is being challenged by a new next-door neighbor, the **National Museum of the American Indian ❽** *(for ticket details, see margin tip on next page)*. Distinctively curvilinear and domed, the limestone-faced building borrows its design from the rocky topography of those lands native to some of the Western hemisphere's indigenous people to help prepare you for the museum's rich and beautiful world. The building faces east toward the rising sun, in keeping with the tradition of many native peoples and, a bit ironically, lines up perfectly with the dome of the US Capitol, the site of 200-plus years of political maneuvering that all but eliminated native cultures and legislated away from the natives so much of their land.

The forests, wetlands, meadows and rocks that formed so much of the natives' habitat are represented here in a work-in-progress landscaping scheme that covers much of the site. It features 40 "grandfather rocks" or boulders quarried in Quebec and blessed by the Montagnais First Nations of Quebec before being installed on the grounds to welcome and remind visitors of the native people's relationship with the earth and, despite all, their staying power.

The centerpiece of the museum's interior is the Potomac rotunda, so called for the tribe that once occu-

Map: pages 70–71

The National Museum of the American Indian.

BELOW: ceremonial garb at the National Museum of the American Indian.

TIP

Like other Smithsonian museums, the **National Museum of the American Indian** is open daily 10am to 5.30pm. Admission is free, but timed tickets are required. First-come first-served same-day passes are available at the east entrance. Advance tickets are available by phone at 1-866-400-6624, www.american indian.si.edu or www.tickets.com (although these tickets incur a service charge).

BELOW:
traditional Native American costume.

upied what is now Washington, DC. It soars 120 ft (37 meters) to a sky-light. The rotunda's floor, fashioned from red granite and marked with the motifs of the solstices and equinoxes, serves as a gathering spot and central staging area for demonstrations of crafts, native dancing and other ceremonial per-formances. The museum is not sim-ply a repository of artifacts, but a place where native culture is kept alive, where its objects and ways "come out from under the glass," as the museum's director, W. Richard West, a member of the Southern Cheyenne, put it.

As for the artifacts themselves, there are more than 800,000 of them, plus 125,000 photographs, formerly the collection of engineer and investment banker George Gus-tav Heye, whose namesake Indian museum is in New York.

Three permanent exhibits – Our People, Our Lives, Our Universe – contain more than 3,500 objects from Heye's collection and include the artifacts of 24 native tribes. There's everything from masks, feather bonnets and other ceremo-nial dress to ceramics, weavings and textiles, totem poles, and works of gold and other metals. The museum showcases the past with its collec-tion of native ivory carvings, bead-work, and hunting implements, and also displays contemporary sculp-tures and works on paper. The per-manent exhibits are augmented with a series of changing displays in other smaller galleries.

There are two well-stocked gift shops, plus a café called Mitsitam, a word borrowed from the Piscataway and Delaware peoples meaning – what else? – "let's eat!"

The National Gallery

Cross the east end of the Mall, which is dominated by the imposing edifice of the Capitol, to Madison Drive and you will run into the West and East Buildings of the **National Gallery of Art** ❾ (Mon–Sat, 10am–5pm; Sun 11am–6pm; closed Dec 25 and Jan 1; tel: 202-737-4215 or visit www.nga.gov).

Incongruous as they seem side by side – the one neoclassical, the other

starkly contemporary – these structures complement one another architecturally as well as artistically. Although the National Gallery is run by the federal government, it relies exclusively on private and corporate contributions for acquisitions and is not part of the Smithsonian.

The seed for a national gallery was planted by the industrialist and Treasury secretary Andrew W. Mellon, who built his collection of 121 Old Masters, including 21 paintings purchased from Russia's Hermitage Museum, with the idea that he would eventually give the collection away. Following Mellon's lead, 1,300 donors have so far given their treasures to the National Gallery since its doors officially opened in 1941.

The esteemed John Russell Pope was commissioned as architect for the **West Building**. Its dome happens to look distinctly like that crowning the Jefferson Memorial, which Pope also designed. Being a traditionalist, Pope chose a classical design – firstly, because official Washington was classical, and secondly, because he believed that it conveyed the appropriate image for a serious art gallery.

Start your visit in the art information room where you can find a listing of current exhibits, lectures, concerts, and special events. Here you'll also find the **Micro Gallery** with its touch-screen monitors to guide you through the museum and allow you to research artists and locate more than 1,700 works in the collection.

From there, you can proceed to the rotunda with its marble columns and fountain centerpiece and then into the the sculpture halls. The **East Sculpture Hall** displays classically inspired marble works while the **West Sculpture Hall** houses works in bronze. Each Hall ends in a garden court, and in the **West Garden Court** on Sunday evenings from October through June you can attend a free concert performed by one of Washington's most distinguished string orchestras (tel: 202-842-6941 or visit www.nga.gov for a listing of concerts).

As for the galleries themselves, the National Gallery has distin-

Detail from Robert Cole's "Voyage of Life – Old Age" in the National Gallery.

BELOW:
garden court at the National Gallery of Art.

The National Gallery of Art's central atrium in spring.

BELOW: intimations of Egypt at the East Building of the National Gallery of Art.

guished itself as a repository of the paintings that plot the evolution of art in the West from the late Middle Ages through the early 20th century. Among the 90 or so galleries, 34 are dedicated to the Italian painters alone. The Dutch and Flemish masters, including Rembrandt and Vermeer, are also represented here, along with several galleries of French and British painters including Turner and Hogarth, and of course the American painters who include Winslow Homer and John Singleton Copley.

In 2002 the Gallery reopened its much anticipated and renovated ground floor **Sculpture Galleries** with 22 oak-floored and Doric-columned rooms displaying 800 sculptures. The Degas display, which includes four versions of his *Little Dancer Aged Fourteen*, is perhaps the collection's highlight and is the largest group of his sculptures to be seen anywhere.

An underground concourse with a moving walkway, a museum shop, a café, and the Mall's only espresso bar, links the West with the **East Building**. When Mellon stipulated that the area to the east of the gallery be reserved for future expansion, the challenge of designing a structure for this odd, trapezoidal lot fell to the creative master architect, I.M. Pei.

He resolved the problem by slicing the trapezoid diagonally and creating two interlocking, symmetrical triangles. He further balanced the site by lining up the central axis of the West Building with the midpoint of the triangular base forming the main block of the East. You don't have to be a mathematician to appreciate this bold and luminous building-as-sculpture, mercurial as the light that plays across its blade-sharp edges and planes.

Pei's brilliant use of triangular geometry infuses the interior with a sense of movement. Open balconies and bridges sweep across the atrium, decried by critics as "wasted space" or Pei-ian self-indulgence. The undeniably dramatic museum exhibits all manner of 20th-century art, from Henry Moore's *Knife Edge Mirror Two Piece* sculpture, displayed outside, to the huge red,

black, and blue mobile by Alexander Calder specially commissioned for the musuem and dominating the low-ceilinged lobby.

There are five floors of European and American masters of the 20th century, including Wassily Kandinsky, Pablo Picasso, and Joan Miró. The ground-floor galleries feature rotating exhibits, the mezzanine galleries hold the larger traveling exhibits, and the concourse galleries are home to the late 20th-century Americans including Robert Motherwell, Andy Warhol, and Roy Lichtenstein.

For more of the gallery's highlights, see the feature on pages 84–85.

Natural History

As you walk west, be sure to pass through the **Sculpture Garden,** which faces the National Archives on Constitution Avenue and features two dozen works from the National Gallery's collection in a peaceful setting of winding paths and flowerbeds. The pool is used as an ice-skating rink in winter (Mon–Thurs, 10am–11pm; Fri–Sat, 10am–

midnight; Sun, 11am–9pm; admission fee) and offers a respite in summer from the heat and crowds.

The **National Museum of Natural History** , subtitled the **National Museum of Man**, is a hulk of a building, and was dubbed the "new" National Museum when it opened in 1910. Be forewarned that it is today one of the more popular museums on the Mall, a fact immediately apparent if you venture into the four-story-high rotunda on a typical summer day. As you wander through its three floors and labyrinthine halls, which exhibit everything under the sun from dinosaur skeletons to the Hope diamond, the biggest blue diamond known to exist, bear in mind that all that you see represents only a fraction of the more than 124 million items stored under the care of the museum's 500 scientists and researchers.

Stop at the information desk near the mall entrance for a map and for information about the IMAX features and the **Immersion Theater** (tel: 202-633-7400; admission charge), where you can manipulate

Security is a concern on the Mall, so expect to have your bags searched when you visit the museums. To speed things up, have your bags ready, don't argue with the guards, and leave any questionable items at home.

BELOW: the rotunda of the National Museum of Natural History.

Map:
pages
70–71

A 1948 Tucker auto in the National Museum of American History.

BELOW:
the Eisenhower years
remembered in the
National Museum of
American History.

the onscreen action with your own control panel.

As you enter the rotunda you'll notice the enormous elephant on display. Even for an African elephant, he's a big specimen, weighing in at 12 tons – about 5 tons more than the average. He was killed in 1955 and his skin was shipped to the Smithsonian where workers mounted it on a wooden frame. Every year, more than 6 million people stop for a look at him.

In the **Dinosaur Hall,** the giant reptile known as "Hatcher" is on display. Discovered by Wyoming bone collector John Bell Hatcher in 1891, this triceratops is shown frozen in battle with a Tyrannosaurus Rex. Encircling the dinosaurs are the **fossil galleries** where you can see evidence of life on display from the Big Bang 4.6 million years ago up to the present.

The second floor holds the **gem and mineral collections**, including the **Hope Diamond**, the largest in the world at 45.5 carats and celebrated for its color and clarity; originally from India, it has had a checkered

history worthy of Hollywood. Other gems include sapphires, rubies, emeralds, and a display of royal jewelry including the 950-diamond necklace that Napoleon presented to Empress Marie-Louise on their wedding day in 1810.

If you have children in tow, be sure not to miss the **Insect Zoo** where the cases are low to accommodate young visitors who can watch a giant mound of African termites at work and catch the popular tarantula feeding (Tues–Fri, 10.30am, 11.30am, 1.30pm; weekend times vary).

American History

The pink marble box next to the National History Museum is the **National Museum of American History** , designed by the Beaux-Arts firm of McKim, Mead and White, and eventually completed in 1964 by Steinman, Cain and White. Originally called the National Museum of History and Technology, it was created to house the Philadelphia Centennial leftovers that would not fit in the Arts and Industries Building.

With its lively focus on *things* – more than 16 million objects – it's aptly called the "nation's attic." Perhaps garage would be a better term, given that exhibits include a Ford Model T automobile and a Conestoga wagon like the kind that pioneers used on the way to the Great Plains and California.

Other exhibits include a display of inaugural gowns worn by presidential wives, the first-ever typewriter, the flag which inspired Francis Scott Key to write the words to America's national anthem, Archie Bunker's armchair, Dorothy's red slippers from the 1939 film *The Wizard of Oz*, Mr Rodgers's zippered cardigan, and George Washington's false teeth. (For more information on the museum, see the feature on pages 30–31.) ❑

MUSEUM CAFES

National Museum of American History

14th Street and Constitution Avenue, NW. Tel: 202-357-2700

Main Street Cafe
Open daily, 11am–4pm.
Food court à la shopping mall, large, noisy; wide selection of American fast food.

The Palm Court and Ice Cream Parlor
Open daily, 10am–5pm
Simple sandwich menu with vintage soda fountain featuring hand-dipped ice cream treats. Adjoins Main Street Cafe.

National Museum of Natural History

10th Street and Constitution Avenue, NW. Tel: 202-357-2700

Atrium Café
Open: Sat–Thur, 11am–6pm; Fri, 11am–4pm & 6pm–10pm
Windows, sunlight and light fare: pizza, burgers, fries, chicken. Near the museum's IMAX theater; Friday evening cocktails, hors d'oeuvres and a few gourmet selections.

Fossil Café
Open : Sat–Thurs, 11am–6pm; Fri, 11am–7pm
Small, tucked at the back of the Dinosaur Hall. A few salads, sandwiches and desserts.

National Gallery of Art Sculpture Garden

9th Street and Constitution Avenue, NW. Tel: 202-737-4215

Pavilion Café
Open: Mon–Thurs & Sat,10am–7pm; Fri, 10am–9pm; Sun,

11am–7pm
Retro-nouveau pavilion overlooks a garden outfitted with modern sculpture near a fountain. Indoor and outdoor seating. Limited cafeteria-style menu features salads, sandwiches, pizza, desserts, beer and wine. Live jazz Friday evenings.

National Gallery of Art, West Building

6th Street and Constitution Avenue, NW. Tel.: 202-737-4215

The Garden Court
Open: Mon–Sat, 11.30am–3pm; Sun, noon–6.30pm
Sit-down service for grown-ups with a limited but tasty menu of soups, salads and sandwiches and a modest buffet.

National Gallery of Art, East Building

4th Street and Constitution Avenue, NW. Tel: 202-737-4215

Cascade Café
Mon–Sat, 10am–3pm; Sun, 11am–4pm.
Everything from pan pizza and macaroni and cheese, to ratatouille, salad nicoise, burgers and soup served in a carved out loaf of sourdough bread, all available cafeteria style. Pleasant dining area adjacent to a glassed-in waterfall.

Terrace Café
Sun, 11am–3pm.
Buffet-style Sunday brunch with live music, overlooking the museum's atrium.

National Museum of The American Indian

4th Street and Independence Avenue, SW. Tel: 202-357-2700

Mitsitam Native Foods Café
Open daily, 10am–5pm.
The café takes its name from a Native American word for "let's eat!" Focuses on traditional native foods authentically prepared.

National Air and Space Museum

6th Street and Independence Avenue, SW. Tel: 202-357-2700.

The Wright Place
Open daily, 10am-5pm.
Food court the size of an airplane hangar; all fast food. Mostly for kids.

Mezza Café
Open daily, 10am–5pm.
Limited sandwich menu, coffee, beer and wine. Usually crowded.

Flight Fare Café
Daily, 8am-5pm, in summer.
Outdoor kiosk on the west side features pastries and hot dogs, ice cream, coffee and soft drinks.

Hirshhorn Museum and Sculpture Garden

7th Street and Independence Avenue, SW. Tel: 202-357-2700

Full Circle Café
Mon–Fri, 11am–4.30pm, in summer.
Outdoor café set among sculpture works offering simple soup and salad combinations, sandwiches, beer, wine.

Arts and Industries Building (the Castle)

900 Jefferson Drive, SW. Tel: 202-357-2700

Seattle's Best Coffee kiosk
Open daily 10am–5pm.
Adjacent to the visitors' information center; excellent coffee and accompanying noshes.

The Commons
Open Sun, 11am–2pm. Tel: 202-371-1083
Members-only dining room open to the public for Sunday buffet brunch. Reservations a must. American regional dishes, plus cheeses, omelets, fruits and more.

United States Holocaust Memorial Museum

100 Raoul Wallenberg Place (15th Street), SW. Tel: 202-488-6151

Café
Open Fri–Mon & Wed, 8.30am–4.30pm; Tues & Thurs, 8.30am–6.30pm.
Small, deli-like with a vegetarian and kosher menu that includes matzah-ball soup.

PRICES

Prices in these museum cafes run generally between **$10** and **$15** for a full meal, excluding beer or wine. Brunches or special evening meals are higher. Coffee, tea, or a soft drink and a light snack run between **$5** and **$10**. Hamburgers, hot dogs and other sandwiches range from **$4** to **$10**.

THE NATIONAL GALLERY OF ART

Some of the world's greatest art, from Da Vinci to Rothko, can be seen here for free, thanks to the largesse of some of America's top collectors

Many of the world's best works of art are in the National Gallery, which is on the Mall but, unlike everything else there, is not part of the government-supported Smithsonian. The Gallery is stocked with the treasures of 1,300 donors who followed Gallery founder Andrew W. Mellon's lead in handing over their collections to the country for the people to enjoy. Federal funds maintain it, but the Gallery's acquisitions come from strictly private sources.

Andrew Mellon was a financier and former US Treasury secretary who built his own collection of 121 Old Masters, which went on display in 1941 in what is now known as the National Gallery's West Building. In 1978 the East Building opened, futuristic, triangular-shaped and home for the works of many of the 20th century's masters. The two buildings, which together cover every era in art, are connected by an underground concourse featuring a waterfall and a café. Just west of the West Building, you can stop at the Gallery's Sculpture Garden, a 6-acre block of greenery featuring several large, modern works with a cooling fountain perfect in the summer heat and a small café.

● *Location, contact details and opening times: page 78.*

ABOVE: everyone stops at the classical marble works that fill the East Sculpture Hall, main floor. You can browse the ancients on your way in and out of the adjacent galleries of French and British art.

LEFT: besides painting them, Edgar Degas also sculpted ballet dancers. This wax study of his famous *Little Dancer Aged Fourteen* is outfitted in a linen bodice, a tutu made of muslin, and satin dance slippers.

ABOVE: the Milanese sculpture Pietro Magni's *The Reading Girl* is one of the ground-floor Sculpture Galleries' most alluring figures.

THE HIGHLIGHTS

Micro Gallery. As you enter the West Building from the Mall, 13 touch-screen computer monitors provide a useful overview which, along with friendly guides, will help you tailor your visit to make it less exhausting.

13th–15th century Italian paintings, in galleries 1–15. Here are works by Botticelli, Raphael, and the only painting of Leonardo da Vinci's found outside Europe. *Ginevra di Benci*, a portrait of a nobleman's daughter, is haunting for the sadness of expression it portrays, owing to Ginevra's presumed break from her lover.

17th-century Dutch and Flemish paintings, in galleries 42–50C. Jan Vermeer's *Girl with the Red Hat* is here, as is Rembrandt's *Apostle Paul* and his 1659 *Self-Portrait*.

The Armand Hammer Collection. American industrialist Hammer's collection of drawings includes works by da Vinci, Picasso and many old and modern masters.

Gilbert Stuart's Washington. The famous American portrait artist rendered the first five Presidents, including GW, his most famous work of all.

West Building Sculpture Galleries. More than 800 statuettes and busts, decorated objects, and rare books, some dating from the Middle Ages, are on display, including several Renaissance bronze figures and works by Auguste Rodin and Edgar Degas.

Sculpture Garden. Huge block of green space adjacent to the West Building features several large-scale sculptures amid trees, shrubs and a fountain big enough to double as an ice-skating rink in winter, plus a café.

Mark Rothko. The East Building's collection, the world's largest, includes 295 paintings and hundreds of sketches of the Russian immigrant's work, including his signature soft-edged and colorful rectangles.

20th-century Masters. The East Building's rotating collections of America's Warhol, Lichtenstein and Pollack, plus Picasso, Magritte, Mondrian and Miró make this heaven for modern art enthusiasts.

Small French Paintings. Small-scale masterpieces by Cézanne, Degas, Matisse and others donated by the banking Mellons and installed in the East Building.

ABOVE: he is best known for his mobiles, but even Alexander Calder's freestanding sculptures have the feeling of movement. Calder was first inspired by the Dutch De Stijl artist Piet Mondrian's bright blocks of color, envisioning them set in motion.

RIGHT: bankrolled by the Medicis, artist and Dominican friar Fra' Angelico teamed with the younger Filippo Lippi to produce *The Adoration of the Magi*, one of the Renaissance's most renowned works. Among the family's vast inventory, this was the most valuable, priced at 100 florins in 1492.

THE MALL WEST

This is sacred ground – the heart of the monumental city. As well as monuments to Washington and Lincoln, this oasis of urban parkland, set apart from the museum-lined corridor across the way, contains a variety of memorials to the dead of America's wars.

South of Constitution Avenue and west of 14th Street to the banks of the Potomac sprawls the tree-shaded westward extension of the Mall. Unofficially, it also takes in the **Ellipse ⓬**, the 52-acre (21-hectare) oval field south of the White House, where the national Christmas tree stands each year.

One of the most enjoyable ways to explore this area is to walk. Miles of paths weave through the trees, around the memorials, and along the riverfront. You may prefer to take a **Tourmobile** shuttle bus (tel: 202-554-7950) which loops through the entire Mall area allowing visitors to get on and off between sites. Distances are farther away than they seem once you strike out on foot.

The Washington Monument

The prevailing vertical in the horizontal city is the **Washington Monument ⓭** (daily Jun–Aug 8am–11.45 pm, the rest of the year daily 9am–4.45pm; closed Dec 25. Tickets are required, but are free at the kiosk or tel: 202-426-6841 or 1-800-967-2283; www.nps.gov/nacc).

This is the essential memorial to the nation's first president, the District's quintessential symbol and landmark – and the invariable object of ribaldry. A few hundred feet west of the monument, you will find the

Jefferson Pier marker, designating the monument's *intended* site at the intersection of the city's east-west and north-south axes – in line with the White House.

The spot proved to be too marshy (Constitution Avenue was at that time part of the C&O Canal), and so the monument had to be constructed on higher and drier ground. However, this threw the true east-west axis off by one degree to the south.

In 1783 the Continental Congress passed a resolution to erect a statue

Map: pages 70–71

LEFT: the Jefferson Memorial.
BELOW: a spring clean for Mr Lincoln.

in honor of George Washington, though what they had in mind was something equestrian. Lack of funds delayed the project and finally in 1833 a group of private citizens raised $28,000. The cornerstone for architect Robert Mills's simpler and more elegant monument was laid July 4, 1848, but construction was delayed again, in part because of the intervening Civil War but also because of additional funding troubles that had the appearance of malfeasance. "A great many citizens of this country will never feel entirely comfortable until they know exactly what has been done with the cart-load of money collected in behalf of Gen. George Washington's monument," wrote a journalist in the *Washington Post* in 1877. "The public ear is elevated to the proper angle in anticipation of a real nice explanation. Will some gentleman arise?"

Work resumed when blocks of stones were donated by several nations, states, and other organizations, inscribed with mottos and good wishes. One large stone donated by Pope Pius IX provoked the anti-Catholic contingent involved in the building, who smashed the stone and threw the pieces into the Potomac.

Ask a National Park Service ranger about the color change in the monument's shaft and you may be told that it is a high-water mark. Or that it is the height to which the monument is folded at night after everyone goes home. Actually, the color change marks the switch from Maryland to Massachusetts marble after construction resumed. When the discrepancy was noticed, building stopped again until a more compatible quarry was found.

Work started up again in 1880 when Congress came up with the needed funds to finish the job, and eight years later, the Washington Monument was finally compled. At 555 ft (169 meters), it was the tallest structure in the world until the Eiffel Tower was completed five years later. An elevator will take you in 70 seconds to the top, where from the observation deck you can have a panoramic view of the city. The monument is crowded, especially in summer, so it's best to arrive early.

Down the slope and off to the side of the monument stands the small outdoor stage of the **Sylvan Theater** ⓮. On sultry summer nights it's a great spot to spread a picnic and enjoy a concert. Beginning at 8pm on every summer evening except Saturday, you can attend free concerts by the US Army Band (tel: 703-696-3399), "The President's Own" Marine Band (tel: 202-433-4011), the US Navy Band (tel: 202-433-2525) , and the US Air Force Band (tel: 202-767-5658), which perform on a rotating schedule.

Money for nothing

While in the vicinity, you might consider a detour down to the "new" **Bureau of Engraving and Printing** ⓯ at Raoul Wallenberg Place (formerly 15th Street) and C Street

TIP

On the day you plan to visit, be sure to line up well before opening, especially in summer, to get the timed tickets at the kiosk for the Washington Monument and also for the Holocaust Museum.

BELOW: lining up to see dollar bills being produced at the Bureau of Engraving and Printing.

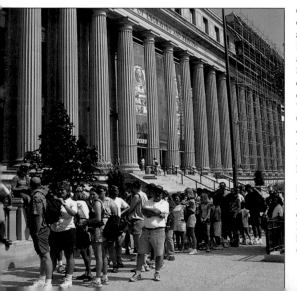

(tours Mon–Fri, 9am–2pm; closed federal holidays; tickets required but free with valid photo ID, and available at the 15th St. kiosk which opens at 8am; tel: 202-874-2330 or 1-800-967-2283). Until World War I, the "old" bureau was housed next door in what is now called the Auditor's Building.

All of the country's paper currency – about $20 billion a year – is produced here, along with treasury notes, postage stamps, White House invitations, and other printed matter. On a tour, you can watch the stuff roll off the presses. This is a popular family attraction and lines can be long.

A sobering experience

The bureau's neighbor at 100 Raoul Wallenberg Place is the privately funded **United States Holocaust Memorial Museum** ⑯ (daily 10am–5.30pm; closed Dec 25 and Yom Kippur; tel: 202-488-0444 for information about timed tickets which may be needed for permanent exhibits, or get in line by 8am to receive a ticket for that day. Advance tickets may be obtained from tickets.com or by phoning 1-800-400-9373, but they carry a service charge. www.ushmm.org). The museum is a sobering tribute to the 6 million Jews and 5 million other victims of the World War II Holocaust.

As its designers intended, this five-story brick and limestone simulated concentration camp with its rough gray surfaces and exposed beams and "watchtowers," delivers an emotionally charged message about one of the world's darkest times. The atmosphere is grim and even when crowded, the museum is unnaturally quiet. The story is told through documentary films, photographs, artifacts and oral histories. To add to the intensity, visitors are given a photo identification card of an actual Holocaust victim, someone of the same age and gender.

Many exhibits focus on Jewish life just before the Holocaust and explain the political and military events leading up to it, but the most powerful are the archival films documenting executions, medical experiments performed on prisoners, and suicide victims.

Collections of personal articles such as shoes, glasses, and eating utensils help to quantify and make tangible the loss of human life and are interspersed with an actual railroad car used to carry prisoners to the camps and a scale model of a gas chamber. One display is devoted to Raoul Wallenberg, a Swedish diplomat who was stationed in Budapest and who led the effort to save the Hungarian Jews.

Particularly moving is the **Hall of Remembrance**, a hexagonal, skylit spiritual space for reflection and contemplation, where visitors can light memorial candles and where a perpetual flame burns for the dead.

There is nothing remotely lighthearted about visiting this museum, nothing that can ease the horror of the subject matter, so plan accord-

Map: pages 70–71

TIP

There are few places to eat in this section of the Mall. The United States Holocaust Memorial Museum does have a cafe, which is included in the Mall East food listings on page 83.

BELOW:
children's tiles at the Holocaust Museum.

The annual Cherry Blossom parade, which attracts up to 200,000 visitors each April, was started by the city in 1935 as a way of attracting tourists. There is a three-hour parade, with bands and floats, and a Miss Cherry Blossom contest.

BELOW:
cherry blossom
by the Tidal Basin.

ingly, especially if you're traveling with young children.

Cherry blossoms

After this, you may be ready for some fresh air and the serenity of the **Tidal Basin** ⓱ nearby. Not a monument but undeniably monumental, this free-form "lake" was created in 1897 to trap the overflow from the estuarial Potomac River and drain it into the Washington Channel. A photographic cliché when the cherry trees are in bloom, it is nevertheless one of the city's beauty spots, great for picnicking, paddleboating, or perambulating.

The **cherry blossom trees**, Washington's most distinctive horticultural image, originally came from Japan. According to one local correspondent who has researched their background, since the trees were planted around 1912, there have been some local difficulties. When President Franklin D. Roosevelt ordered ground broken for the Jefferson Memorial in 1938, bulldozers went into the cherry groves and found some local matrons

chained to the trunks in protest. During World War II, there were spasmodic ax attacks on this symbol of Imperial Japan, and such vandalism was made a federal offense. Occasionally, a hapless tourist trying to break off some blossoms is giving a stern warning of imprisonment by one of the vigilant Park Police.

Bill Anderson is the chief scientist for the National Park Service, and it is his annual duty to stroll through the groves to establish which is the day to announce peak blossoming, which he reckons at 70 percent in bloom on 70 percent of the trees. Mr Anderson explains that this is a tricky calculation because the Japanese cunningly sent two varieties of cherry tree. Roughly two-thirds are Yoshino, and these bloom an average 10 days earlier than the other variety, the Kwanzan. March 16, in 1990, was the earliest day ever recorded for peak blossoming. Nevertheless, Washington's Cherry Blossom Festival kicks off the first weekend in April, whether there are blossoms or not (check the *Washington Post* Friday "Weekend" section for information on scheduled events).

If you want to join the annual pilgrimage, walk in, or use public transportation. A nocturnal stroll under the glowing trees, set off by stunning views of the monuments, is a magical experience, but it's best to exercise caution if strolling around once the sun has gone down.

The Jefferson Memorial

The Basin's shoreline path will lead you to the steps of the domed and graceful **Jefferson Memorial** ⓲ (daily 8am–11.45pm; closed Dec 25; tel: 202-426-6841 or visit www.nps.gov/nacc) arguably one of Washington's prettiest monuments, especially at night.

Designed by John Russell Pope, architect of the National Gallery of Art and the National Archives, and

landscaped by Frederick Law Olm-sted, Jr, the monument-in-the-round recalls the Roman Pantheon, a nod to Jefferson's own fondness for that ancient structure and similar to the president's designs for his own home, Monticello.

Built on the soft site of a dredged marsh which characterized much of the Mall, the memorial, completed in 1943, needed a foundation of con-crete-filled steel cylinders sunk 135 ft (41 meters) down to bedrock. The domed building is ringed by 54 Ionic columns. Not everyone loved the monument. Critics decried its form as too "feminine," or as a "cage for Jefferson's statue," a 19-ft-high (5.8-meter) bronze sculpted by Rudolph Evans. The memorial marks the southern point of the Mall's north-south axis, with the White House forming the counterpoint.

To the south is **East Potomac Park**, a peninsula that dangles between the Potomac River and the Washington Channel, and which forms the southern half of a 700-acre (280-hectare) riverside park. The views are superb, and you can

watch planes take off and touch down across the river at Virginia's Reagan National Airport. This is also a good place to enjoy the springtime cherry blossom trees, where there are fewer crowds than around the Tidal Basin.

You'll also see the new **George Mason Memorial** ⑲ (tel: 703-550-9220 or visit www.gunstonhall.org), dedicated in 2002 to the memory of Virginian and patriot George Mason whose Virginia Declaration was the basis for the Bill of Rights. Mason refused to sign the original constitution, drawn up in 1787, because it did not guarantee freedom of the press and of religion, and freedom from unreasonable searches and the right to a fair and speedy trial.

Thanks to his efforts, the Bill of Rights was finally added in 1791 and form the basis of American democracy and political freedom. Mason's restored plantation home, **Gunston Hall**, is in Virginia, about 20 miles (32 km) south of DC, and is open for tours (*see page 187*).

The peninsula's tip, **Hains Point**, holds a wonderful surprise: a giant

Map: pages 70–71

Jogging by the Potomac can get noisy near Reagan National Airport.

BELOW:
cherry blossoms overlooking the Jefferson Memorial.

figure breaking through the earth. The sculpture, *The Awakening* by J. Seward Johnson, Jr, was installed in 1980 as part of a citywide sculpture show. Climbing on the sculpture is encouraged by the artist.

The FDR Memorial

Stay a northwestern course into **West Potomac Park** and you'll reach the **Franklin Delano Roosevelt Memorial** ⓴ (daily 8am–11.45pm; closed Dec 25; tel: 202-426-6841; www.nps.gov/nacc). The memorial was opened in 1997, although there already existed a monument to Roosevelt, a stone slab on Pennsylvania Avenue in front of the National Archives that was, according to wishes he expressed to his friend and Supreme Court Justice Felix Frankfurter, no bigger than his desk. This one, designed by Lawrence Halprin, is much grander.

Spread over 7½ acres (3 hectares), this memorial to the nation's 32nd president, who helped lift the country out of the Depression and guided it through World War II, combines sculpture and natural landscape. Soft red South Dakota granite walls constitute four open-air rooms, each signifying one of Roosevelt's four terms of office. Shade trees and waterfalls are interspersed, with quotes and carvings on the walls. A 9-ft. (2.7-meter) bronze statue shows Roosevelt seated with Fala, his faithful Scotch terrier, by his side.

The Lincoln Memorial

Continue further into the park and you'll reach the incomparable shrine to Abraham Lincoln: a neo-classical temple of gleaming, white marble cresting its acropolis. Familiar as the image that graces the back of the penny and the $5 bill, Henry Bacon's design for a **Lincoln Memorial** ⓴ (open daily 8am–11.45pm; closed Dec 25, tel: 202-426-6841 or visit www.nps.gov/nacc) was selected over John Russell Pope's and was dedicated on Memorial Day in 1922. It was a sad irony that day that a key speaker, the black president of Tuskegee Institute, was ushered away from the speaker's platform and seated in the segregated black section of the audi-

Franklin Delano Roosevelt (1882–1945) is remembered for his New Deal, designed to alleviate the effects of the Depression in the 1930s. He was the first president to stand for – and win – a third term, and he went on to win a fourth shortly before his death. Later, the constitution was amended to limit presidents to two consecutive terms.

BELOW:
the FDR Memorial.

ence across the road. On Easter Sunday 1939 operatic singer Marian Anderson sang from the steps for an audience of 75,000, having been denied permission to perform at DAR Constitution Hall because she was black. The First Lady, Eleanor Roosevelt, arranged for the outdoor concert, then resigned her own DAR membership.

Similar to Athens' Parthenon, the building is fronted by a colonnade of 36 Doric columns, the exact number of American states in the Union at the time of Lincoln's death. The columns slope inward to avoid looking out of proportion. Above the columns is a frieze with the names of these 36 states; higher still are the names of the 48 states that were in the Union at the time the monument was dedicated.

Daniel Chester French designed the famous figure of Lincoln, the tallest president, seated inside the memorial. If this marble Lincoln were to stand up, he would measure 28 ft (8.5 meters). When it was discovered that Lincoln's naturally-lit face was nearly obscured, General Electric was called in to install special artificial lighting to create the shadows on his hair, brows, cheeks, and chin. Adding a personal touch to his masterpiece, French, who had a deaf son and who knew American sign language, so shaped Lincoln's hands so that the left holds the sign for "A," and the right "L."

From the memorial, you can savor Lincoln's magnificent view across the **Reflecting Pool**, the elegant, 2,000-ft (600- meter) waterway and promenade inspired by Versailles and the Taj Mahal, to the Washington Monument and beyond to the Capitol. Attractive at any time, the scene is most dramatic in the light of dawn or at dusk.

War memorials

To the south of the Reflecting Pool is the **Korean War Veterans Memorial ㉒**, (daily 8am–11.45pm; closed Dec 25, tel: 202-426-6841; www.nps.gov/nacc) dedicated to those who served in the conflict which, although it lasted from 1950 until 1953, was never officially declared a war. Regardless, 1½ mil-

Map: pages 70–71

BELOW: listening to Abe inside the Lincoln Memorial.

The man

who gave

meaning,

honor, and

purpose

to the Nation

s still.

lion Americans served, with more than 54,000 killed, 110,000 captured or wounded, and another 8,000 declared missing. The site features an American flag at the point of a triangle which thrusts into a circular pool. Nineteen statues of soldiers, sculpted by Frank Gaylord and a mural with many faces, the work of Louis Nelson, are also featured.

Sandwiched between the Reflecting Pool and Constitution Avenue is the green swath known as **Constitution Gardens**. After the last of the temporary wartime structures was demolished in 1966, President Richard Nixon proposed that the area be developed as a Disneyesque amusement park. The idea was soundly vetoed. Instead, you will find a tranquil setting of shady trees and bench-lined paths which meander alongside an artificial lake. A lovely little island in the lake contains a memorial to the signers of the Declaration of Independence.

Vietnam Veterans

The most subtle and emotionally powerful of the Mall's monuments,

the **Vietnam Veterans Memorial ㉓**, (daily 8am–11.45pm; closed Dec 25; tel: 202-426-6841 or visit www.nps.gov/nacc) stands just a short distance away through the trees to the west of the lake. It was a Vietnam vet who proposed the idea of a memorial, which Congress authorized in 1980.

Jan Scruggs came up with the idea for the memorial after he saw Michael Cimino's 1978 movie *The Deer Hunter*, which addressed the struggles returning vets had faced. To raise funds, Scruggs founded the Vietnam Veterans Memorial Fund which he still operates from a downtown office, raising funds for upkeep and overseeing an educational program.

Selected from nearly 1,500 entries in an open design competition, the contemplative V-shaped wall of names – 58,229 casualties – in polished black granite was designed by Maya Lin, a 21-year-old Yale University architecture student and the daughter of Chinese immigrants, who explained: "The design was purposefully simple

BELOW: the Korean War Memorial.

Map: pages 70–71

because embellishment upon something so moving [as the war] would only diminish its effect."

To assuage the critics of Lin's abstract "rift in the earth," a representational statue of three soldiers by sculpture Frederick Hart and a memorial flagpole were erected. The names are inscribed on the wall in chronological order in which the soldiers died. At the two entrance ramps leading down into the memorial, visitors can locate the names of the deceased alphabetically and find the exact location of each soldier's name on the wall. More than 40 million Americans have come to the wall to find solace and closure, making it the country's most popular memorial.

Veterans' groups have set up makeshift shelters and tents near the memorial which are used as 24-hour vigil sites. In addition to selling mementoes and advertising their political grievances, the groups and shelters are there for the vets themselves, who come to reclaim the wall in the privacy of night. By day the wall belongs to the public – who file reverently by to gaze, to discover their own reflections, to touch a name, to leave flowers or a poem, or to make a wall rubbing.

Nearby is another Vietnam War memorial, this one to the 265,000 women who served either in the military or as volunteers with such organizations as the USO and the Red Cross. **The Vietnam Women's Memorial ㉔** was dedicated in 1993 and features a 7-ft (2.1-meter) high bronze statue of three women tending a wounded soldier – most of the women who served were nurses.

World War II remembered

With all the memorials that were been erected on the Mall in commemoration of those who served in America's wars, the Iwo Jima Memorial in Arlington, which pays tribute to those who served in World War II, suddenly seemed insufficient. In 2001 Congress approved the 7.4-acre (3-hectare) site just west of 17th Street as the location for the **National World War II Memorial ㉕** (open 24 hours daily; tel: 1-800-639-4992; www.wwii memorial.com). Of the 16.4 million

The Vietnam Women's Memorial.

BELOW: the Vietnam Veterans Memorial, with the Washington Monument reflected.

Map: pages 70–71

The National World War II Memorial.

BELOW: the National World War II Memorial.

Americans who served in the war, fewer than 4 million are alive today, and most of those will be dead within a decade. So why the delay in creating this memorial, more than half a century after the war ended? The fact is that controversy has always dogged plans for even the best known monuments, and bringing this one into being took 12 years of public hearings, fundraising, design disputes, and construction.

The memorial, the work of Friedrich St Florian, an Austrian-born architect and former dean of the Rhode Island School of Design, is more a plaza than a monument. It is meant as a place of rest and contemplation, unmistakably classical.

You descend a wide staircase through a ceremonial entrance lined with 24 bas-relief panels depicting America's agricultural, industrial, military and human resources. These are the work of architect and sculptor Raymond Kaskey. Once on the plaza itself, you can see that it extends beyond a reflecting pool, once neglected but now restored and cleverly incorporated into the cen-

terpiece of the design. The plaza is in turn encircled with 56 stone pillars, one for every state and territory making up the US during the war. The decorative bronze wreaths on each pillar are also Kaskey's work, as are the four bronze eagles inside the memorial arches that anchor each end of the plaza. In their classical and graceful way, these arches – one for the Pacific, one for the Atlantic – are meant to mark the two theaters of war and, situated on either end, serve to remind visitors of the war's wide and terrible reach.

Opposite the entrance, on the other side of the pool, is the Freedom Wall, majestic, curved and situated between two waterfalls. It has been outfitted with 4,000 gold stars, each hand-made and affixed to the wall in memory of the 400,000 US service men and women who died.

The memorial to end memorials? Not quite. A 4-acre (1.6-hectare) site on the northwest edge of the Tidal Basin is to be the home of the **Martin Luther King, Jr. National Memorial** once funds for its building have been secured. ❑

A Monumental City

A t last count, Washington had 750 monuments, with more on the way. Besides the memorials everyone visits, there are other lesser known, even obscure monuments.

Take, for instance, the monument to Taras Shevchenko, a 19th-century Ukrainian serf turned poet and revolutionary, whose enormous bronze statue on P Street between 22nd and 23rd was erected in 1964 as a Cold War-era snub to the Soviets, for whom Shevchenko's most famous work *The Bard* was a threat. The Lebanese poet Khalil Gibran, best known for *The Prophet*, is remembered with a statue at Normanstone Park near Observatory Circle. There's a memorial to Maine lobstermen on Water Street, one to the Boy Scouts on the Ellipse, and one to Joan of Arc on Meridian Hill.

A former French ambassador, Jean Adrien Antoine Jules Jusserand, has a memorial in Rock Creek Park. A bird-watching buddy of President Theodore Roosevelt's, the ambassador was also a fellow skinny-dipper in the Potomac, although – unlike T.R. – the more modest Jusserand, as the story goes, was always careful to wear his gloves so as not, technically, to be caught naked.

The craze for monuments began with Congress in 1815 when it decreed that the grave of every senator or representative buried in Congressional Cemetery be marked with a shrine. Sixty years and 200 monuments later, the practice was stopped as space ran out. But that didn't stop the monuments and memorials from coming.

Americans have needed to mark the people and places connected with the events that have most defined them as a nation, regardless of how humble those places might be. Nothing could be more modest than the building on H Street, near 5th, once a tavern and boarding house and now a Chinese restaurant. It figured prominently in Lincoln's assassination because its owner, Mary Sarratt, unwittingly rented a room to his killer, John Wilkes Booth. For this, she was hanged for conspiracy, the first woman in America to be officially executed.

One of the more striking monuments is in Rock Creek Cemetery (off North Capitol Street near Rock Creek Church Road, not to be confused with Rock Creek Park on the other side of town). The bronze statue of a young woman by Augustus Saint-Gaudens was commissioned in 1890 by writer Henry Adams as a memorial to his wife Clover, a suicide. The figure, cloaked and seated on a rough stone, evokes such a sense of remorse that, even though the memorial bears no inscription or title, she has always been known simply as Grief.

It's hard to miss the rather glorious Columbus Memorial Fountain by Lorado Taft that's been in front of Union Station since 1908, but inside, in the West Hall, is a lesser known memorial to William Frederick Allen, who made the trains run on time. In the 1880s, the country had 50 different railroad time schedules, none coordinated, all confusing, and sometimes the cause of tragic accidents when trains simultaneously found themselves on the same tracks. To alleviate the problem, Allen divided the country into four time zones, a system that since 1883 has kept more than just the railroads running like clockwork. ❏

RIGHT: Gandhi statue outside the Indian Embassy.

THE MEMORIALS THAT MATTER

Of the many monuments and memorials, the three dedicated to Washington, Jefferson and Lincoln form the essential Washington experience

ABOVE: the Washington Monument, from the Lincoln Memorial.

ABOVE: Some who objected to the Jefferson Memorial's classical style – domed and ringed by 54 Ionic pillars – tied themselves to the famous cherry trees in protest. It was completed in 1943.

Nothing conveys the spirit of Washington, DC more tangibly or marks those moments of American history that have so defined it as a nation, both its triumphs and disgraces, quite like the city's many monuments. There are hundreds of them scattered across DC, marble statuary ornate to the point of excess and dedicated to long-forgotten generals, down to lowly brass plaques affixed to the walls of some of the city's oldest buildings.

But of all of the markers erected to the memory of its people and events, there are three that seem to say "This is Washington!" best; three that capture most viscerally the men and ideals that have so indelibly shaped and defined the American democratic narrative. Although the trio of monuments erected in the name of Washington, Jefferson and Lincoln are fixtures in the city, eternally popular with the millions who come here, the design and construction phases of all three were marked by long controversies and sharp criticism.

● *Contact details, opening times: pages 87, 90, 92.*

ABOVE: the Lincoln Memorial took more than 50 years to complete, and when it was finished in 1922 it was dismissed by critics as outdated and not representative of America's taste.

ABOVE: the Washington Monument took nearly 100 years to plan and build (1783–1888). Fund raising, changes in construction plans and an episode of fiscal malfeasance all delayed the project.

THE MEN BEHIND THE MONUMENTS

ABOVE: George Washington shown ascending to heaven after he died in 1799 (artist unknown).

The challenges involved in building the monuments seemed to parallel the upheaval that marked the lives of the very men they were meant to memorialize. Their place in America's mythology secure, the country's three most famous citizens were nevertheless anything but perfect. Washington, as Revolutionary War general, lost more battles than he won, then served as president with some reluctance; Jefferson, though he espoused freedom for all men, stubbornly persisted in his refusal to accept the glaring immorality of slavery; and Lincoln, though credited with sparing the Union, did so less in response to a moral imperative as to mounting political expediencies that would not tolerate a permanently divided nation.

Imperfect as they may have been, however, each stood, and stood erect, to meet the challenges of his age – Washington to lead the fractious colonies to form a republic; Jefferson to craft its first body of laws; Lincoln to guide it through its first true test. Whatever else they may have contributed, the qualities these three Americans exemplified most, what their memorials stand in testament of, are dignity, courage and strength – qualities that the memorials serve to remind are inherent in us all.

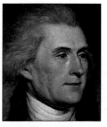

ABOVE: Thomas Jefferson

ABOVE: Abraham Lincoln

CAPITOL HILL AREA

The Hill's few short blocks, which contain two of the three branches of the federal government, the legislative and judicial, form the critical mass of Washington's political scene. As well as the Capitol building itself and the Supreme Court, the elegant Library of Congress is also located here.

From the long green sweep of the Mall, the **US Capitol** ❶ floats like a white mirage above the city. Icon of the federal republic and symbol of Washington, the Capitol has been the center of the city's political life since 1800 when the first joint session of Congress was called to order. Today, nearly 20,000 Congressional staff members, hordes of lobbyists and camera-carrying and notebook-toting members of the media swarm like bees around the Capitol hive.

The building is open Mon–Sat, 9am–4.30pm; closed Sun, Thanksgiving and Dec 25, but open federal holidays. Tours are by free timed tickets only from the West Front facing the Mall at the **Capitol Guide Service kiosk** near the Garfield traffic circle at Independence Avenue and First Street; tickets are distributed from 8.15am on a first-come first-served basis (tel: 202-225-6827 or visit www.aco.gov). Senate and House chambers are not included.

Capitol classic

The original land patent for what would become Capitol Hill was granted in 1663 to a George Thompson and eventually passed to the prominent Carroll family of Maryland. Known then as Jenkins Hill, this 500-acre (200-hectare) plot

above the Potomac was renamed Federal Hill by city architect Pierre L'Enfant who described it in a letter to George Washington as "a pedestal waiting for a superstructure." The superstructure L'Enfant had in mind was the Capitol, which he envisioned as the center of a thriving neighborhood of elegant shops and homes, though absurdly high real estate prices thwarted development. Even George Washington lost his original investment on a pair of townhouses he had built near the

Map on page 102

LEFT: the Great Welcoming Hall of the Library of Congress.
BELOW: the US Capitol at Christmas.

"It could be probably be shown by facts and figures that there is no distinctly native American criminal class except Congress."

—MARK TWAIN
FOLLOWING THE EQUATOR
(1897)

Capitol. Only since the 20th century has this section of the city really come into its own, displaying the elegance L'Enfant intended.

He envisioned the Capitol as the geographical centre of the city, the heart of the four equally developed quadrants, but the city developed primarily westward instead. Although the Capitol itself is surrounded by beautiful grounds and massive marble buildings, this grandeur doesn't extend much beyond Lincoln Park. The Capitol Hill neighborhood includes many of Washington's most important sites and a small historic district of townhouses located east of North and South Capitol streets and behind the Capitol. Here, you'll also find clusters of restaurants and bars – and more of the city's lower-income housing. Caution is advised, especially at night, since these neighborhoods between Lincoln Park and the Anacostia River have contributed significantly to DC's high crime rate.

A new **Capitol Visitors Center** will make it much easier to accommodate the crowds, which can exceed 18,000 curious tourists in a day. The three-story underground Center, with exhibit space, conces-

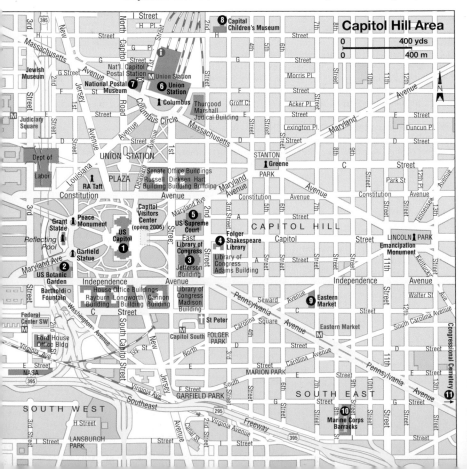

sions and restrooms and convenient access to the Capitol, is scheduled to open in 2006.

Design by committee

Dr William Thornton, an amateur architect and physician from the Virgin Islands, designed the original US Capitol after, as he put it, he "got some books and worked a few days." Nevertheless, Washington, who had chosen Thornton's plan from among the 16 submitted in a design competition for the Capitol, praised the plan for its "grandeur" and "simplicity." Construction commenced when Washington, using a silver trowel and a marble-headed gavel in the traditional Masonic style, laid the cornerstone in 1793. Thornton's casual attitude, however, soon cast doubt on his ability to carry through with the project and he was replaced by the runner-up in the competition whose egotism soon got the better of him. James Hoban, who won the competition to build the president's house, was called in to save the day, and by November 1800 enough of the work was com-

plete to enable Congress to meet in the north wing, the original Senate chamber, for the first time.

Jefferson then called in his friend Benjamin Henry Latrobe, a professional and by this time the Capitol's fourth architect, to supervise construction of the south wing, the House's original chamber. Except for the U-shaped gap between the two wings, the Capitol was more or less complete. But, on August 24, 1814, British Admiral George Cockburn torched "this harbor of Yankee democracy," leaving it a ruin. Latrobe once again set to work to restore the Capitol.

Temperamental and outspoken, Latrobe eventually fell victim to politics and his own indiscretions and was forced to resign his post. He was replaced by Charles Bulfinch, a New England architect noted not only for his brilliance but also for his tact and even-handedness in dealing with difficult congressmen who saw the Capitol not as a place to conduct the nation's business but as a monument to their own egos. "Architects expect criticism," the

A statue of President James A. Garfield stands to the west of the Capitol.

BELOW:
the Capitol in 1850.

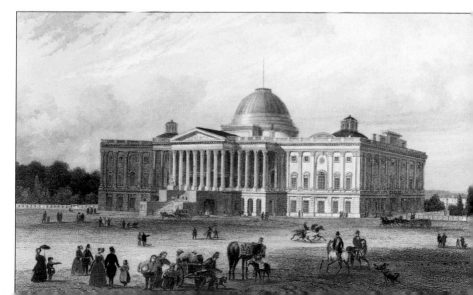

self-effacing Bulfinch wrote, "and must learn to bear it patiently."

He managed to link the two wings that Thornton and Latrobe had built before abandoning the project and was responsible for adding a 55-ft (17-meter) high dome, the Capitol's first.

Bulfinch also finished the **old House Chamber**, which was in use until 1857 when it was vacated for larger quarters and eventually became **Statuary Hall** where each state has on display a statue commemorating favorite sons and daughters. (The story goes that the Missouri delegation would have included Mark Twain but decided against it after the famous author wisecracked, "Suppose you were an idiot. And suppose you were a member of Congress. But I repeat myself.")

By 1850, Congress had clearly outgrown the Thornton-Latrobe-Bulfinch building and ordered an expansion, which included a bigger dome. This dome, the one you see today, is the work of Philadelphia architect Thomas U. Walter and con-

sists of two trussed cast-iron shells, one superimposed upon the other, and painted to resemble marble.

Oddly enough, the Civil War, which should have slowed construction, didn't, even though Union soldiers (who referred to it as the "Big Tent") were bivouacked under the dome. Lincoln insisted that construction on the Capitol continue on the theory that "if people see the Capitol going on… it is a sign we intend the Union shall go on."

In 1863, Thomas Crawford's 19-ft (5.8-meter) bronze **Statue of Freedom** was lifted into place atop the dome. The statue features a robed woman, her right hand on the sheath of her sword, her left holding a laurel wreath and a shield with 13 stripes, one for each of the original colonies.

Spectacular view

Inside, the dome forms the Capitol's **Great Rotunda**, 180 ft (55 meters) high, where painter Constantino Brumidi's *Apotheosis of Washington* depicts George Washington and other colonial statesmen mingling with a bevy of loosely robed allegorical fig-

The Statue of Freedom crowns the Capitol's dome.

BELOW:
touring the Capitol.

ures. Brumidi, born in Rome in 1805, worked at the Vatican before arriving in the US in 1852. "My one ambition," he wrote, "is that I may live long enough to make beautiful the Capitol of the one country on earth in which there is liberty."

Unfortunately, he didn't live long enough to see his wish fulfilled. At the age of 72, as he was working on the ceiling, his chair slipped from the scaffolding and he was left dangling 60 ft (18 meters) above the floor until he could be rescued. This proved too much of a strain, and a few months later he died. The grisaille frieze around the base of the dome, begun by Brumidi, runs a total length of 300 ft (90 meters) and depicts 400 years of American history. It was finally completed in 1953 by American artist Allyn Cox. A little closer to eye level, you'll notice the Rotunda walls, decorated with paintings by John Trumbull, an aide to General Washington during the Revolutionary War.

You can also visit **Statuary Hall**, whose semi-circular and half-domed shape amplifies the slightest sound,

an unintended consequence of the original design and a feature that many of the members of the House of Representatives who met here originally objected to for obvious political reasons. In the **Hall of Columns** you'll find the overflow of works from Statuary Hall. Running parallel to that is the **Hall of Capitols**, decorated with murals by Allyn Cox which depict historical and everyday moments in American life.

The handsome **Old Senate Chamber** features a Rembrandt Peale portrait of George Washington. The **Old Supreme Court Chamber** was used by the court between 1810 and 1860 and contains many original furnishings.

Beneath the Rotunda is the **Crypt**, intended originally to enshrine the body of George Washington. His survivors insisted instead that he be laid to rest at Mt Vernon. The crypt also features a landmark embedded in the floor marking the zero point from which the city's quadrants were drawn. There is also on display a bust of Lincoln by Mt Rushmore sculptor Gutzon Borglum who

Map on page 102

The Old Senate Chamber.

BELOW LEFT:
the Capitol's rotunda is 180ft (55 meters) high.

Grant's Statue

Look for the statue of General Ulysses S. Grant astride his horse. It's outside at the base of the Capitol. As equestrian statues go, it's the second largest in the world, at 40 ft/12 meters high (only Victor Emmanuel's, the first king of modern Italy, is bigger), and the work of the little known sculptor Henry Shrady, a law school drop-out and failure in the match stick business. His father was one of Grant's physicians. Sited directly in line with the Lincoln Memorial, the statue was intended to anchor the east end of the Mall.

In 1885 Grant's funeral drew a million mourners who turned out to pay homage to the general who, as commander in chief of the Union's forces, quite literally saved the country. He served two terms in the White House and, despite the scandals that marred his presidency, his popularity was still holding steady when in 1922, after 21 years of work, Shrady's statue was finally ready to be unveiled. That April day, federal offices were closed and cheering crowds lined the streets as units from the army, navy, and marines ceremoniously marched from the White House to the statue. Yet, these days, with the Capitol looming behind it, the General is seldom noticed.

chose to leave off the president's left ear, this to symbolize Lincoln's unfinished life.

On either side of the Capitol are the buildings that house the offices and committee rooms where the everyday work of Congress takes place. On the House side of the Capitol, running along Independence Avenue, are the Cannon, Longworth and Rayburn buildings. The Senate office buildings, the Russell, Dirksen, and Hart buildings, are on the north side of the Capitol along Constitution Avenue.

On the Capitol's **West Terrace**, free summer concerts are offered by the armed services bands on many evenings beginning at 8pm. (Check the listings in the *Washington Post* or phone the US Army Band (tel: 703-696-3399), "The President's Own" Marine Band (tel: 202-433-4011), the US Navy Band (tel: 202-433-2525) , and the US Air Force Band (tel: 202-767-5658) for schedules.)

There is no more quintessential Washington entertainment than to sit on the Capitol steps, tap your feet to a Sousa march, and watch the sun set behind the Washington Monument.

Take time to stroll the **Capitol grounds** – a former mud flat filled with alders and transformed into a shady parkland by the landscape architect Frederick Law Olmsted, Jr, in 1874. Now encompassing 200 acres (80 hectares), the grounds include 5,000 trees, some planted in the late 1800s, and in spring a magnificent display of red and yellow tulips and jonquils.

For more of the lush life, visit the **US Botanic Garden ❷** (First Street and Maryland Avenue; entrance on Maryland Avenue; open daily 10am–5pm; free admittance; tel: 202-225-8333) on the southwest side of the Capitol. The gardens were originally established to hold the specimen plants brought back from South America and the Pacific by the congressionally mandated Wilkes Expedition in 1842. A conservatory was erected in 1933 as the collection expanded and has recently been renovated to include a huge glass atrium packed with tropical plants and flanked by two smaller pavilions.

The gardens make a great stop on cold, rainy days and during special seasonal shows. Across the street, in a charming pocket park (open daily, dawn to dusk), is the city's graceful bronze **Bartholdi Fountain**, designed by Frederic August Bartholdi (of Statue of Liberty fame) and installed here in 1877.

The Library of Congress

The favorite room of many a Washingtonian is the Main Reading Room at the **Library of Congress ❸**, located inside the stunning **Thomas Jefferson Building** just behind the Capitol (open Mon–Sat, 10am–5.30pm; closed Sunday and federal holidays; free guided tours of the Jefferson Building available by ticket Mon–Sat, 10.30am, 11.30am, 2.30pm, 3.30pm from the Visitors Center at the First Street

The Longworth Building was named for House Speaker Nicholas Longworth who served from 1925 to 1931. He was better known as the husband of the irreverent Alice Roosevelt, daughter of T.R. Outspoken Alice once quipped at a dinner party: "If you can't say anything good about someone, sit right here by me."

BELOW: the Bartholdi Fountain, facing the Botanic Garden.

entrance; tel: 202-707-5000 or 202-707-9779 or visit www.loc.gov).

At the foot of the Jefferson Building, by the entrance, is the **Neptune Fountain**, designed by Roland Hinton Perry. Inside is an impressive two-story white marble **Great Hall** decorated with murals and sculptures and gold leaf. To enter the Great Hall is to be taken back to the Renaissance with its white Italian marble, its arches, its generously applied 23-karat gold-leaf, and its 75-ft (23-meter) high ceiling with a marble mosaic portrait of Minerva, the ancient Roman goddess of wisdom who forms the library's central motif, presiding over what has become the largest library in the world. A grand staircase leads to the second-floor gallery where changing exhibit showcase some of the Library's vast collection.

The original library was housed in the Capitol and intended only for the legislators. When the library was destroyed in the fire of 1814, Thomas Jefferson offered his own 6,500 volumes to Congress, which they bought for $24,000, roughly half the price he would probably have received at auction. Jefferson's hand-sewn and leather-bound books on botany, astronomy, history, literature, philosophy and more formed the core of a library that quickly grew, overflowing its quarters in the newly rebuilt Capitol to become "the greatest chaos in America," as the then librarian described it.

Once more, in 1851, fire broke out, this time the result of a faulty fireplace flue. This disaster reduced to ashes what before had been simply chaos and destroyed most of Jefferson's collection.

Congress once again allotted money for the rebuilding of the Library, a Beaux-Arts gem and probably the city's most beautiful public building, opened in 1897. As a way to increase its holding, the Library gradually opened its doors to the public and now has more than 150 million books, rare manuscripts, maps, musical scores, recordings and musical instruments, films, photographs, and other materials. Among its many treasures are a Gutenberg Bible, a rough draft of

Map on page 102

TIP

The Library of Congress offers a free concert series in its beautiful Coolidge Auditorium. Performances usually begin at 8pm and include jazz, folk, string quartets and early-music groups. Call the Library for a schedule.

BELOW: cleaning up a statue at the Library of Congress.

Jefferson's Declaration of Independence, and Abraham Lincoln's Gettysburg Address.

In the Jefferson Building's circular Main Reading Room, with its massive wooden desks arranged in rings, you're in for still more treasures. It takes dedicated readers to concentrate on their research in this room with its 160-ft (49-meter) high domed ceiling.

All gold-leafed and hand-painted with clusters of richly veined marble columns, the center of the ceiling displays allegorical murals painted by Edwin Blashfield and is composed of a dozen figures representing the great ages of Western Civilization.

Just above that, in the stained-glass cupola where the sun refracts so colorfully on a bright day you'll notice, if you happen to be seated at one of the desks while waiting for a librarian to bring your selections from the stacks, another of Blashfield's classical figures, this of a winsome female gazing down thoughtfully at everyone. This is a lyrical depiction of the principle of human understanding, the guiding force behind the Library.

Only some its holdings, which are increasing at the rate of several thousand new items every week, are housed in the Library's main Jefferson Building. The rest are contained in the squat limestone **John Adams Building**, directly behind the main Library, in the modern and boxy **James Madison Memorial Building**, across Independence Avenue, and in an assortment of warehouses scattered across town.

The Library of Congress also offers concerts by noted musicians, lectures by historians and important public figures, readings by some of the country's best fiction writers and poets (it appoints the nation's Poet Laureate), and other events, all of them free. Check at the Visitors Center or phone the main information line for a schedule.

Folger Shakespeare Library

The austere Art Deco exterior of the nearby **Folger Shakespeare Library ❹** (201 East Capitol Street, SE; Mon–Sat, 10am–4pm; closed

The Main Reading Room of the Library of Congress.

BELOW: the Folger Library, Capitol Hill.

Map on page 102

federal holidays; tel: 202-544-4600, or visit www.folger.edu) belies the cozy, Elizabethan-style interior of this great library, museum, and center of literary and performing arts. Previously the site of 14 overpriced townhouses erected in 1871 that never sold and then fell into disrepair, the Folger was built by Standard Oil president Henry C. Folger who bought the land in 1928 with the idea of building a library to hold his expansive collection.

The Folger, which opened in 1932, houses the world's largest collection of Shakespeare's printed works, including a set of precious First Folios from 1623. The Elizabethan and Renaissance worlds are brought to life in the **Great Hall** where many of the Folger's treasures are displayed. It's easy to imagine this hall full of mead-drinking, boar-eating revelers feasting at sturdy banquet tables.

The intimate Elizabethan-style **Folger Theatre** presents performances of medieval and Renaissance music, and other educational programs. The handsome **Reading Room** is open to the public during events such as the Poetry Series, the PEN/Faulkner Fiction Readings, and Shakespeare's birthday celebration. Herbs and flowers grown in Shakespeare's time are planted in the secluded Elizabethan garden, a place to contemplate "nature's infinite book of secrecy."

The Supreme Court

"Oyez! Oyez! Oyez!" With this dramatic cry the **US Supreme Court** ❺ is brought to order (open Mon–Fri, 9am–4.30pm; closed major holidays; sessions open on a first-come first-served basis; lectures and guided tours are offered when the Court is not in session; tel: 202-479-3211 or visit www.supremecourt.gov). This imposing marble edifice at 1st and East Capitol streets wasn't opened until 1935 and, with just nine members, houses the smallest branch of the federal government.

The Court was established by the US Constitution to balance the federal and legislative branches of government and to act as court of last appeal. It first met in 1790 in New

Doorway to the US Supreme Court.

BELOW:
the Supreme Court.

About the Justices

During the Supreme Court's first two centuries, only 107 persons, nominated by the President and confirmed by the Senate, have served as justices. Of these, two are women (Sandra Day O'Connor and Ruth Bader Ginsburg), and two African-American (the late Thurgood Marshall and Clarence Thomas). All but 14 have been Protestants, most have been educated at Harvard, though one (Stanley F. Reed who served from 1938 to 1957) had no law degree at all. Justices have come from 31 of the 50 states, most often from New York, which has sent 16 justices. In 1967, President Lyndon Johnson nominated the first black justice, Thurgood Marshall, a noted civil rights lawyer who won quick Senate confirmation. The same wasn't true for the second black justice, Clarence Thomas, a George Bush, Sr. conservative nominated in 1991 who was humiliated when former colleague Anita Hill testified to his sexual harassment of her. President Ronald Reagan nominated the first woman justice, Sandra Day O'Connor, in 1981. In 1993, President Bill Clinton nominated Ruth Bader Ginsburg, the Court's second woman and the first Democratic appointee in over 35 years.

There is no J Street in Washington because in the script style of the 19th century, I and J looked too much alike. In fact I Street is sometimes written as Eye Street, for clarity. There are no X, Y or Z streets either, and as for the two B streets, which once ran on the north and south sides of the Mall, they became Independence and Constitution avenues.

BELOW:
dinners and inaugural balls are held in Union Station's marble hall.

York, and for its first 145 years had no permanent home. Taverns, hotels, private homes, and the Capitol itself served as a gathering place for the justices. Finally, in 1928, William Howard Taft, the only president to also serve as a justice on the court, convinced Congress to allocate funds for the building, which was designed by architect Cass Gilbert. A broad staircase flanked by the *Contemplation of Justice* and the *Authority of Law*, both sculpted by James Fraser, leads up to this mammoth marble building. Carved into the pediment are the words "Equal Justice Under the Law."

In interpreting the Constitution, the Court has effectively shaped the course of American democracy by ruling in such pivotal cases as Brown v. the Board of Education of Topeka, which in 1954 ended school segregation. In the 1966 case of Miranda v. Arizona, the Court ruled that arresting police officers must inform suspects of their legal right to counsel. In 1973, the Court ruled in favor of making abortion legal in the case of Roe v. Wade.

Other historic cases the Court has heard include Marbury v. Madison, which in 1790 established the Court's ability to declare certain acts of Congress unconstitutional, and the 1857 Dred Scott decision in which the Court declared that Congress had no right to limit the spread of slavery and that slaves were chattel and not citizens and therefore not entitled to protection under the law. More recently, the outcome of the 2000 presidential election was controversially decided by the Court when it ruled in favor of the constitutionality of the electoral procedures.

From the first Monday in October through April, the court hears oral arguments. Of the 7,000-plus requests it receives each year, it actually only hears between 75 and 100. Most case arguments are scheduled for just one hour, each attorney having half an hour to present the case. The justices then withdraw to deliberate. In May and June it delivers its opinions.

Union Station

North of the Supreme Court on Massachusetts Avenue is one of the

Map on page 102

city's great successes of architectural preservation: **Union Station ❻** (50 Massachusetts Avenue, NE; tel: 202-371-9441). This glorious Beaux-Arts train station was built in 1908 by architect Daniel Burnham and when it opened was the largest train station in the world at 750 ft by 344 ft (229 by 105 meters). With the decline of train travel, it had fallen into serious disrepair by the 1970s. In 1981, private and public funds provided $160 million for a rescue job. In 1988 Union Station's former grandeur and the romance of the rail were restored. Today, 25 million visitors a year pass over its platforms and through its marble hallways.

The entrance features a grand triple-arched portico modeled after the Arch of Constantine. In the Main Hall – inspired by the Roman Baths of Diocletian – Amtrak passengers, Metrorail riders (there's a Metro stop here), lunching Capitol Hill staffers, shoppers and visitors surge and flow in perpetual motion. Several cafés and first-class restaurants, plus a 9-screen movie theater, and dozens of shops and fast-food stands keep the station lively day and night.

Next to Union Station is another stately Beaux-Arts building, the old City Post Office building, now home to the **National Postal Museum ❼** (Massachusetts Avenue and First Street, NW; open daily 10am–5.30pm; closed Dec 25; free admittance; guided tours available daily at 11am and 1pm; tel: 202-357-2991 or visit www.si.edu). The museum, operated by the Smithsonian Institution, was opened in 1993 to house an interesting but otherwise worthless collection of Confederate postage stamps and has since grown to become the world's largest philatelic collection. The museum charts America's mail service from its Pony Express days, and features three vintage mail planes suspended from the 90-ft (27-meter) glass atrium ceiling, a walk-through railroad car, and six galleries with changing exhibits.

A museum for children

Behind Union Station at 800 3rd Street is the **Capital Children's Museum ❽** (open late May–early Sept daily 10am– 5pm; remainder of the year Tues– Sun, 10am–6pm; closed Thanksgiving, Dec 25, New Year's Day; admission fee; tel: 202-675-4120 or visit www.ccm.org). The exhibits here are designed to let children learn through experiences as diverse as play-riding a bus or taxi or learning about the Mexican culture by making tortillas and hot chocolate. The museum's greatest accidental PR event is staged near closing time when parents begin coaxing their children away from the museum's captivating gizmos and gadgets.

Kids can learn Morse code and how to type on a Braille typewriter, print a poster on a Ben Franklin printing press, and star in a cartoon. Experience is the theme at this museum whose motto is a Chinese proverb: "I

Old mail planes in the National Postal Museum.

BELOW: the Capital Children's Museum.

Map on page 102

Eastern Market.

BELOW: kids at play in Eastern Market.

see and I forget. I hear and I remember. I do and I understand."

Eastern Market

Once, Washington had several fresh food emporiums, but **Eastern Market ❾** at 7th and C streets, SE is the only survivor and the unofficial center of the neighborhoods surrounding the Capitol. This block-long building dates from 1873 and houses vendors selling fresh produce, meat, poultry, seafood, and cheeses every day but Sunday. Prices aren't exactly cheap, but the old-market atmosphere and the quality of the goods are worth every penny.

Get in line at **Market Lunch** (open Tues–Sat, 7.30am–3pm; Sun, 11am–3.30; tel: 202-547-8444), famous for its hearty breakfasts, crab cakes, and oyster sandwiches. On Saturdays and Sundays, vendors set up shop outside and sell baked goods, flowers, antiques, clothing, jewelry, and a variety of junk.

Stirring sounds

On the south side of Pennsylvania is the **Marine Corps Barracks ❿**

(tel: 202-433-6060) at 8th and I streets, home of the "Eighth and Eye Marines." Make reservations early for the Friday evening Marine Corp parade held here in summer. With unmatched precision and patriotism, the Band, the Drum, and the Bugle Corps as well as the silent drill team assemble within the quadrangle for a stirring ceremony. The sight of a solitary, spotlighted marine playing "Taps" from the parapet of the main tower sends chills up some spines and brings tears to some eyes. The Marines' distinguished band first came to worldwide notice under the baton of John Philip Sousa *(see below)*.

Ten blocks east of the barracks is **Congressional Cemetery ⓫**, at 1801 E Street. Opened in 1807, these burial grounds include the graves of senators, diplomats, prominent members of Congress as well as Capitol architect William Thornton, "March King" John Philip Sousa, Civil War photographer Matthew Brady, FBI director J. Edgar Hoover, and Choctaw chief Pusha-ma-ta-ha. ❏

John Philip Sousa

One of 10 children, Sousa was born in Washington, DC in 1854 to a Portuguese immigrant and his Bavarian-born wife. When he tried to run away to join a circus when he was 13, his father enlisted him into the US Marines. After his discharge in 1875, Sousa, then an accomplished violinist, joined up again in order to conduct the Marines' band.

After he finally left the Marines, Sousa formed his own band and was as wildly popular as any rock star today. His best-known compositions include the famous *Washington Post March* (written for that newspaper's publicity campaign) and *The Stars and Stripes Forever*, now the US's national march. He died in 1932.

RESTAURANTS & CAFETERIAS

Restaurants

American

America
Union Station, 50 Massachusetts Ave., NE. Tel: 202-682-9555. Open: L & D, daily; Sun brunch. $$
The huge menu celebrates US ethnically-inspired cooking.

B. Smith's
Union Station, 50 Massachusetts Ave., NE. Tel: 202-289-6188. Open: L & D, daily; Sun brunch. $$$
Upscale Southern Creole; gumbos, jambalaya, crawfish, and sweet potato-pecan pie.

Bullfeathers
410 First St., SE. Tel: 202-543-5005. Open: L & D, daily; Sun brunch. $–$$
When Teddy Roosevelt was hungry he'd cry, "Bullfeathers!," hence the name. Pub scene; good burgers.

Capitol View Restaurant and Lounge
In the Hyatt Regency, 400 New Jersey Avenue. Tel: 202-783-2582. Open: D, Tues–Sat. $$–$$$
Indulge in the Chocoholics Bar; great view of the Capitol Building and Hill area.

Hawk and Dove
329 Pennsylvania Ave., SE. Tel: 202-543-3300. Open: L & D, daily. $$
Excellent burgers, good choice of brews. Long time Hill favorite.

Market Lunch
225 7th St., SE (inside Eastern Market). Tel: 202-547-8444. Open: Tues–Fri 7:30am–3pm; Sat & Sun, 11am–3:30pm. $
Bare-bones lunch counter serving fresh meats and seafood from the market. Busy at lunch.

The Monocle
107 D St., NE. Tel: 202-546-4488. Open: L&D, Mon–Sat; D only Sun. $$
Clubby, popular among Republican Hill staffers. Near the Senate side of the Capitol.

Two Quail
320 Massachusetts Avenue, NE. Tel: 202-543-8030. Open: L & D, Mon–Fri; D only Sat–Sun. $$
Among the Hill's oldest eateries, crammed with Victoriana; chops and grilled offerings.

French

Bistro Bis
Hotel George, 15 E St, NW. Tel: 202-661-2700. Open: B, L & D, daily. $$$
Classic bistro and bar; pates, cheeses, good wine list, constantly changing menu.

La Colline
400 N. Capitol St., NW. Tel: 202-737-0400. Open: B, L & D, Mon–Fri; D only Sat.. $$–$$$
Consistently good French fare; gathering spot for schmoozers and celebs.

Montmartre
327 7th St., SE. Tel: 202-544-1244. Open: L & D, Tues–Sun. $$–$$$
Lively bistro, small, popular, seasonal menu; all-French wine list.

German

Café Berlin
322 Massachusetts Ave., NE. Tel: 202-543-7656. Open: L & D, Mon–Fri; D only Sat–Sun. $
Short, excellent list of German specialties; goulash, schnitzel, sauerbraten. Good pastries.

Indian

White Tiger
301 Massachusetts Ave., NE. Tel: 202-546-5900. Open: L & D, Mon–Sat; D only Sun. $$
Small, finely prepared menu includes vegetarian, lamb, chicken, papri chaat and traditional tandoori.

Irish

Dubliner
520 N. Capitol St., NW. Tel: 202-737-3773. Open: L & D, daily; bar open until 2am. $
The bar's the draw here; Irish ale and lager; fish and chips; often live music.

Italian

Barolo Ristorante
223 Pennsylvania Avenue, SE. Tel: 202-547-5011. Open: L & D, Mon–Fri; D only Sat. $$$–$$$$
Elegant and tasty, especially the seafood. Handmade pasta; menu changes often.

Cafeterias

Operated by the government primarily for Congress and staffers, these cafeterias serve tasty and reasonably priced meals and are also open to the public, generally 8am–2pm weekdays. Security concerns and congressional schedules may restrict availability, so it's best to check first.

Dirksen Senate Office Building
1st St & Constitution Ave., NE. Tel: 202-224-4249.
There are two cafeterias here, one the Senators' Dining Room with white tablecloths and friendly service.

Library of Congress
James Madison Building, First St and Independence Ave, SE. Tel: 202-707-8300 or 202-707-5000.

Reflectory
US Capitol Building, Senate Side. Tel: 202-224-4870.
Offers take-away sandwiches and other light fare until 3.30pm

House of Representatives Restaurant
US Capitol Building, Room H118. Tel: 202-225-6300.

Canon House Office Building Cafeteria
First St and Independence Ave., SE. Tel: 202-225-1406.

Longworth House Office Building Cafeteria
South Capitol and C sts, SE. Tel: 202-225-4410.

Rayburn House Office Building Cafeteria
Independence Ave and South Capitol St., SW. Tel: 202-225-7109.

Supreme Court Cafeteria
Supreme Court Building First St., NE. Tel: 202-479-3246

PRICE CATEGORIES

Prices for three-course dinner per person with a half-bottle of house wine, tax and tip:
$ = under $25
$$ = $25–$40
$$$ = $40–$50
$$$$ = more than $50

DOWNTOWN

Downtown Washington is as much a concept as a locale. Geographically, it stretches roughly between Foggy Bottom and Chinatown, runs from the White House north toward P Street, and includes much of Pennsylvania Avenue.

R evitalized after long neglect, downtown burns with power, glitters with wealth, and oozes with culture. It's power-lunching at upscale restaurants such as The Palm and The Caucus Room *(see page 127),* and dealing with panhandlers on street corners. It's K Street lawyers, Pennsylvania Avenue bureaucrats, and a new young breed of moneyed professionals taking up residence in the new Penn Quarter along the 7th Street corridor, fresh with pricey condos, shops, and the Shakespeare Theatre *(see page 122).* It's limos stretched curbside and young professionals at their happy-hour haunts. Side by side and overlapped, it's all downtown.

A walk in the park

The best place to start is **Lafayette Square ❶**, directly across Pennsylvania Avenue from the White House. Thanks to that populist Thomas Jefferson, this once-private presidential park is enjoyed by chess players, office workers on their lunch breaks, tourists, and, alas, the homeless, whom you'll notice camped out with their shopping carts and placards. Most are harmless, though they may seem intimidating. If you want to help, see the sidebar on page 26.

Contrary to popular belief, Lafayette Square is not named for the French major-general whose statue you'll see tucked into the southeast corner and who served in Washington's army during the Revolutionary War, but rather for the day itself when in 1824 the Marquis visited Washington and the adoring crowds overflowed into the park just to get a glimpse. The main sculptural feature of the square is actually the statue of General Andrew Jackson – the first equestrian statue, by the way, erected in America. As a tribute to the General, Congress

Map on page 116

LEFT: the Great Hall of the National Building Museum.
BELOW: exuberant staff at The Palm.

resolved that the statue include metal from the brass guns which Jackson captured when he defeated the British in the War of 1812 at the Battle of Pensacola, in Florida, and then finally in New Orleans in 1815.

Among the landmarks ringing the park and facing the **Hay-Adams Hotel** (One Lafayette Square; tel: 202-638-6600) on the corner of H and 16th streets is the pretty yellow-and-white **St John's Church** ❷ (Mon–Sat, 9am–3pm; Sun 8am–3pm; tel: 202-347-8766) with its adjacent Federal-style **Parish House**. Completed in 1816, the socially-correct Episcopal church has been visited by every US president since James Madison, earning it the accolade "Church of the Presidents." Pew 54 is reserved as the "President's Pew," should he decide to drop by.

The brick townhouse across H Street and Jackson Place and facing the Square is the 1818 **Decatur**

Genral Andrew Jackson's statue in Lafayette Square.

House ❸ (748 Jackson Place, NW; Tues, Wed, Fri, Sat, 10am–5pm; Thur, 10am–8pm; closed Mon, Jan. 1, Thanksgiving, Dec 25; free admission; tel: 202-842-0920). This was the first private residence on the Square. Stephen Decatur, a wildly popular 19th-century naval hero, had the house built near the White House, where he was frequently a guest, reputedly because he had designs on the executive mansion himself. Unfortunately, he only lived here for 14 months before he was killed in a duel.

After Decatur's death, several notable statesmen and diplomats lived in the house before Edward Fitzgerald Beale bought it. An adventurer, Beale was the messenger who brought news from California twice, first in 1847 to announce the state's accession into the Union, and then, after a 47-day mad dash across the country on horseback, to

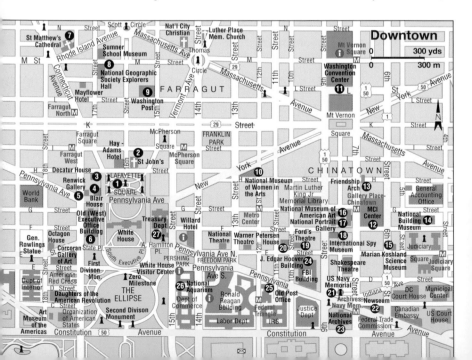

announce the discovery of gold there. The first floor of the house displays furnishings and possessions from the Decatur era, and the second floor is resplendent in Victoriana.

Head back toward the White House and turn right and you'll reach the **Blair House ❹** at 1651 Pennsylvania Avenue. It's not open to the public, but is where visiting dignitaries and other presidential guests stay when they're in town. The house was originally the property of Francis Preston Blair, a 19th-century publisher. It was here that the command of the Union Army at the start of the Civil War was offered to General Robert E. Lee, who refused the post.

The government purchased the house in 1942, and during the Truman renovation of the White House, the president and his family lived here. In 1950, two Puerto Rican nationalists attempted to assassinate the president while he was inside. In the ensuing shoot-out on the street in front of the house, one guard was killed along with one of the intruders. The other was sent to prison where he remained until, by presidential decree, he was released in 1979 and returned to Puerto Rico.

Anchoring the block on the corner of Pennsylvania and 17th Street is the palatial **Renwick Gallery ❺** (open daily 10am–5:30pm; closed Dec 25; tel: 202-357-2700 or visit www.si.edu), an extension of the Smithsonian's National Museum of American Art, devoted to crafts and decorative arts from the traditional to the contemporary and beyond. Built in 1859, it was the District's first art gallery. When William Corcoran commissioned James Renwick to design an avant-garde museum for his art collection, he unwittingly set an architectural trend responsible for the likes of the overdone French Second-Empire-style Old Executive Office Building across the street.

A grand red-carpeted staircase leads to the Renwick's second floor **Grand Salon**, all very red-velvet Victorian and stacked with paintings à la Louvre that include Rembrandt Peale and George Catlin, best known for his portraits of Native Americans. Also notable is the six-

Map on page 116

Decatur House.

BELOW:
the Renwick Gallery.

*Scott Circle. where
Rhode Island Avenue
and Massachusetts
Avenue intersect, is
named after General
Winfield Scott (1786–
1866), a Virginian
and a Mexican War
hero whose statue
(one of more than 30
equestrian statues in
the city) adorns it. To
the west is a statue of
New Hampshire con-
gressman Daniel
Webster (1782–1852),
whose oratory skills
fired the anti-slavery
argument and made
the case for
preserving the Union.*

BELOW: reflected glory
of the Old Executive
Office Building.

sided **Octagon Room**, designed to display Hiram Powers' notorious nude, *The Greek Slave*. Victorian etiquette dictated that men and women view this sculpture separately. The statue is now shamelessly on display at the Corcoran Gallery of Art *(see page 133)* just down the street. The rest of the museum is devoted to American crafts, everything from basketry and clay, to wood and fiber, with five galleries on the first floor reserved for changing exhibits.

Across the street from the Renwick is the **Old Executive Office Building** ❻ a Second Empire style "wedding cake" designed by Alfred Mullett and built in 1888. It was originally the home of the State, War, and Navy departments until each gradually moved out to bigger quarters. In 1947, the Executive Office of the President took it over as a much-needed annex to ease its own crowded office space, but little was done in the way of upkeep. Largely neglected, the building underwent a wholesale restoration in the 1980s, and now stands as the country's

finest example of this architectural style. There are more than 500 rooms here, occupied today by the Office of Management and Budget, the National Security Council, and the Office of the Vice President.

Downtown favorites

Walk north through **Farragut Square** and up Connecticut Avenue and you'll come to the sumptuous **Mayflower Hotel** (1127 Connecticut Avenue, NW; tel: 202-347-3000), a Washington institution completed just in time to serve as the site of Calvin Coolidge's inaugural ball in 1925. FDR stayed here while his rooms were being readied at the White House, FBI director J. Edgar Hoover dined here nearly every night for 20 years, and cowboy actor and singer Gene Autry once rode his horse Champion right through the middle of the banquet room. More recently, famed Clinton paramour Monica Lewinsky bunked here when she was in town testifying before Special Prosecutor Kenneth Starr.

Just off Connecticut on Rhode Island Avenue is the deceptively plain edifice of **St Matthew's Cathedral** ❼ (1725 Rhode Island Avenue, NW; tel: 202-347-3215), which President John F. Kennedy attended. The interior, a profusion of mosaic and marble, displays an altarside marker where Kennedy's casket rested during his funeral Mass in 1963.

Monopolizing the M Street block between 16th and 17th streets is the imperious, three-building HQ of the **National Geographic Society** ❽ (Mon–Sat, 9am– 5pm; Sundays and holidays, 10am–5pm; closed Dec 25; free admission; tel: 202-857-7588; www.nationalgeographic.com). Oddly, the Grosvenors, the conservative first family of the society, hired Edward Durell Stone, the avant-garde architect of New York's Museum of Modern Art and the Kennedy Center,

to design the modernist 17th Street building. The society, characteristically, documented the construction with a time-lapse camera.

Inside, **Explorers Hall** tackles exactly what you'd expect of National Geographic, everything from weather and biology, to anthropology and outer space, and regularly changes its exhibits. Free films, usually well-done National Geographic productions, are shown on Tuesdays at noon, and the gift shop has a large stock of videos and books. Perfect for kids, but just as engaging for adults.

Next, head over to **The Washington Post ❾** (1150 15th Street, NW; free guided tours on Mondays must be booked two to six weeks in advance; tel: 202 334-7969). Second only to *The New York Times* in journalistic influence, the *Post*, in print since 1877, outshined them all with its legendary Watergate coverage in the early 1970s which led eventually to President Richard Nixon's resignation in 1974. News junkies will appreciate the tour of the newsroom and pressroom.

Walk through **McPherson Square** on your way to the **National Museum of Women in the Arts ❿** (1250 New York Avenue, NW; open Mon–Sat, 10am–5pm; Sun, noon–5pm; closed Jan 1, Thanksgiving, Dec 25; admission fee; tel: 202-783-5000; www.nmwa.org). Housed in a former Masonic Temple, a National Historic Landmark, the museum opened in 1987.

There are more than 2,700 pieces of art here, all the work of women, everything from *Portrait of a Noble-woman* by Lavinia Fontana, a 16th-century Italian considered the first professional woman artist, and Elisabeth Vigee-Lebrun, court painter to Marie Antoinette, to renowned Impressionist Mary Cassatt and 20th-century painters Helen Frankenthaler and Lee Krasner.

Nearby is the **Washington Convention Center ⓫** (801 Mt Vernon Place, NW; tel: 202-789-1600), which opened in 2003. Its dramatic 100-ft (30-meter) high curved glass entrance gives onto more than 2 million sq. ft. (186,000 sq. meters) of space and it is expected to draw 3

Check the *Post* for performances of the Capitol Steps, a Gilbert-and-Sullivanesque troupe made up entirely of Hill staffers. Their hilarious song-and-dance spoofs spare no one and take on all issues.

BELOW:
the National Museum of Women in the Arts.

million visitors a year to conventions and trade shows.

In the old days, Washington, like big cities across America, had a thriving downtown anchored by more than one department store to draw crowds. Those days, of course, are gone, but one lone survivor, the **Hecht Company** (corner of 12th and G streets, NW; tel: 202-628-6661), spruced up and catering mainly to visitors who stay at the new hotels nearby, offers shoppers an array of choice soft goods. The centerpiece of this revitalized neighborhood is the **MCI Center** ⑫ (601 F Street, NW; tel: 202-628-3200), a 20,000-seat sports arena complete with shops and restaurants and which serves as the home of the Washington Wizards basketball team and the Capitals hockey team.

Chinatown

At the Gallery Place Metro station at 7th and H streets, NW, you'll notice the striking red pagoda-styled **Friendship Arch** ⑬ marking the beginning of Washington's **Chinatown**. It's definitely not San Fran-

TIP

Tickets to see the Washington Wizards basketball team – known formerly and rather unfortunately, considering the city's high murder rate, as the Washington Bullets – cost from $35 to $175 and can be bought at the MCI Center (202-628-3200) or through Ticketmaster (202-432-7328).

BELOW:
a Chinatown chef.

cisco or New York and only spans the few blocks between 5th and 9th streets, but the restaurants are authentic, and the shops offer lots of imported products, including a wide selection of teas.

From Chinatown, you're not far from the **National Building Museum** ⑭ (401 F Street, NW, Mon–Sat, 10am–5pm; Sun noon–5pm; closed Jan 1, Thanksgiving, Dec 25; tel: 202-272-2448; www.nbm.org), which occupies an entire city block and commemorates American architecture in a series of changing exhibits. In the 19th century, the building was the headquarters of the Pension Bureau, a federal agency charged with distributing pension funds to war veterans and their families. The building was declared a National Landmark, in part because of its terra-cotta frieze, the work of sculptor Casper Buberi, that extends around the entire outside of the structure and which depicts Civil War scenes. Inside, 75-ft (23-meter) high Corinthian columns mark the enormous space, the setting for the inaugural balls of several presidents.

The **Marian Koshland Science Museum** ⑮ (6th and E streets, NW; tel: 202-334-1201; www.koshland-science-museum.org; Wed–Mon 10am–6pm; fee), a new attraction, is intended to make science more fun and accessible. It is part of the National Academy of Sciences, which has offices right round the corner on 5th Street (as well as its original offices on C Street in Foggy Bottom). There's a small but excellent bookstore in the lobby, stocked with titles from its own Joseph Henry Press, which publishes new science works, from oceanography to outer space, with intelligent lay readers in mind.

Named for the wife of wealthy benefactor, the museum focuses on what's new, exciting and challeng-

ing in the scientific world, and tries to reduce science's fear factor. It features exhibits on global warming and DNA, and tries to be very much hands-on and interactive.

Art collections

The Old Patent Office Building on 8th Street at F and G streets, NW is home to two of the Smithsonian's best off-the-Mall museums, the **Smithsonian National Museum of American Art** and the **National Portrait Gallery** ⑰. Both are getting much-need facelifts, and both, unfortunately, are closed until at least 2006, though their collections are traveling around the country, and you can take a virtual tour by visiting www.si.edu.

The building, which housed the Patent Office, the agency that issued patents to inventors, dates from 1867, and at the time it was opened was the city's largest. In 1958, Congress officially gave the building to the Smithsonian. The American Art Museum began as a mix of private and public collections put on display in the office in 1841. The collection is dedicated strictly to American art and has in its holdings more than 30,000 objects.

The adjacent Portrait Gallery, a sort of national family photo album, took up residence in the Patent Office in 1968 and counts among its 15,000 portraits, sculptures, photos, and drawings of American men and women of significance one of the celebrated Landsdowne portraits of George Washington.

Where the spies are

Across the street is the **International Spy Museum** ⑱ (800 F Street, NW; open daily 10am-8pm; closed Jan 1, Thanksgiving, Dec 25; admission fee; tel: 202- 393-7798; www.spymuseum.org). As soon as they walk through the door, visitors are put under surveillance and assume a "cover" identity to get a sense of what it's like to live as spies do, constantly on red-alert.

The emphasis here is on the Cold War with exhibits on the Rosenbergs and Gary Powers, the U-2 pilot shot down over Soviet airspace in 1960, though spies from others eras are represented, including everyone from Mata Hari to the Navajo Codetalkers of World War II. James Bond, Maxwell Smart, and Austin Powers also get billing. Turncoats Aldrich Ames and former FBI agent Robert Hanssen make their mark here amid the cases of spy gadgetry, including a tube of lipstick that doubles as a miniature pistol. Note that lines can be up to three hours long, according to the museum itself. To avoid the crowds, visit after 4pm, and stop for dinner at **Zola** (tel: 202-654-0999), the museum's classy eatery.

Where Lincoln was shot

In the middle of 10th Street between E and F Streets, NW is **Ford's Theatre** ⑲ (open daily for tours 9am–5pm; closed Dec 25 and during rehearsals and performances; tel: 202-426-6924 or visit

Map on page 116

Its location isn't a well-kept secret.

BELOW: the National Portrait Gallery, now being refurbished.

The play's the thing...

BELOW:
the presidential box
at Ford's Theatre.

www.nps.gov/foth). It was here that Abraham Lincoln was shot on April 14, 1865. The theater was then just two years old, lavishly outfitted in the Victorian style, and considered one of the finest theaters in the country. Five days after the end of the Civil War, President and Mrs Lincoln were enjoying a performance of the English comedy *Our American Cousin* when John Wilkes Booth, a popular actor and impassioned Southern sympathizer, crept into the presidential balcony box and fired a bullet into Lincoln's head, just behind the left ear. Booth then leapt for the stage, snagged his foot in the draped flag and broke his left leg. But he still managed to escape on horseback.

While Booth galloped toward Maryland to make his crossing at Port Tobacco into safe territory in Virginia, the unconscious Lincoln was carried across the street to a boarding house owned by tailor William Petersen. Lying in a back room diagonally across a bed because he was too tall to fit in it, Lincoln succumbed to his wound at 7.22am the following morning. On April 26, a detachment of soldiers, in search of Booth, surrounded a Virginia tobacco barn where the assassin had holed up. Refusing to surrender, Booth shot himself.

After the president's death, the theater was closed by the government, which ultimately bought it, then re-opened it in 1932 as a museum. Restored to its original condition, it reopened as a theater in 1968. Check the *Washington Post* for a schedule of plays, usually comedies and seasonal classics such as *A Christmas Carol*, a Ford's Theatre annual tradition. The presidential box is as it was on the day Lincoln was shot, and many artifacts from the assassination are displayed in the basement museum.

The small and humble **Petersen House** ⓴ across the street at 516 10th Street, NW, offers tours in conjunction with the museum at Ford's and remains open when the theater itself is closed for tours due to its performance schedule.

One of the city's best theaters is the new **Shakespeare Theatre** (450 7th Street, NW; tel: 202-547-1122 or visit www.shakespearetheatre.org) whose resident company gives new life to the bard's classic tales. Next door is **Olsson's Books and Music** (418 7th Street, NW; tel: 202-638-7610), a well-stocked chain with knowledgeable staff and several locations across the area, including a branch at Dupont Circle (1307 19th Street, NW; tel: 202-785-1133).

The nation's main street

As part of city architect Pierre L'Enfant's link between Capitol Hill and the White House, **Pennsylvania Avenue** was designed to be the center of its commercial activity, lined with farmers' markets, shops, government offices and residences. The avenue thrived well into the 20th century until the growth of the sub-

Map on page 116

urbs after World War II drew business and housing away from the city. By the 1960s, the avenue, the traditional inaugural parade route of presidents, was an embarrassment, lined with ramshackle buildings and dreary government offices. Not any more. Improvement has been gradual, but Pennsylvania Avenue is restored, and once again worthy of being "the nation's main street."

Continue your downtown circuit by heading up Pennsylvania Avenue toward the White House. Those with an interest in things nautical will enjoy the **US Navy Memorial** ㉑ (7th Street and Pennsylvania Avenue; open Tues–Sat, 9:30–5pm; free admission; tel: 202-737-2300 or 1-800-723-3557 or visit www.lone-sailor.org). It charts the Navy's story since the War of Independence. Those who have served can add their names to the memorial's register, call up photos of their ship on a computer, and connect with their shipmates. On summer evenings, the Navy and Marines stage free concerts on the plaza.

Where Pennsylvania and Consti-tution avenues come together, you'll notice the very modern and gleaming glass wedge that serves as the **Canadian Embassy** (501 Pennsylvania Avenue, NW; tel: 202-682-1740), and across from it at 6th Street and Pennsylvania Avenue what will eventually be the **Newseum** ㉒ (tel: 703-284-3544 or 1-888-639-7386; www.newseum.org), a museum for serious news aficionados scheduled to open in 2007.

For five years, the Newseum was a popular attraction in the headquarters building of the Gannett newspaper chain in nearby Rosslyn, Virginia. When it outgrew its space, newspaper executives also decided that a move into the city proper would add to its prestige. All glass with a 90-ft (27-meter) high atrium, the building will come equipped with a large LED media screen attached to its exterior, a sort of giant television facing the nation's main street, to project a constant flow of up-to-the-minute breaking news. It will also feature a 60-ft (18-meter) high slab of stone engraved with the words of the First Amendment,

Pennsylvania Avenue, DC's main street, got its name after that state failed to win the bid to have the nation's capital located in Philadelphia. The street back then was little more then a lane, muddy and scrub-lined.

BELOW: the US Navy Memorial.

The National Archives.

BELOW: checking out the constitution in the National Archives.

which guarantees freedom of the press, lest anyone on Capitol Hill, deliberately within clear sight of the new building, have ideas otherwise. Inside, the museum promises to be an "interactive museum of news" with videos, photo displays, a 500-seat auditorium, the requisite museum store, and a "news café."

The National Archives

As the federal government's repository of records essential to the country, the **National Archives ㉓** (Pennsylvania Avenue between 7th and 9th streets, NW; tel: 202-501-5000) has everything from the original US Constitution and census records to materials related to the Kennedy assassination and more. The display of the Constitution and the Bill of Rights is the centerpiece, and artist Barry Faulkner has restored the impressive *Declaration of Independence* mural by the entrance. Gallery space has been upgraded and expanded to showcase some of the Archive's rich store of holdings, and there's a theater with a schedule of timely documentaries.

Next is the **J. Edgar Hoover Building ㉔**, home of the Federal Bureau of Investigation (tours unavailable at press time; to check availability, tel: 202-324-3000 or visit www.fbi.gov). Opened in 1975 and named for the bureau's most famous leader *(see panel)*, this stark and cold-looking building, erected in the off-putting architectural style known as New Brutalism, is meant to give an impression of no-nonsense, though that doesn't quite match the bureau's tarnished image of the past few years. The tour, a hit with children, has traditionally focused on gangsters and has included a short firearms demonstration. Plans are in the works for a new tour, which promises to bring things a little more up-to-date.

Spared the wrecker's ball during the city's revitalization campaign, the imposing castle-looking granite building across the street is the **Old Post Office ㉕** (Pennsylvania Avenue and 12th Street, NW; tel: 202-606-8691; open Easter through early Sept, 8am–10.45pm; the remainder of the year 9am–4.45pm).

Hoover's Snooopers

The legendary J. Edgar Hoover, director of the FBI for 48 years until his death in 1972, is said to have kept his job for so long because of the secret files and tape recordings he kept on everyone else in the power game. Looking for elusive evidence of Martin Luther King's Communist Party links, the FBI instead collected tapes of King's bedroom activities. Hoover's collection of evidence about the sex life of President John F. Kennedy and Attorney-General Robert F. Kennedy ensured that the FBI director was unsackable. After he died, reports leaked out that the chaste, no-nonsense and unimpeachable Hoover had a secret, too: a penchant for dressing in women's clothes.

The 1899 building has been converted into space for offices and trendy shops. Take the elevator 270 ft (82 meters) to the top of the tower for a commanding view of the city, especially if you've missed the timed tickets for the Washington Monument. The food court below offers good, inexpensive choices.

Next door is **Federal Triangle**, a modern office complex including the **Ronald Reagan Building**. Across Pennsylvania are two of the city's oldest theaters, the **National** (1321 Pennsylvania Avenue, NW; tel: 202-628-6161), on this site since 1864, and the **Warner** (1299 Pennsylvania Avenue, NW; tel: 202-783-4000).

Stop to rest in **Freedom Plaza**, all flags, fountains and pavement into which has been embedded L'Enfant's original plan for the city, then head over to the Department of Commerce where tucked away in the basement is the **National Aquarium** (14th Street and Constitution Avenue; daily 9am–5pm; closed Dec 25; admission fee; tel: 202-482-2825; www.national aquarium.com). Although not the biggest or the splashiest, it is the country's oldest aquarium. Every day at 2pm, the keepers feed either the sharks, the piranha, or the alligators, which you're welcome to watch, and give impromptu talks. Children like it here, and it's a good place to stop when the Washington heat becomes unbearable.

Nearby **Pershing Park**, a pleasant city green space, offers shade on a hot day. The pond attracts ducks, and in winter you can ice skate. (Rink open Mon–Thurs, 10am–9pm; Fri–Sat, 10am–11pm; Sun 10am–7pm; admittance fee; tel: 202-737-6938).

A renowned hotel

At 14th Street and Pennsylvania Avenue is the **Willard Hotel** (tel: 202-628-9100), built in 1901 as a replacement for the original Willard built on this site in 1801. Lincoln stayed here while he was awaiting the White House to be readied for him. Charles Dickens was a guest here, as was Edward VII when he was Prince of Wales. Julia Ward Howe was a guest of the hotel during the Civil War when she composed *The Battle Hymn of the Republic.* The Willard also gave us the term "lobbyist" since it was in the lobby of this grand hotel during the 19th century that White House office seekers and others pressing their cases in Congress routinely gathered.

Lastly, at 15th Street on the east side of the White House, a gray and rather impenetrable looking building seems vaguely familiar. This is the **US Treasury Department Building** and it's pictured on the back of the $10 bill. Designed in the Greek Revival style by Robert Mills, who also designed the Washington Monument, it dates from 1833. The Treasury Department itself was set up in 1789. Several government bureaus, including the Mint, the Internal Revenue Service and the Secret Service, fall under its purview. ❑

Map on page 116

TIPS

● Stop by the main Visitors Information Center in the Ronald Reagan Building on Pennsylvania Avenue for maps, brochures, and helpful advice.

● Stop by the Woodrow Wilson Plaza outside the Ronald Reagan Building any summer evening. There's a regular schedule of free concerts and other performances.

BELOW: formal high tea in the Willard Hotel's Crystal Room.

RESTAURANTS

American

Butterfield 9
600 14th St., NW. Tel: 202-BU9-8810. Open: L & D, Mon–Fri; D only Sat & Sun. $$$–$$$$
Name comes from the telephone exchange in the Thin Man movies; wins consistent raves.

Breadline
1751 Pennsylvania Ave., NW. Tel: 202-822-8900. Open: L & D, Mon–Fri until 7pm. $
Freshly made breads, sandwiches, fries, soups, desserts. Busy.

Capital Q
707 H St., NW. Tel: 202-347-8396. Open: L&D, Mon–Sat. $
Popular spot for US-style barbecue.

Corduroy
In the Sheraton Four Points Hotel, 1201 K St., NW. Tel: 202-589-0699. Open: B, L & D, Mon–Fri; B & D Sat & Sun $$$–$$$$
Quality ingredients simply prepared in a comfortable setting; elegant desserts.

David Greggory
2030 M St., NW. Tel: 202-872-8700. Open: L & D, Mon–Fri; D only Sat; Sun brunch. $$$
Casual spot features the work of local artists and classic entrées with Latin twist.

DC Coast
1401 K St., NW. Tel: 202-216-5988. Open: L & D,

PRICE CATEGORIES

Prices for three-course dinner per person with a half-bottle of house wine, tax and tip:
$ = under $25
$$ = $25–$40
$$$ = $40–$50
$$$$ = more than $50

Mon–Fri; D only Sat. $$$
Mix of New Orleans gumbos, California modern, crabcakes and other seafood fare.

District Chophouse and Brewery
509 7th St., NW. Tel: 202-347-3434. Open: L & D, daily; bar closes midnight. $–$$
Burgers, beers, billiards; casual brew pub near the Shakespeare Theatre and MCI Center.

15 Ria
Washington Terrace Hotel, 1515 Rhode Island Ave., NW. Tel: 202-742-0015. Open: B, L, D, daily. $$$
Upscale comfort food, seafood and steaks.

Georgia Brown's
950 15th St., NW. Tel: 202-393-4499. Open: L & D, Mon–Fri; D only Sat; Sun brunch & D. $$$
What your grandmother would serve if she were Southern: fried favorites and biscuits.

The Jefferson Room
In the Jefferson Hotel, 1200 16th St., NW. Tel: 202-833-6206. Open: B, L & D, daily; Sun brunch. $$$
Cozy, elegant; menu of upscale American fare changes often. Afternoon tea daily, 3–5pm.

Lafayette
In the Hay-Adams Hotel on Lafayette Square, 800 16th St., NW. Tel: 202-638-2570. Open: B, L & D, daily. $$$$
Long-time city favorite features an elegant dining room, classic menu, top service.

McCormick & Schmick's Seafood
1625 K St., NW. Tel: 202-861-2233. Open: L & D, daily. $$–$$$
Pacific Northwest chain

known for its fresh fish and crustaceans.

Occidental Grill
1475 Pennsylvania Ave, NW. Tel: 202-783-1475. Open: L & D, daily. $$–$$$
Clubby watering hole since 1906; sandwiches and meat-and-potatoes dishes.

Old Ebbitt Grill
675 15th St., NW. Tel: 202-347-4800. Open: L & D, daily; Sun brunch. $$–$$$
Essential Washington eatery since 1856; fine burgers, seafood.

Oval Room
800 Connecticut Ave., NW. Tel: 202-463-8700. Open: L & D, Mon-Fri; D only Sat. $$–$$$
Tony Washington institution; new-American menu; popular at lunch.

Poste
In the Hotel Monaco, 555 8th St., NW. Tel: 202-783-6060. Open: B, L & D, daily. $$$$
Former post office gone modern with top service, classic menu choices, good wine list.

Reeves Restaurant and Bakery
1306 G St., NW. Tel: 202-628-6350. Open: B & L, Mon–Sat, closes at 6pm. $
Famous since 1886 for pies and comfort foods.

701
701 Pennsylvania Ave., NW. Tel: 202-393-0701. Open: L & D, Mon–Fri; D only Sat & Sun. $$$
Upscale, white tablecloths, reputation for good fish. Near the Shakespeare Theatre.

Sky Terrace
In the Hotel Washington, Pennsylvania Ave at 15th St., NW. Tel: 202-638-5900. Open: 11am–midnight, daily;

closed in winter. $
Light fare unexceptional, though the views of the Mall and White House are great.

The Willard Room
In the Willard Hotel, 1401 Pennsylvania Ave, NW. Tel: 202-637-7440. Open: B, L & D, daily; Sun brunch. $$$–$$$$
Elegant dining in the hotel where 19th-century lobbyists got their start. Coffee shop less expensive.

Zola
In the International Spy Museum, 800 F St., NW. Tel: 202-654-0999. Open: L & D, Mon–Fri; D only Sat & Sun. $$$$
American classics with an international flair.

Asian

Full Kee
509 H St., NW. Tel: 202-371-2233. Open: L & D, daily. $, cash only
Offers some of the city's best. Try the shrimp dumpling soup or the oyster casserole.

Nooshi
1120 19th St., NW. Tel: 202-293-3138. Open: L & D, Mon–Sat. $
Authentically prepared noodle dishes with an extensive sushi menu.

Teaism
400 8th St., NW. Tel: 202-638-6010. Open: B, L & D, daily. $
Order from the Japanese-inspired menu at the counter. Many teas.

Ten Penh
1001 Pennsylvania Ave., NW. Tel: 202-393-4500. Open: L & D, Mon–Fri; D only Sat. $$$
Asian-Pacific inspired menu includes inventive desserts. Classy setting.

Tony Cheng's Seafood Restaurant and Mongolian Barbecue
621 H St., NW. Tel: 202-371-8669. Open: L & D, daily. $–$$
Popular, crowded; family-friendly; enormous menu; a DC institution.

Caribbean/Latin/ Mexican/Spanish

Andale
401 7th St., NW. Tel: 202-783-3133. Open: L & D, Mon–Sat. $$
New, serving regional Mexican dishes. Near Shakespeare Theatre.

Café Atlantico
405 8th St., NW. Tel: 202-393-0812. Open: L & D, Mon–Sat; D only Sun. $$$
Upscale Latin and Caribbean cuisine; menu changes often. Near Shakespeare Theatre.

Ceiba
701 14th St., NW. Tel: 202-393-3983. Open: L & D, Mon–Fri; D only Sat. $$
Contemporary menu of Latin-inspired meats, fish, sandwiches. Good appetizers, bar menu.

Jaleo
480 7th St., NW. Tel: 202-628-7949. Open: L & D, daily. $$
Jaleo is Spanish for "commotion." Loud tapas spot. No booking.

Red Sage
605 14th St., NW. Tel: 202-638-4444. Open: 11.30am–11.30pm Mon-Sat; 4.30pm–11pm Sun. $
Tex-Mex standards well done, plus sandwiches, beers, mixed drinks.

French

Bistro D'OC
518 10th St., NW. Tel: 202-393-5444. Open: L & D, daily. $$$

Regional French cooking; cassoulet, veal, roasted chicken. Three-course value pre-theater dinner. Near Ford's Theatre.

Café 15
In the Sofitel Hotel near Lafayette Square, 806 15th St., NW. Tel: 202-730-8800. Open: B, L & D, daily. $$$
Small, modern setting; simply prepared entrées; good wine list and winning desserts.

Gerard's Place
915 15th St., NW. Tel: 202-737-4445. Open: L & D, Mon–Fri; D only Sat. $$$$
One of the city's best with a signature lobster dish. Prix-fixe lunch menu is good value.

Les Halles
1201 Pennsylvania Ave., NW. Tel: 202-347-6848. Open: noon to midnight, daily. $$
Well done French steakhouse; good fries. Try the classic cassoulet. Cigar bar.

German

Café Mozart
1331 H St., NW. Tel: 202-347-5732. Open: B, L & D, daily. $–$$
Down home European; kielbasa, knockwurst, hearty soups, good beer selection.

Indian

Bombay Club
815 Connecticut Ave, NW. Tel: 202-659-3727. Open: L & D, Mon–Fri; D only Sat; Sun brunch. $$$
Regal atmosphere, near the White House; menu includes Indian wine list.

Irish

Fado
808 7th St. NW. Tel: 202-789-0066. Open: L & D, daily. $$

Hearty Irish fare in Chinatown; many beers.

Mediterranean

Zaytinya
701 9th St., NW. Tel: 202-638-0800. Open: L & D, daily. $$
The name means "olive oil" in Turkish; features mezze, appetizers combined to make a meal.

Steakhouses

Bobby Van's Steakhouse
809 15th St, NW. Tel: 202-589-0060. Open: L & D, Mon–Fri; D only Sat. $$$$
Porterhouse steak and side dishes are the hits.

Capital Grille
601 Pennsylvania Ave., NW. Tel: 202-737-6200. Open: L & D Mon–Sat; D only Sun. $$$$
Republican hang-out; steak, chops, gossip.

The Caucus Room
401 9th St., NW. Tel: 202-393-1300. Open: L & D, Mon–Fri; D only Sat. $$$$
Seafood, steaks, white linen tablecloths; popular with powerbrokers.

The Palm
1225 19th St., NW. Tel: 202-293-9091. Open: L & D, daily. $$$$
Politicos gather here for steaks, lobsters, martinis, cigars, gossip.

Smith & Wollensky
1112 19th St., NW. Tel: 202-466-1100. Open: L & D, Mon–Fri; Wollensky Grill open until 2am. $$$$
Very good steaks, salads and wines.

Food Courts

Walk-up counters and cafeterias offering sandwiches, wraps; ice cream, yogurt; Asian, Greek, pizza, chicken, steak, desserts and more. Seating available.

Old Post Office Pavilion
1100 Pennsylvania Ave, NW. Open: 10am–8pm Mon–Sat; noon-7pm Sun. $

Ronald Reagan Building and International Trade Center
1300 Pennsylvania Ave., NW. Open: 7am–7pm Mon–Fri; 11am–6pm Sat; noon–5pm Sun. $

LEFT: the food court at the Old Post Office.

FOGGY BOTTOM AND THE WEST END

This area is a mix of 19th-century townhouses, the modern George Washington University, the oddly placed Kennedy Center, the quirky Watergate complex, magnificent marble edifices, government buildings, new hotels, and a ganglion of poorly marked highways.

Croaking frogs, marshy lowlands, and smoke-belching industry – such were the salient features of Foggy Bottom in the mid-1700s. By the early 20th century, much of this soggy land along the Potomac River was filled in to accommodate the expanding city. Centered around **Washington Circle**, Foggy Bottom's slow and awkward growth created not a few disputes between developers and preservationists. The successes and failures of these groups have created a neighborhood seemingly at odds with itself.

Unusual attractions

This section of DC is bounded by the Potomac River, Constitution Avenue, 17th Street, and N Street. Tourism really isn't big business in Foggy Bottom as it is on the nearby Mall. Entrances are often oblique, reservations for tours may be required weeks in advance, admission might be granted only by showing a photo identification. But the extra effort pays off in the form of smaller (if any) crowds and the feeling you're discovering some unusual attractions just off the beaten path.

To see Washington like a diplomat, begin at 23rd and C streets for one of the city's lesser-known but worthwhile attractions, a guided tour of the **State Department's Diplomatic Reception Rooms** (2201 C Street, NW; tel: 202-647-3241 to arrange in advance for a guided tour, available Mon–Fri, 9.30am, 10.30am, and 2.45pm). These five drawing rooms and dining rooms are where the Secretary of State entertains distinguished foreign guests several nights a week. The exquisite 18th- and 19th-century-style rooms contain a collection of donated antiques, including the mahogany desk upon which

Map on page 130

LEFT:
on the march for
a state occasion.
BELOW:
Einstein's memorial
at the National
Academy of Sciences.

TIP

You can visit the Diplomatic Rooms of the State Department on one of the best "insiders" tours – and it's free. Security concerns dictate availability, and you'll have to book well in advance, but it's worth the effort.

Thomas Jefferson drafted the Declaration of Independence, one of John Jay's punch bowls and a portrait by John Singleton Copley. The oddest item in the collection is the *Landing of the Pilgrims*, a work that depicts a British man-of-war flying the US flag, redcoats as pilgrims, and a dangerously rocky Massachusetts coast lined with welcoming Indians. More sublime scenes of the Mall and the Potomac River beyond are framed by the south rooms' graceful Palladian windows.

Secluded in a grove of elm and holly trees at the corner of 22nd and Constitution is the **Einstein Memorial** at the National Academy of Sciences. The memorial consists of a 7,000-lb (3,200-kg) bronze statue of Albert Einstein seated casually before a circular sky map. The granite map is embedded with 2,700 metal studs representing the planets, sun, moon and stars visible to the naked eye. So endearing is this avuncular Einstein that most people can't resist climbing up onto his lap to pose for a photograph.

The seldom-visited **National Academy of Sciences ❷** (2201 C Street, NW; tel: 202-334-2000) building features a Foucault's Pendulum in the ornate Great Hall, two-story-high window panels illustrating the history of scientific progress, and an auditorium where free Sunday afternoon concerts are frequently held.

At the **Federal Reserve ❸** (20th and C streets; Mon–Fri, 11am, 1pm, and 3pm with 24-hour pre-registration required; tel: 202-452-3778 www.federalreserve.gov), which sets the country's monetary policies, you'll find a changing art exhibit in the building's central atrium. Here you might see anything from 19th-century formal portraiture to an on-the-spot graffiti artist armed with a spray can. The Fed's board meetings are sometimes open to the public, so if you just can't resist sitting in on a discussion of inflation, prime interest, or bank discount rates, check the website for schedules.

Americana

The **Department of the Interior ❹** building at 18th and C streets (Mon–Fri, 8.30am–4.30pm with valid photo ID; closed weekends and federal holidays; tel: 202-208-4743) houses one of the more eclectic museums. The department is charged with overseeing America's public lands and natural resources, including everything from its coal mines to its national parks, and its American Indian reservations and US territories, and as a result it has in its possession a little bit of everything. Dioramas depict an Indian trading post and scenes from the 19th-century Oklahoma land rush, and there are collections of artifacts from the Oceanic peoples of the Marshall Islands and American Samoa. The **Indian Craft Shop**

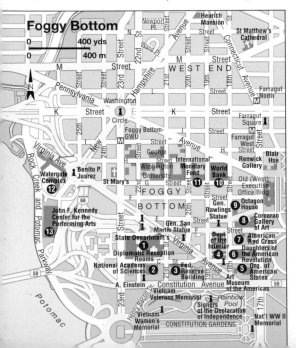

(Mon–Friday and the third Sat of every month, 8.30am–4.30pm) across the hall sells museum-quality turquoise and silver jewelry, baskets, sculpture, weavings and other fine works produced by the artisans of 45 Native American tribes.

In the exact geographical center of DC, at 17th Street and Constitution Avenue, is the **Organization of American States ❺** (Tues–Sun, 10am–5pm; tel: 202-458-3000). The OAS, a largely ceremonial coalition of 35 North and South American countries, also occupies one of the city's most ornate Beaux-Arts buildings. The interior courtyard, with its pre-Columbian-style fountain and jungle of tropical trees, provides respite from the summer heat and a south-of-the-border getaway in the winter. Ascend the grand staircase to the **Hall of the Americas**, a magnificent room with barrel-vaulted ceiling and Tiffany chandeliers. Behind the building is the slightly neglected **Aztec Garden** and, on 18th Street, the OAS-operated **Art Museum of the Americas** (Tues–Sun, 10am–5pm; closed major holidays; guided tours Tues–Friday with reservations; tel: 202-458-6016 or visit www.museum.oas.org) – a treasure house devoted to contemporary Caribbean and Latin American art and also offering a series of films and lectures.

Continental Hall at 1776 D Street (Mon–Fri, 8.30am–4pm, Sun 1pm 5pm; closed major holidays; tel: 202-879-3241 or visit www.dar.org) serves as the headquarters and museum of the **Daughters of the American Revolution ❻**. The organization, founded in 1890 by a group of women descendants of Revolutionary War patriots, has more than 170,000 members. The **DAR museum** contains 34 period rooms furnished to evoke the state-by-state and historical differences in interior design in the United States. You'll see a California adobe-style parlor from 1850; a New Hampshire attic full of children's dolls and toys of the 18th and 19th centuries; and a nautical-style New Jersey room with a chandelier made from the recast anchor and chains from a British frigate.

The DAR's **Library of Geneal-**

Map on page 130

Known originally as Hamburgh, Foggy Bottom got its name from the incessant fog that rolled in off the Potomac, combined with a nearby smoke-belching brewery, glass factory and gas works. The air has been clear since the 1950s, but the name has stuck.

BELOW: the Department of the Interior's museum.

Art Treasures

Washington is not just about politics and marble monuments. There's art here, too, and plenty of it, as one would expect in a capital city. The National Gallery, in particular, is packed floor joists to rafters with some of the world's best.

The city's first art gallery, the Corcoran (now the Renwick), which opened in 1859, and the smaller private museums such as the Kreeger Museum (modern European paintings and sculptures from an insurance tycoon's private collection) and the Phillips Collection *(see page 152)*, claim prizes of their own. The good news is that there's so much to see here that Washington's been able to slough off its image as a cultural backwater to become one of the world's most important centers of art. The bad news is that there's so much to see here that you can't possibly cover it all, certainly not in one visit.

Of course, seeing it all isn't the point. The point is to choose what pleases you and come away from the experience restored, inspired and reminded that "art," as operatic singer Beverly Sills once said, "is the

signature of civilization." Here's just a smidgen of what you'll find.

The National Gallery *(see pages 78–81)* has the only painting by Leonardo da Vinci outside of Europe, the haunting portrait of *Ginevra di Benci* (c. 1480), whose expression he seems to have perfectly captured after she was, so the story goes, deserted by her Venetian lover. It is his earliest known portrait. Several of the Dutch masters are here, too, including Jan Vermeer. Not much is known about the man from Delft beyond the fact that he fathered 11 children, died bankrupt, and produced only a few paintings, among them the lively *Girl with the Red Hat* (1665–67). Enter the Gallery's modern East Wing and you'll see Alexander Calder's massive *Mobile* (1978) suspended from the ceiling and gently paddling the air.

Visit the Corcoran Gallery *(see opposite page)* to see Frederick Church's *Niagara* (1857). A major figure in the Hudson River School, which celebrated American landscape, Church's grand painting was a tribute to the Falls, at one time regarded as a place for spiritual renewal. *The Luncheon of the Boating Party* (1881) by Pierre-Auguste Renoir is in the Phillips Collection. Depicting the comforts and pleasures of good friends and good wine on a pleasant afternoon, this is one of the best loved in the gallery and a favorite of founder Duncan Phillips.

"I am the dog," sculptor Albert Giacometti said of his famous elongated and existential creature *The Dog* (1951), which you can see in the Hirshhorn Sculpture Garden *(see page 75)*. If you stop at the National Museum of Women in the Arts *(see page 119)*, you'll find the Impressionist Mary Cassatt's *Mother Louise Nursing Her Child* (1899), a loving reminder of the special link between mother and child.

For those who prefer browsing, and perhaps even buying, the area around Dupont Circle offers more than two dozen galleries. Many coordinate special showings between 6pm and 8pm on the first Friday of the month (except July–Aug). For the latest details, check www.artgalleriesdc.com ❑

LEFT: the Freer Gallery's Peacock Room.

ogy and Local History is the second largest in the country. Visit this four-story library if only to gaze up at its skylight ceiling that sheds light over a cascade of balconies and onto the tomes perused by diligent researchers below. This room served as the DAR's convention hall until 1920 when the annual convention outgrew this space. In 1929, **Constitution Hall**, designed by architect John Russell Pope, opened next door on 18th Street to accommodate the DAR assembly. DC's second largest auditorium also hosts a variety of public lectures and concerts.

Just north of the DAR at 17th and D streets is the **American Red Cross** ❼ (Visitors Center Mon–Friday, 8.30am–4pm; tours Tues and Fri, 9am, by appointment; tel: 202-639-3038). Here you'll find a trio of stained-glass windows by Louis Comfort Tiffany in the upstairs board room. These beautifully iridescent, opalescent windows feature St Filomena, famed for her healing powers, plus gallant knights of the Red Cross and fortitudinous Una from Spenser's *Faerie Queene*.

The Corcoran Gallery

One block north on 17th Street is the city's oldest and largest private art museum, the **Corcoran Gallery of Art** ❽ (Wed–Mon, 10am–5pm, Thurs until 9pm; closed Jan 1, Thanksgiving, Dec 25; fee; tel: 202-639-1700; www.corcoran.org). The present gallery was opened in 1888 to house the expanding collection of William Wilson Corcoran, a Washington philanthropist and banker, which had outgrown its original red-brick quarters near the White House. That original gallery, now the Renwick Gallery, was begun in 1859. Construction stopped at the outbreak of the Civil War when Corcoran, a Southern sympathizer, found himself unwelcome in Washington and headed off for Europe.

The museum, finally opened in 1874, was hailed as one of the country's first major art galleries, only surpassed 14 years later by the "new" and bigger Beaux-Arts gem that is the gallery's permanent home. As you enter the Corcoran, look up at the frieze where 11 names, chosen by the architect, are carved: PHIDIAS,

Map on page 130

LEFT:
Tiffany window in the Red Cross building.
BELOW:
the Corcoran Gallery.

Octagon House.

BELOW: the Corcoran
Gallery of Art.

GIOTTO, DURER, MICHELANGELO, RAPHAEL, VELASQUEZ, REMBRANDT, RUBENS, REYNOLDS, ALLSTON, and INGRES.

The trustees discovered too late that the much-lesser talent, Washington Allston, was an uncle of the architect's mother. Correcting in print what they can't in stone, gallery publications have replaced Allston with the more deserving Da Vinci.

Inside is a comprehensive collection of 19th- and 20th-century American art as well as European carpets, tapestries, marble sculptures, and European paintings including those by well-known artists such as Rembrandt, Rubens, Renoir, and Degas. Perhaps the best known work is a nude sculpture by artist Hiram Powers, *The Greek Slave*, which scandalized Victorian museum-goers when first unveiled.

In 1925 Senator William Clark of Montana bequeathed to the Corcoran his extensive European collection, including tapestries and stained glass. He also donated an entire French salon, the *Salon Dore*, considered one of the finest examples of late French-Rococo interior design.

Just west of the Corcoran is the **Octagon House** ❾ (Tues–Sun, 10am–4pm; closed Jan 1, Thanksgiving, Dec 25, admission fee; tel: 202-638-3105 or visit www.archfoundation.org) designed in 1798 by Dr William Thornton, the first architect of the Capitol, for Colonel John Tayloe, a wealthy Virginian and friend of George Washington's. Although its name suggests eight sides, this Federal-style structure, which is now the headquarters of the American Institute of Architects, actually has only six.

The city's second largest land holder (after the federal government) is **George Washington University**, occupying 20 square blocks from Washington Circle south to G Street. The school settled here in 1912 and expanded into the surrounding town homes, converting them into classrooms, dormitories, and offices. The university's well-known law library at 718 20th Street is an elegant brick and concrete structure and an improvement over GW's prosaic campus style.

If you see an ocean liner run aground in a row of townhouses, you're at **2000 Pennsylvania Avenue**, a modern office building fronted by the **Lion's Row town houses**. The building houses offices, several restaurants, and a number of other mall-type shops. Also in the neighborhood are the little-known private **international galleries** run by the arts societies of the **World Bank** (1818 H Street, daily 9am–5pm; tel: 202-477-1234), which features sculpture, jewelry, and paintings by bank staffers and the **International Monetary Fund** (720 19th Street, NW; open Mon–Friday, 10am–4.30pm; tel: 202-623-6869) which displays member countries' currency and showcases international artists.

On the north side of Washington Circle, between Georgetown and Downtown, is DC's newly developed **West End**. The main strip along M Street is dominated by glitzy hotels and new office buildings.

Watergate

Moving south toward the Potomac you'll come upon the round and lay-ered **Watergate complex** and the adjacent rectangular Kennedy Center. Distinctive if unattractive, they've been described together as a "wedding cake and the box it came in." Now infamous as the site of the break-in at the offices of the Democratic National Committee that ultimately resulted in the resignation of Republican president Richard Nixon in 1974, the ultra-modern curvaceous Watergate is a complex of apartments, offices, shops and restaurants – and the Watergate Pastry Shop (2534 Virginia Avenue, NW; tel: 202-342-1777) where you can feast on scandalously rich desserts.

The Kennedy Center

The John F. Kennedy Center for the Performing Arts (tel: 1-800-444-1324 or 202-467-4600; www.kennedy-center.org for information, schedule and box office) pays a more positive tribute to a former president. It serves as a living memorial to Kennedy's belief that the US should be remembered not for its "victories or defeats in battle or in politics," but for its "contribu-

Map on page 130

Washington loves conspiracy theories. One argued that the CIA framed Nixon over Watergate to divert attention from its own covert activities. Russia said the US military-industrial complex had undermined Nixon because he had become too friendly with the Soviet Union. And China said the Russians were behind it all because they believed Nixon had become too close to Beijing.

BELOW: the Watergate complex.

Map on page 130

Plans to make the Kennedy Center more accessible over the next decade include linking it with the Mall, with a four-block plaza stretching over existing roadways and a new terrace surrounding the building and hanging over the Potomac.

BELOW:
JFK's 7-ft (2.1-meter) bronze bust in the Kennedy Center.
RIGHT:
the Kennedy Center's Hall of Nations.

tion to the human spirit." Legislation establishing the center was actually signed into law by President Dwight D. Eisenhower in 1958 and was designated a memorial to President Kennedy following his assassination in 1963. Angular and flat-roofed, the building was designed by Edward Durrell Stone, and opened for its first performance in 1971.

Isolated by careless urban planning and a tangle of roadways, this imposing monument contains six theaters presenting opera, ballet, musical theater, chamber music, jazz concerts, silent films, recitals, workshops, and children's theater. The Concert Hall, its largest performance space with more than 2,400 seats, is home to the National Symphony Orchestra.

There are free performances at 6pm every evening at the **Millennium Stage** (actually two stages, one at either end of the Grand Foyer). Afterwards, you can take the elevator to the **Roof Terrace** for a fine view of the city and a bite to eat in one of two restaurants (tel: 202-416-8555 for reservations and hours).

You can take a free guided tour (Mon–Fri, 10am–5pm; Sat–Sun, 10am–1pm; tel: 202-416-8524) to see the inside of the theaters, the glamorous **Hall of Nations**, which displays the flags of all the nations with which the US has diplomatic relations, and the **Hall of States**, where the flags of the states are displayed in the order that they entered the Union. The tour includes the **Performing Arts Library** and the **Grand Foyer,** one of the world's largest rooms at 630 ft (192 meters) long, 60 ft (18 meters) high, and 40 ft (12 meters) wide. It contains the Robert Berks sculpture of President Kennedy and 18 one-ton Orrefors crystal chandeliers. There's an interactive "John F. Kennedy, His Life and legacy" exhibit.

Note that parking is limited and expensive. The easiest option is to take Metro to the Foggy Bottom/ George Washington University station and catch the free shuttle bus, which operates every 15 minutes between 9.45am to midnight, Mon–Sat, and noon–8pm on Sundays and public holidays. ❑

RESTAURANTS

American

Aquarelle
In the Watergate Hotel, 2650 Virginia Ave, NW. Tel: 202-298-4455. Open: B, L & D, daily; Sun brunch. $$–$$$
Upscale with a Mediterranean slant. Near the Kennedy Center; offers a pre-theater menu.

Blackie's
In the Washington Marriott, 1217 22nd St., NW. Tel: 202-333-1100. Open: L & D, daily. $$$$
Veteran DC establishment focuses on beef served up any way you like it.

Circle Bistro
One Washington Circle, NW. Tel: 202 293-5390. Open: B, L & D, daily; Sun brunch. $$$
Casual, upscale dining features top desserts; claim a stool at the long glossy bar for a drink after the show at the Kennedy Center.

The Grill
In the Ritz-Carlton Hotel, 1150 22nd St., NW. Tel: 202-835-0500. Open: B, L & D, daily; Sun brunch. $$$
Elegant hotel restaurant with a casual feel, American-style fish and meat entrées, good champagne Sunday brunch.

Melrose
In the Park Hyatt Hotel, 1201 24th St., NW. Tel: 202-955-3899. Open: B, L & D, daily; Sun brunch. $$$
Overlooks a courtyard. Try the crabcakes; save room for dessert. Jazz combos and dancing on weekends.

Nectar
In the George Washington University Inn, 824 New Hampshire Ave., NW. Tel: 202-298-8085. Open: D only, Tues–Sat..$$$
Few tables, fewer entrées, tasty and billed by the attentive staff as "progressive American cooking".

The Prime Rib
2020 K St., NW. Tel: 202-466-8811. Open: L & D, Mon–Fri; D only, Sat & Sun. $$$$
Tuxedoed waiters, baby grand, prime rib, dependably excellent, DC institution.

Roof Terrace Restaurant
The Kennedy Center, 2700 F St, NW. Tel: 202-416-8555. Open: D, on performance evenings; supper and dessert afterwards; Sun brunch. $$–$$$
Perfect before or after the show; gorgeous rooftop view of the city. Classic, well-done American entrées. In a hurry? Try the salad bar/sandwich line before the show at the refurbished KC Café.

600 Restaurant at the Watergate
600 New Hampshire Ave, NW. Tel: 202-337-5890. Open: L & D, Mon–Fri; D only, Sat & Sun. $$$
Go before a Kennedy Center show and sample the appetizers and salad entrées, or order the double lamb chops, venison or even ostrich. Revives the top-notch cookery of a former favorite at this location.

French

Marcel's
2401 Pennsylvania Ave NW. Tel: 202-296-1166. Open: D daily. $$$$
Pre-theater dinner includes limo service to the Kennedy Center. Return afterwards for dessert and a drink at the piano bar.

Italian

Galileo
1110 21st St., NW. Tel: 202-293-7191. Open: L & D, Mon–Fri; D, Sat & Sun. $$$$
Long one of the city's best; menu changes daily. Lunch at the bar is a less expensive treat.

Latin

Agua Ardiente
1250 24th St., NW. Tel: 202-833-8500. Open: L & D, Mon–Fri; D, Sat & Sun. $$–$$$
Top-notch latin-style dining in a former church complete with altar.

Dishes include garbanzo-bean bread wraps and many tapas.

Seafood

Legal Sea Foods
2020 K St., NW. Tel: 202-496-1111. Open: L & D, Mon–Fri; D only Sat. $$$
One of a national chain known for fresh food.

Kinkead's
2000 Pennsylvania Ave., NW. Tel: 202-296-7700. Open: L & D, daily. $$$$
Fresh seafood finely but simply prepared; live jazz daily; opt for a light meal at the bar.

PRICE CATEGORIES

Prices for three course dinner per person with a half-bottle of house wine, tax and tip:
$ = under $25
$$ = $25–$40
$$$ = $40–$50
$$$$ = more than $50

RIGHT: Washington, DC is renowned for its seafood.

GEORGETOWN

Georgetown has the commercial bustle of a 19th-century port city, the youthful energy of a college town, the international style of a diplomatic community, and the wealthy mien maintained by its resident population of lawyers, socialites and members of the media.

Georgetown is the pedestrian heart of Washington. Shaded streets, brick and cobblestone sidewalks, row houses, and low-rise commercial buildings create an atmosphere that is quaint and on a distinctly human scale. It is inaccessible by Metro, thanks to the residents who argued when the tunnels were being dug that a subway stop would only crowd the streets with the hoi polloi, so you'll be forced to either hoof it the 10 minutes or so it takes from Foggy Bottom, the nearest Metro stop, or spring for a cab.

Georgetown's traffic gridlocks are legendary and its limited parking a source of frustration. It is also a place of rowdy just-legal imbibers cruising M Street and Wisconsin Avenue, of Halloween madness and of mayhem after a Redskins victory. Georgetown hosts a not-trivial number of muggings and burglaries that make some quiet side streets unsafe after dark.

Port authority

Originally a part of Maryland, Georgetown was settled in 1703 on the banks of the Potomac River. Wharves, warehouses, and factories – many structures still extant – lined the riverbank of this flourishing port that shipped tobacco and flour world wide. The square-mile town was probably named after King George

II (two owners of the original land grants were also named George and historians still squabble over who among the Georges the area was really named for). It was soon populated by plantation owners from Maryland and Virginia, merchants from New England, and a great number of slaves and laborers. In the 1780s, Georgetown's gracious homes, inns and taverns made it an ideal staging area for the planning of the nation's permanent capital city.

George Washington, Thomas Jef-

Map on page 140

LEFT: reflecting in a Georgetown market.
BELOW: joggers in Georgetown, near the C&O Canal.

Students on campus.

BELOW:
Georgetown University.

ferson, John Adams, and a slew of architects, governors and foreign envoys frequented Georgetown, many establishing permanent homes. In the late 1780s Bishop John Carroll founded Georgetown Seminary – an institution that added to Georgetown's distinction. The seminary grew into **Georgetown University** ❶, the oldest Catholic college in the country. Two of George Washington's nephews were enrolled here, as was a grandnephew of Andrew Jackson. The gothic spires of the university's **Healy Hall** dominate the skyline of Georgetown from its perch at 37th and O streets. The building was named for Father Patrick J. Healy, a black man who served as the university's president between 1874 and 1882. The university's School of Foreign Service has turned out some of the nation's top diplomats, and its law school is among the best in the country.

Georgetown thrived as a cos-

mopolitan city, industrial center, and shipping canal terminus until the advent of the railroad and of steam navigation, which required deeper waters than the town's port could provide. The growth of the new capital after the Civil War sealed Georgetown's fate, especially after its territory was swallowed by Washington in 1871. By the end of the 19th century, Georgetown fell into neglect, but never lost its sense of a separate identity. In 1950, the area was declared a National Historic District, paving the way for restoration of many of the original Federal-style homes. Many of Washington's most powerful live here, conducting much of the business of government and politics at their exclusive private parties.

Georgetown is ringed like a walled city by Rock Creek Park, the Potomac River, Georgetown University and Whitehaven and Dumbarton Oaks parks. Though most of the trade here is conducted in shops and

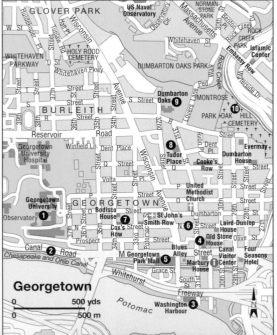

Georgetown

restaurants along M Street and Wisconsin Avenue, Georgetown's waterfront retains some of its earlier bustle.

To reach the waterfront from the higher levels, movie fans may like to take the 97 "Exorcist Steps" from the junction of 36th and Prospect Street. William Peter Blatty, *The Exorcist*'s author, had been a student at Georgetown University and the steps where the priest met his fate featured in the 1973 film that Billy Graham said had "a power of evil."

Touring and shopping

The 185-mile-long (300-km) **Chesapeake & Ohio Canal ❷** *(see panel, page 165)* begins in Georgetown and is easily accessible from several points here. Commuters, strollers, dog walkers and weekend athletes use the serene and shaded canal and its towpath. **Mule-drawn boat rides** from the Foundry Mall take you back to a more leisurely age.

On the Potomac River at 31st Street is **Washington Harbour ❸**, a modern monstrosity housing not-so-notable shops, eateries and offices. But it's worth a visit if only

for its computer-choreographed fountain, sculptures and riverside promenade.

At 30th and M streets you'll find the **Old Stone House ❹** (3051 M Street, NW; open Wed–Sun, 10am–4pm; closed major holidays; tel: 202-426-6851), one of the city's oldest and quaintest buildings. Built in 1765, this six-room house was used as a carpentry shop and home by its original owners. The architecture and furnishings reflect the modest lifestyle of the pre-Revolutionary days. Behind the house is a small and wonderfully wild garden where fruit trees and densely planted borders of flowers bloom with abandon spring through fall. This is a perfect retreat for lunchtime picnickers and weary pavement pounders.

At the west end of M Street is the oft-promoted **Georgetown Park ❺** mall. This $100-million Victorian-style mall is a success story of architectural preservation, but its 85 international boutiques and specialty shops can't hold a candle to the more interesting (and less pricey) stores along M Street and Wisconsin

Interpreting the past on the C&O Canal.

LEFT: restaurants flourish in Georgetown's harbor. **BELOW:** Georgetown Park shopping mall.

Map on page 140

Georgetown's busy main street.

BELOW: Halcyon House, in Prospect Street, was built by Benjamin Stoddert, the first secretary of the navy, in 1783. It is not open for visits.

Avenue. These streets are lined with opportunities to buy everything from expensive Italian suits, cheap shoes, antiques, surplus military wear, household goods, coffees and spices, and American crafts.

Famous residents

Georgetown's greatest charm is its architecture – street after street of elegant town homes, best seen on foot. In particular, look for the fine Federal-style historic homes on **N Street ⑥**. The **Laird-Dunlop House** at **number 3014**, originally the home of a wealthy tobacco merchant, was owned by Abraham Lincoln's son, Robert Todd. The house at **number 3017,** built in the 1790s by a descendant of an original Georgetown landowner, was where Jacqueline Kennedy lived after her husband's assassination. Before he was president, Jacqueline and John Kennedy lived at **number 3307** in the stately **Marbury House.** The houses from numbers 3327 to 3339 are known as **Cox's Row ⑦**, named for Colonel John Cox, Georgetown's first mayor, who served for

22 years and lived at **number 3339**.

Evermay is a spectacular private residence you can admire from the sidewalk at 1623 28th Street, along with **Cooke's Row**, four whimsical Victorian town homes on the 3000 block of Q Street.

One of the grandest residences in the neighborhood is **Tudor Place ⑧** at 1644 31st Street (by guided tour only with advance reservations; Feb–Dec, Tues–Fri 10am, 11.30am, 1pm, 2.30 pm, and Sat on the hour 10am–3pm; closed major holidays; donation required; Christmas tours available in December; garden open year round Mon–Sat, 10am–4pm, no reservation needed; tel: 202-965-0400 or visit www.tudorplace.org).

From 1805 to 1983, this neoclassical mansion was occupied by generations of the same family. Martha Custis Peter, a granddaughter of Martha Washington, purchased a city-block's worth of property with $8,000 left to her by the Washingtons. Martha and her husband Thomas hired Dr William Thornton, architect of the original US Capitol and the Octagon House, to design

their home. As a friend of Thomas Jefferson, Thornton created a gracious home with some clever Monticello-esque features. The rooms are eclectically decorated with formal neoclassical portraits, Civil War-era daguerreotypes, moderately masterful paintings by "artistic" family members, and modern snapshots.

Dumbarton Oaks

Just north of Tudor Place is **Dumbarton Oaks ❾** (Tues–Sun, 2pm–5pm; closed major holidays; tel: 202-339-6401; www.doaks.org) a museum-house and garden that is beautiful in every season. The 1801 home and property were bought in 1920 by Mr and Mrs Robert Woods Bliss as a "country retreat in the city." Mr Bliss, a former ambassador to Argentina, was a collector of Byzantine and pre-Columbian art. His wife Mildred, and noted landscape gardener Beatrix Farrand, designed 10 acres (4 hectares) of formal gardens.

In 1940, the Blisses donated their property, library, and collections to Harvard University, which subsequently opened it to the public. Several famous musicians performed for the Blisses and their guests in the lavish **Music Room**, including Igor Stravinsky whose *Dumbarton Oaks Concerto* was commissioned by the couple for their 30th wedding anniversary. In 1944, amid the room's Flemish tapestries and frescoes and under its hand-decorated ceiling, representatives from the US, the UK, China, and the Soviet Union gathered for talks that led to the formation of the United Nations.

The museum's **Byzantine collection** is comprised of some 1,500 artifacts, including textiles, mosaics, crosses and other liturgical items, plus 12,000 Byzantine coins, making it an exceptionally complete collection. The **pre-Columbian collection** is housed in eight exquisite glass pavilions designed by Philip Johnson. The glass invites the leafy green outdoors in to envelope the brilliant gold jewelry, jade statues, and stone masks on display.

What was envisioned for Dumbarton Oaks' neglected grounds was nothing short of brilliant. The old barnyards, cow paths, and steep

In summer the river can get as crowded as the roads.

BELOW: Dumbarton Oaks gardens.

Map on page 140

TIP

Although exclusive Georgetown doesn't have a Metro station, two small buses offer a service every 10 minutes to and from three Metro stations. One runs from Foggy Bottom along Wisconsin Ave. and K St., and the other between Dupont Circle and Rosslyn along M St. Details: www.wmata.com

BELOW: Blues Alley.

slopes were replaced by terraced gardens, boxwood hedges, 10 pools, nine fountains, an orangery, a **Roman-style amphitheater**, a pebble garden, and three seasons of blooming flowers. A full-time crew of a dozen gardeners work year-round to maintain the gardens, whose beauty and number of visitors peak with the blooming of bulbs, forsythia, and cherry trees in the spring.

Nearby **Oak Hill Cemetery** ❿ provides the perfect classroom for an education in urban landscaping, local history, and the architecture of the afterlife. In continuous use since 1849, this comfortable place includes the graves of John Howard Payne (author of *Home, Sweet Home*), statesmen Edwin M. Stanton and Dean Acheson, and socialite Peggy O'Neill. The gatehouse offers a brochure with a map locating the graves of other Washingtonians.

A stroll down the brick paths and mossy steps leads you past a **Gothic-style chapel**, a miniature **Temple of Vesta**, marble obelisks, pensive angels, and forlorn women carved in Phidian robes.

Dumbarton House (2715 Q St; tours Tues–Sat 10:15am, 11:15am, 12:15pm, 1:15pm; tel: 202-337-2288; www.dumbartonhouse.org), HQ of the National Society of the Colonial Dames of America, displays Federal-period furniture and art. It shows how life was lived by the well-to-do in the early 1800s. Dolley Madison *(see page 61)* stopped here when fleeing from British troops.

Georgetown's nightlife

By night, Georgetown is where you'll find the greatest variety and densest concentration of restaurants *(see opposite page)*. While the local bar scene tends to be run-of-the-mill, one nightclub is worth seeking out. **Blues Alley** (in the alley at Wisconsin Avenue below M Street; tel: 202-337-4141; www.bluesalley.com) is DC's oldest and most prominent jazz club where top stars such as Dizzy Gillespie, Wynton Marsalis and Nancy Wilson have performed. Reservations are essential, and the better tables go to patrons who show up early for dinner, which features Louisiana Creole cuisine. ❏

RESTAURANTS

American

Austin Grill
2404 Wisconsin Ave, NW. Tel: 202-337-8080. Open: L & D, daily; Sat & Sun brunch. $
Top Tex-Mex standards; known for its crabmeat quesadilla.

Booeymonger
3265 Prospect St., NW. Tel: 202-333-4810. Open: daily 8am–midnight. $
Long-time favorite deli and hangout with extensive sandwich list; order one of theirs, or build your own. Espresso bar.

Clyde's
3236 M St., NW. Tel: 202-333-9180. Open: L & D, daily; Sun brunch. $–$$
G-town anchor; comfortable bar; friendly service; good burgers, seafood.

Martin's Tavern
1264 Wisconsin Ave., NW. Tel: 202-333-7370. Open: L & D, daily. $$
70-year-old watering hole to the famous; casual; comfort food, steaks; JFK proposed to Jackie here.

Mendocino Grille and Wine Bar
2917 M St., NW. Tel: 202-333-2912. Open: L & D, Mon–Sat; D only Sun. $$
California east; salads, sandwiches; Asian-influenced menu with good wine bar.

PRICE CATEGORIES

Prices for three-course dinner per person with a half-bottle of house wine, tax and tip:
$ = under $25
$$ = $25–$40
$$$ = $40–$50
$$$$ = more than $50

Nathan's
3150 M St., NW. Tel: 202-338-2000. Open: L & D, daily; Sun brunch. $$
Clubby landmark with bar and white-tablecloth service; good burgers and fish; Sunday brunch best.

1789
1226 36th St., NW. Tel: 202-965-1789. Open: D, daily. $$$–$$$$
New-American in elegant Federal-style townhouse; true DC classic.

Sequoia
3000 K St., NW, at the Washington Harbour. Tel: 202-944-4200. Open: L & D, daily; Sun brunch. $$$$
Terrace offers best view of the Potomac; tony, new-American.

Tony & Joe's
3000 K St., NW, at the Washington Harbour. Tel: 202-944-4545. Open: L & D, daily. $$$
Casual, upscale; seafood favorites on a waterfront location.

Asian

Asia Nora
2213 M St., NW. Tel: 202-797-4860. Open: D, Mon-Sat. $–$$
Small, quiet, good fish; try the sample entrées which combines bites of various dishes.

Ching Ching Cha
1063 Wisconsin Ave, NW. Tel: 202-333-8288. Open: L and tea, daily. $–$$
Peace and quiet with ceremonious tea service and light meals.

Miss Saigon
3057 M St., NW. Tel: 202-333-5545. Open: L & D,

daily. $$$
Fine Vietnamese with exceptional seafood.

Ethiopian

Zed's
1201 28th St., NW. Tel: 202-333-4710. Open: L & D, daily. $$
Top fare includes doro watt (spicy chicken) and gomen (collard greens) in upscale setting.

French

Bistro Français
3124 M St., NW. Tel: 202-338-3830. Open: L & D, daily; open until 4am. $–$$
Onion soup, omelets, lamb and more; perfect for post-party lingering.

Bistro Lepic
1736 Wisconsin Ave., NW. Tel: 202-333-0111. Open: L & D, Tues–Sat. $–$$
Intimate, authentic bistro with a following; also offers some international dishes.

Michel Richard Citronelle
In the Latham Hotel, 3000 M St., NW. Tel: 202-625-2150. Open: B, L & D, Mon–Fri; B & D Sat & Sun. $$$$
Sophisticated, French-inspired menu changes often, regarded as the city's best.

Italian

Pizzeria Paradiso
3282 M St., NW. Tel: 202-223-1245. Open: L & D, daily. $
Love pizza? Stop here. Crust a winner; every topping you can name.

Café Milano
3251 Prospect St. Tel: 202-333-6183. Open: L & D,

daily. $$–$$$
The food's excellent but it's the bar scene that draws DC café society here.

Filomena
1063 Wisconsin Ave. Tel: 202-338-8800. Open: D daily. $$$
Elegant and long a favorite; popular with Kennedy Center goers.

Middle Eastern

Café Divan
1834 Wisconsin Ave. Tel: 202-338-1747. Open: L & D, daily. $
All the favorites; stuffed grape leaves, baba ghanoush, fried feta, lamb and beef kebabs in a stylish setting.

Fettosh
3277 M St., NW. Tel: 202-342-1199. Open: L & D, daily. $
What your mother would serve if she were Lebanese; kebabs, hummus, 32 appetizers.

RIGHT: serving up the local brew at Martin's Tavern.

DUPONT CIRCLE TO ADAMS MORGAN

Dupont Circle is Washington's artiest neighborhood, packed with galleries, eateries, small museums, and a bevy of Beaux-Arts mansions. Adams Morgan, a sort of Latin Quarter and Greenwich Village rolled into one, is best known for its ethnic mix.

Dupont Circle ❶ – where Connecticut, Massachusetts, and New Hampshire avenues intersect – is the heart of the artsy neighborhood that goes by the same name. Since the 1960s the circle has been a rallying point for demonstrations and a stage for ad hoc concerts and impromptu happenings. When the sun shines, the circle is a veritable theater-in-the-round, whose colorful cast of characters includes chess players, lunchtime picnickers, lovers and potential lovers, the generally wacky and weird – and the down and out.

The circle, originally known as Pacific Circle, was part of the neighborhood colorfully named The Slashes after Slash Run, a stream used as the dump for the aromatic offal of several nearby slaughterhouses. Thanks to the massive public works projects of the 1870s, Slash Run was finally diverted into a sewer system and buried, and Connecticut Avenue, until then a muddy lane, was widened and paved, making the area suddenly attractive to wealthy real estate developers.

Architecturally, Dupont Circle is a treasure. The town houses lining its shady side streets are infinitely, and often whimsically, outfitted with English-style gardens, keyhole porticoes, stained- and leaded-glass windows and – if you look up –

slate roofs, turrets and copper bays.

In 1882 the circle was renamed for Admiral Samuel F. Dupont, a member of the famous Delaware chemical family, who gave the Union its first naval victory of the Civil War when he captured Port Royal, South Carolina. Put in charge of the new ironclad fleet, Dupont then went off to take Charleston from the Confederates, but failed miserably, was relieved of his command, and died in disgrace in 1865. His widow Sophie worked to revive

Map on page 148

LEFT
wall art in the style of Toulouse-Lautrec.
BELOW:
Dupont Circle.

Kramerbooks: a place for browsing and shmoozing.

her husband's honor, which eventually led to Congress's approving the funds for the **fountain** you see in the circle's center and which commemorates the admiral. The fountain was dedicated in 1921 and designed by the team of Daniel Chester French and Henry Bacon, collaborators on the Lincoln Memorial, and features upper and lower basins connected by nautically inspired marble figures representing the sea, the stars, and the wind.

Architectural attractions

An antidote to Washington's monumental and decidedly conservative tendencies, Dupont Circle is comfortably human-scaled and playfully trendy, with a European touch. Two dozen **art galleries**, which hold a joint **open house** the first Friday of each month are scattered throughout (check the *Washington Post* or visit www.artgalleriesdc.com for a current list of openings and events). You'll

also find myriad outdoor cafés, bistros, and bars such as **Kramerbooks and Afterwords Café** (1517 Connecticut Avenue, NW; Sun–Thurs, 7.30am–1am; Fri–Sat 24 hours; tel: 202-387-1400), Dupont Circle's Grand Central for browsing, cruising, or shmoozing. You'll also find funky shops, chic boutiques, and a good second-hand bookstore, **Second Story Books** (2000 P Street, NW; tel: 202-659-8884). This is also the hub of DC's gay community.

The Beaux-Arts style

The Dupont Circle area offers wonderful examples of the classically inspired Beaux-Arts style of architecture that characterized so many of the homes of America's 19th-century industrialists. Before the advent of income tax, when those with money were less concerned with having to shelter it, wealthy Americans put their money into their homes. In Washington, the elite looked to architects Waddy Butler Wood, Nathan C. Wyeth, George Oakley Totten, Jr. and others who studied in Paris, where the movement began, to erect their ornately decorated and elegantly symmetrical residences. Though arguably monuments to capitalism's excesses, the houses, with their carvings and porticos and mansard roofs, stand as fine examples of American artistry and craftsmanship.

Two palatial landmarks front Dupont Circle, both typical of the neighborhood's fashionable heyday. The ornate Patterson House at number 15 – now the **Washington Club**, a private women's social club – temporarily housed the Calvin Coolidges during White House renovations in 1927. When Charles Lindbergh returned from Paris, he received his presidential welcome here. The **Sulgrave Club**, another private social club housed in the triangular manse at Massachusetts and

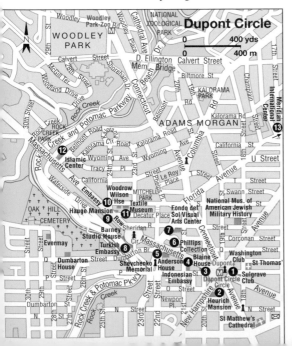

P Street, was named after George Washington's English ancestral home.

If you follow New Hampshire Avenue to 18th Street, you'll find an unusual pocket park cornering Church Street. With its backdrop of 19th-century ruins from the original Gothic-style **St Thomas' Episcopal Church** (1772 Church Street, NW; tel: 202-332-0607), it conjures romantic images of the English countryside. Toward the middle of this narrow, gas-lighted Victorian street is the **Church Street Theater** (1742 Church Street, NW; tel: 202-265-3748), a "rental house" to local and non-local companies, which stages plays, dance and readings from works of literature.

Another impressive Beaux-Arts landmark commands the corner of 18th and Massachusetts. Now the headquarters of the **National Trust for Historic Preservation**, the original McCormick Apartments, built in 1917, were once *the* prestige address in town. Each of its six apartments – one per floor – featured such amenities as silver- and gold-plated door-

knobs, wine closets, and silver vaults. Andrew Mellon, one of many notable residents, amassed the art collection here which spawned the National Gallery of Art. The Trust bought the building in 1977 from its think-tank neighbor on Massachusetts Avenue, the **Brookings Institution**.

Historic brewing

When the German brewer and entrepreneur Christian Heurich came to Washington in 1871, he founded the successful Heurich Brewing Company in Foggy Bottom on the present site of the Kennedy Center and subsequently built a 31-room, Romanesque-Revival castle on the corner of New Hampshire and 20th. Today the lavish **Heurich Mansion ❷** (1307 New Hampshire Avenue NW; Mon–Sat, 10am–4pm; free admission; tel: 202-785-2068), fully restored down to the wallpaper, stands as a monument to Victoriana. In the late 1980s Heurich's grandson reincarnated the family business as the Olde Heurich Brewing Company. While the new designer version of the family lager

Map on page 148

TIP

The *Washington Blade* is the gay community's best news source. Free copies are available in many shops in the Dupont Circle area.

BELOW:
artist at work, Dupont Circle.

Diplomatic Pleasures

One of Washington's hidden treasures is the on-going season of embassy-sponsored cultural events open to the public. As one cultural attaché quoted in the *Washington Post* put it, "Culture is the bearer of the most important information about a country. This is how we can really make ourselves understood."

Until the Great Depression forced many of Washington's wealthiest to sell their Massachusetts Avenue mansions, much of the city's diplomatic community was concentrated in the Meridian Hill section. In 1931, Great Britain and Japan built new embassy compounds along the avenue and were soon followed by several diplomatic missions, which bought the formerly private residences, thereby dubbing the area Embassy Row.

The embassies offer everything from jazz concerts and violin recitals to Warhol retrospectives (his parents were Slovakian immigrants), wine tastings, benefit dinners, plays, films, operas, birthday celebrations, rugby matches, mime performances, art exhibits and more. You can enjoy a glass of Burgundy or a Perugina chocolate, experi-ence Finnish silk or Australian glass, taste an authentic Viennese pastry or a Polish kielbasa.

The embassies also stage culture events at venues such as public parks and art galleries and in cooperation with various other organizations such as the Russian Cultural Institute (1825 Phelps Place, NW; tel: 202-265-3840; www.russianembassy.org) and Germany's Goethe Institute (814 7th Street, NW; tel: 202-289-1200).

Besides being enjoyable, the embassy-sponsored events are a good way to meet new and interesting people, and to learn a little something else about the world. For schedules of events and details, check the following websites: www.EmbassyEvents.com; www.EmbassySeries.org; www.embassy.org; or contact the Inter-American Development Bank's Cultural Center at 1300 New York Avenue, NW, tel: 202-623-3558; www.iadb.org.

Some of the most active embassies are: **Australia**, 1601 Massachusetts Avenue, NW; tel: 202-797-3176; www.austemb.org
Austria, 3524 International Court, NW; tel: 202-895-6776; www.austria.org
Canada, 501 Pennsylvania Avenue, NW; tel: 202-682-7712; www.canadianembassy.org
Ecuador, 2535 15th Street, NW; tel: 202-234-7200; www.ecuador.org
Egypt, 3521 International Court, NW; 202-895-5463; www.embassyofegyptwashingtondc.org
France, La Maison Française, 4101 Reservoir Road, NW; tel: 202-944-6091; www.la-maison-francaise.org
Italy, Instituto Italiano di Cultura, 2025 M Street, NW, Suite 610; tel: 202-223-9800; www.italcultusa.org
Japan, The Japan Information and Culture Center, 1155 21st Street, NW; tel: 202-238-6949; www.usemb-japan.go.jp/jicc/calendar
Korea, The Korean Cultural Service, 2370 Massachusetts Avenue, NW; tel: 202-797-6343; www.koreaemb.org
Switzerland, 2900 Cathedral Avenue, NW; tel: 202-745-7900; swissemb.org
United Kingdom, www.britainusa.com/arts/events (contact by web only).   ❑

LEFT: taking tea on Embassy Row.

is now bottled in Utica, New York, DC claims Heurich as its own – and only – brew.

At 2000 Massachusetts Avenue is the **Blaine House ③**, Dupont Circle's oldest surviving mansion. It was built in 1881 by Maine Senator James G. Blaine, co-founder of the Republican Party, two time secretary of state, and unsuccessful Republican presidential candidate (he lost to Grover Cleveland). In 1901, the inventor George Westinghouse bought the house and lived there until his death in 1914. In the 1920s Blaine House was the site of the Japanese legation, and today it houses several professional offices.

Diplomat's alley

Fittingly, Massachusetts Avenue west of Dupont Circle is known as **Embassy Row**, where Washington's diplomatic community is concentrated. Colorful flags and coats-of-arms of more than 175 nations decorate the embassies and chanceries, both on and off the avenue. While most of the embassies are open only for official business, several offer concerts and other cultural events *(see opposite page)* to which the public is invited. If you call ahead you may be invited inside for a tour of the opulent **Indonesian Embassy ④** at 2020 Massachusetts Avenue (tel: 202-775-5200), the former home of Thomas Walsh, an Irish immigrant who struck it rich in the gold mines of Colorado. Walsh's daughter Evalyn – the last private owner of the Hope Diamond, which is now on display in the National Museum of Natural History – sold the home to the Indonesian government in 1951.

When the diplomat Larz Anderson and his wife planned their 50-room palace at 2118 Massachusetts Avenue, it was with the idea that it would become the future headquarters for the Society of the Cincinnati,

an elite fraternity founded by Revolutionary War officers and restricted to their male descendants. The facade of the **Anderson House ⑤** (2118 Massachusetts Avenue NW; open Tues–Sat, 1pm–4pm; free admittance; tel: 202-785-2040) only hints at the impossibly opulent interior of this turn-of-the-century house-museum, filled with the couple's astounding international collection of art and furnishings, and the ghosts of privilege and power. The first floor houses Revolutionary War artifacts and a library of reference works on the war and local history, and the second remains as it was originally furnished with 18th-century paintings, Belgian tapestries, and enormous chandeliers.

The prestigious and private **Cosmos Club** across the street occupies the former mansion of railroad tycoon Richard Townsend. In contrast to Dupont Circle's typical lavish style is the austere **Friends Meeting House** (2111 Florida Avenue, NW; tel: 202-483-3310), built in 1930 for Quaker President Herbert Hoover, a few blocks away.

Map on page 148

The Cosmos Club.

BELOW: chefs' market at Dupont Circle.

TIP

Although the area is usually safe, a recent crime wave between Dupont and Logan circles means you should take care, especially at night. When riding Metro's station escalators, especially the Dupont Circle station escalator (the world's longest), the best way to avoid being fingered as a tourist is to stand to the right and let others pass.

BELOW:
the Phillips Collection.

The plain interior has a traditional "facing bench," designed for "weighty" Friends to pronounce their messages.

An intimate museum

Of all the museums in Washington, the **Phillips Collection** at 21st and Q streets, (open Tues–Sat, 10am–5pm; Sun, noon–7pm; Thurs until 8.30 pm; closed Mon, Jan 1, July 4, Thanksgiving, Dec 25; admission fee; tel: 202- 387-2151 or visit www.phillipscollection.org) across from the Ritz-Carlton Hotel, is certainly the homiest and most intimate.

Indeed, the country's oldest museum of modern art started out in 1921 as a two-room gallery in Duncan and Marjorie Phillips's brownstone. Duncan was the grandson of a Pittsburgh steel magnate who put his fortune into his eclectic art collection, some 2,500 works that include everything from Degas and Renoir (*Luncheon of the Boating Party*, the museum's most renowned treasure, is here) to Picasso, Marin, O'Keeffe, and Rothko. The Cubist pioneer Georges Braque has 13 works on display, including *The Round Table*, and the Paul Klee room contains whimsical canvases such as *Arab Song* and *Picture Album*. Horace Pippin's naïf *Domino Players* is a perennial favorite.

There is a café next to the museum shop downstairs, and free concerts are held in the grand music room. Call for details about the museum's popular program of "Artful Evenings," held on Thursday nights and featuring lectures and discussion groups, concerts, and receptions.

In a different vein, a block up on R Street is the **Fondo del Sol Visual Arts Center** (2112 R St., NW; open Wed–Sat, 12.30pm–5.30pm; $5 donation; tel: 202-483-2777) three floors of exhibits, art and video providing a cultural history of the Americas with a Hispanic focus. The museum was founded by a group of pan-American artists and writers to highlight the region's multicultural heritage. The gallery showcases work by contemporary artists and craftspeople, but it also has an eclectic collection of folk and pre-Columbian art.

Map on page 148

Kalorama

Massachusetts Avenue makes an elegant turn to the west at **Sheridan Circle**, the embassy-ringed and tightly secured nucleus of the **Kalorama** neighborhood. Formerly a diplomat's country estate, the name means "beautiful view" in Greek. A few blocks to the north, the quiet streets of this exclusive neighborhood, epitomized by **Kalorama Circle**, are a feast of elegant Tudors, Normans, and Georgians dating from the 1920s.

In front of the **Romanian Embassy** (1607 23rd Street, NW), a curbside memorial marks where a car bomb killed the Allende-appointed Chilean ambassador Orlando Letelier and, unintentionally, his passenger Ronni Moffitt, on September 21, 1976; the job was linked to Chilean secret police and army officials in the Pinochet regime.

Moving clockwise around the circle to 1606 23rd Street, NW, you'll come to the **Turkish Embassy ❽**, one of Washington's grandest mansions and the former home of Edward Everett who made his mil-

lions by, prosaically enough, inventing the bottle cap. Mrs Everett, an opera singer and popular Washington hostess, gave performances here and was joined by world-renown divas of the day.

On the circle at number 2306 Massachusetts Avenue, NW, is the **Alice Pike Barney Studio House**, a special but little-known landmark. At the turn of the 20th century, Barney, a flamboyant artist, playwright, and producer, decided to liven up Washington's dull cultural life, and so she commissioned Waddy Butler Wood to design an all-purpose home and studio, where for years she ran the only Paris-style salon in town. In 1960 Barney's daughters gave the well-used Studio House to the National Museum of American Art, which serves as custodian but does not offer tours to the public.

At 2349 Massachusetts Avenue is the stately **Hauge Mansion ❾**, now the **Cameroon Embassy.** Designed by George Oakley Totten, Jr., one of Washington's team of Beaux-Arts architects, it was first the home of Christian Hauge, Norway's first

The Cameroon Embassy.

BELOW: summer in the city.

minister to the US. Hauge's American widow Louise hosted some of Washington's grandest parties in this home with its tower and candle-snuffer roof inspired by a 16th-century French château. In the 1930s the Czechoslovakian government established its foreign mission here, then in 1972 sold the home to Cameroon.

Woodrow Wilson House

The brick Georgian Revival town-house at 2340 S Street, NW, the work of Waddy Butler Wood, is the **Woodrow Wilson House** ❿ (open Tues–Sun, 10am–4pm by guided tour only; admittance fee; closed major holidays; tel: 202-387-4062 or visit www.woodrowwilsonhouse.org). It was the home of Woodrow and Edith Wilson after they left the White House in 1921.

The 28th president, who led the nation during World War I and in 1918 proposed the formation of the League of Nations to foster world peace, bought the house as a surprise for his second wife, presenting her with a piece of earth from the garden and the front door key, in Scottish tra-

dition. Mrs Wilson lived here until she died in 1961.

Next door is the **Textile Museum** ⓫ (2320 S Street, NW; open Mon–Sat, 10am–5pm, Sun 1pm–5pm; closed major holidays; $5 donation; tel: 202-667-0441 or visit www.textilemuseum.org), a fabulous private museum dedicated to the display and study of international textile arts, both historic and contemporary. Its collection of Oriental carpets is unmatched, thanks to the museum's founder, George Hewitt Myers, who became hooked after buying his first rug for his Yale dorm room. He opened the museum in 1925 next door to his home and kept right on collecting.

Today the museum has 1,400 carpets and 13,000 textiles, and its muted galleries feature permanent and special exhibits. The gift shop has a superb collection of books on textile arts, along with crafts, jewelry, and yarn. The small research library contains more than 13,000 volumes. Curators will personally advise about your own textiles, but it's best to call ahead.

BELOW AND RIGHT: the Woodrow Wilson House.

You'll pass **Mitchell Park** if you continue up the hill. It was named for Mrs E. N. Mitchell who, in 1918, bequeathed the land to the city in exchange for the perpetual care of her pet poodle's grave. Dear Bosque's grave, an unmarked and unimpressive cement block encircled by a blue chain, is in the playground.

Across from Mitchell Park is a charming architectural interlude, a sweet spot, a secret garden called **Decatur Terrace**. The formal stairs and fountain, which the neighbors generously refer to as the "Spanish Steps," link 22nd and S streets.

Along Massachusetts Avenue, near Rock Creek Park, is the **Islamic Center** (tel: 202-332-8343) at Massachusetts and Belmont Road. This is the spiritual and cultural mecca for Washington's estimated 65,000 Muslims. Designed by the Italian architect Mario Rossi, a convert to Islam, it's also Embassy Row's most exotic structure featuring the minaret, which rises to 160 ft (49 meters). The mosque itself, situated to face Mecca as all mosques do, is embellished with 7,000 deep blue Turkish tiles, a two-ton chandelier from Egypt, Persian carpets and Iraqi stained glass.

Ethnic interest

In the mid-1950s a neighborhood organization was formed to promote cooperation among racially segregated residents. The group took its name by combining the names of two area elementary schools: the all-white Adams and the all-black Morgan. The Adams Morgan organization left its name as a legacy to and symbol of this uniquely diverse community just north of Dupont Circle. Every September in honor of **Adams Morgan Day**, the neighborhood throws a giant street party, with music stages, ethnic food stands, crafts, and major crowds.

Along with the artists and bohemians, who moved in in the 1960s, came an influx of Hispanic refugees and immigrants, establishing Adams Morgan as DC's Latin quarter and Greenwich Village, rolled into one. The entire community comes out to celebrate itself, joined by thousands, during the **Hispanic Festival**, which is traditionally held the last weekend in July and features pan-Latin food, the sizzling sounds of salsa and marimba bands, wonderful African crafts, and a colorful parade of nations.

The heart of Adams Morgan is at the "T" intersection of **18th Street and Columbia Road**. The closest Metro stop is Woodley Park. Follow Calvert Street across the **"Duke" Ellington Memorial Bridge** – named, of course, for the preeminent jazzman and native son – and you're here.

The plaza by the Suntrust Bank is the village green of Adams Morgan. By day on Saturdays, when the neighborhood is a delight to explore, it becomes a **farmer's market**. On summer evenings you can expect to see anything from Andean panpipers to West African stilt-walkers,

Bargain-hunting at Adams Morgan's annual street fair.

BELOW:
Adams Morgan Day.

Map on page 148

A striking mural, pictured below, of Parisian artist Henri de Toulouse-Lautrec (1864–1901) was painted in 1980 on a restaurant at 2461 18th Street, NW by its then owner, André Neveux. Although the premises have changed owners several times since then, the mural still enlivens the district.

BELOW:
distinctive decor
in Adams Morgan.

a kids' bucket-drum combo to a Delta-blues harmonica player, young rappers to Michael Jackson types.

Inevitable development ("George-townization") has transformed the once higgledy-piggledy stretch of 18th Street into a funky-hip quarter, where exotic aromas – especially Ethiopian and Eritrean – waft from myriad ethnic restaurants. The flavor here is decidedly Left Bank à la Washington, an international smorgasbord of sidewalk cafés, trendy bars and clubs, bookstores and specialty shops, antique and rummage stores, and galleries.

Alas, Adams Morgan is in danger of becoming a victim of its own success. Clubs, bars and restaurants spring up with regularity, only to close down or be taken over by someone else a few months later. **Idle Time Books** (2410 18th Street, NW; tel: 202-232-4774), however, has stayed put and is well-stocked with second-hand treasures.

Hispanic quarter

East of 18th Street, Columbia Road changes abruptly. Salsa blares from

boom-boxes, Latino shops, and vendors' booths, and Spanish is the language of the street.

North of here Adams Morgan flows into the residential neighborhood of **Mount Pleasant**. The heart of Washington's poor and dispossessed Hispanic community is also undergoing block-by-block gentrification, though progress is slow. Seedy and with little to offer visitors, it's a section of the city best avoided.

A quiet refuge away from the fray is provided by **Meridian International Center** ⓭ (1624–1630 Crescent Place, NW; Wed–Sun, 2pm–5pm; closed Mon, Tue, and major and federal holidays; admission free; tel: 202-939-5568), which crowns the ridge between Crescent Place and Belmont Street, off 16th Street. Set on the magnificently landscaped hillcrest are two historic mansions designed by the prolific John Russell Pope. The one is a very French Louis XVI-style château, whose lovely pebbled garden is lined with pollarded Spanish linden trees, while the other recalls an English country manor. Both now belong to this international educational and cultural foundation, whose galleries and concerts are open to the public.

Medical museum

Hypochondriacs should avoid the **National Museum of Health and Medicine**, on the campus of Walter Reed Army Medical Center a few miles north of Adams Morgan (6900 Georgia Avenue and Elder St., NW AFIP, Building 54; tel: 202-782-2200; www.nmhm.washingtondc.museum; daily 10am–5:30pm; free, but security is tight). More than 350 collections cover medicine since the Civil War, and there are thousands of medical instruments, skeletal specimens and preserved organs – many, such as a leg swollen by elephantiasis, not for the faint-hearted. ❑

RESTAURANTS

American

Arbor Restaurant and Wine Bar
2400 18th St., NW. Tel: 202-667-1200. Open: D only, Tues–Sat.; Sun brunch. $$–$$$
Inventive menu features upside-down pizza; patio good for people-watching.

Brickskeller
1523 22nd St., NW. Tel: 202-293-1885. Open: L &D, Mon–Fri; D only Sat & Sun. $
Over 1,000 beers; standard pub fare; favorite DC gathering spot.

Cashion's
1819 Columbia Rd., NW. Tel: 202-797-1819. Open: D, Tues–Sun.; Sun brunch. $$$
Upscale, contemporary menu, one of the best.

The Diner
2453 18th St., NW. Tel: 202-232-8800. Open: 24 hours, daily. $
Burgers, fries, meatloaf, bacon and eggs at 3am; whatever you want.

Florida Avenue Grill
1100 Florida Avenue, NW. Tel: 202-265-1586. Open: B, L & D, Tues–Sat. $
Serving made-from-scratch Southern fare since 1944. Neighborhood can be iffy.

Iron Gate Inn
1734 N St., NW. Tel: 202-737-1370. Open: L & D, Mon–Sat. $$–$$$
Tucked behind rowhouses; trendy fare with a Middle Eastern twist.

Johnny's Half Shell
2002 P St., NW. Tel: 202-296-2021. Open: L & D, Mon–Sat. $$$$
Their motto: "Seafood Specialties, Strong Drink." Lively bar scene.

Nora
2132 Florida Ave., NW. Tel: 202-462-5143. Open: D, Mon–Sat. $$$$
Organic, free-range ingredients carefully prepared and served in elegant townhouse setting.

Perry's
1811 Columbia Rd., NW. Tel: 202-234-6218. Open: D daily; Sun brunch. $$$$
Hip neighborhood rooftop restaurant; drag queen show with Sunday brunch buffet.

Rocky's Café
1817 Columbia Rd., NW. Tel: 202-387-2580. Open: D only Mon–Sat; Sun brunch. $
No frills dining room; spicy Creole favorites include gumbo and po'boy sandwiches.

Tabard Inn
1739 N St., NW. Tel: 202-331-8528. Open: L & D, daily; Sun brunch. $$$
Long-time favorite with an eclectic menu, mismatched furnishings and a pleasant garden.

Tryst Coffee Bar and Lounge
2459 18th St., NW. Tel: 202-232-5500. Open: 6.30am–2am Mon–Sat; Sun open 8am. $–$$
Artsy people-watching spot good for coffee and a hearty sandwich with a full-service bar.

Vidalia
1990 M St., NW. Tel: 202-659-1990. Open: L & D, Mon–Fri; D only Sat. & Sun. $$$
High-tone Southern menu; chicken and dumplings, pork chops, roasted vidalia onions.

Asian

City Lights of China
1731 Connecticut Ave., NW. Tel: 202-265-6688. Open: L & D, daily. $–$$
Basement-level restaurant with good Szechuan and Cantonese cooking.

Teaism
2009 R St., NW. Tel: 202-667-3027. Open: B, L & D, daily. $
Dozens of tea choices; limited selection of tasty bento-box entrées, soups, and breakfast.

Topaz
In the Topaz Hotel, 1733 N St., NW. Tel: 202-393-3000. Open: B & D, daily $$–$$$
Asian-inspired menu, quiet setting; the bar is a neighborhood gathering spot.

Brazilian

Grill from Ipanema
1858 Columbia Rd., NW. Tel: 202-986-0757. Open: D daily; Sat & Sun brunch. $$$
Neighborhood institution. Try Brazil's national dish, feijoada, a stew of beans, meats, greens.

French

Bistrot du Coin
1738 Connecticut Ave., NW. Tel: 202-234-6969. Open: L & D, daily. $$–$$$
The usual Paris café standards. Crowded bar.

La Fourchette
1419 18th St., NW. Tel: 202-332-3077. Open: L & D, Mon–Fri; Sat & Sun brunch & D. $$–$$$
Cozy neighborhood favorite with all the usual French selections.

Italian

i Ricchi
1220 19th St., NW. Tel: 202-835-0459. Open: L & D, Mon–Sat. $$$–$$$$
Tuscan-style grill famous for its fish, game and shrimp entrées.

Obelisk
2029 P St., NW. Tel: 202-872-1180. Open: D, Tues–Sun. $$$–$$$$
Delicious Italian-inspired menu with fresh ingredients. Only a few tables.

Pasta Mia
1790 Columbia Rd., NW. Tel: 202-328-9114. Open: D daily. $
All varieties of pastas, excellent sauces, generous portions. Very busy.

San Marco
2305 18th St., NW. Tel: 202-483-9300. Open: D only, Mon–Sat. $$–$$$
Excellent classics include desserts; good wine selection.

Middle Eastern

Mama Ayesha's
1967 Calvert St., NW. Tel: 202-232-5431. Open: L & D, daily. $$
Tasty selections in open, cheery dining room.

Meze
2437 18th St., NW. Tel: 202-797-0017. Open: D daily; Sat & Sun brunch. $–$$
Combine appetizers to make a full meal. Busy.

Tex-Mex

Mixtec
1792 Columbia Rd., NW. Tel: 202-332-1011. Open: L & D, daily. $
Authentic Mexican fare. Good and inexpensive.

PRICE CATEGORIES
Prices for three-course dinner per person with a half-bottle of house wine, tax and tip:
$ = under $25
$$ = $25–$40
$$$ = $40–$50
$$$$ = more than $50

THE UPPER NORTHWEST

This pleasant stretch of country in the middle of the city includes Rock Creek Park's shady acres and all creatures great and small at the National Zoo.

"**B**ut in the country" was how Washingtonians, weary of the city's heat and humidity, described Upper Northwest until well after the Civil War. Here, in this rural retreat above Rock Creek, woodland was dense and temperatures were decidedly cooler than downtown. On hot summer evenings, Presidents Van Buren, Tyler, Buchanan, and Cleveland came here by carriage from downtown to their gracious country "cottages."

With the completion of the first trolley bridges over Rock Creek at the turn of the 20th century, the city expanded northward. Cleveland Park and Woodley Park became fashionable year-round communities and luxury hotels and grand apartment buildings soon graced the broad Connecticut, Wisconsin, and Massachusetts avenues. Today, Upper Northwest – a triangle of land formed by 16th Street, Massachusetts Avenue, and DC's western border with Maryland – retains much of its original rural appeal. Despite commercial centers rapidly rising and expanding around Metro stations, unspoiled swaths of woodland, sylvan parks, and tree-lined streets give gracious sanctuary to the natural world.

Rock Creek Park

Threading through the entire neighborhood is the city's largest park and prime natural attraction, **Rock Creek Park** ❶ (open daylight hours; free admission; tel: 202-895-6000 or visit www.nps.gov/rocr). The park's 1,754 acres (710 hectares) were purchased by Congress in 1890 for its "pleasant valleys and deep ravines, primeval forests and open fields… its repose and tranquility, its light and shade…" About 4 miles (6.5 km) long and up to a mile wide, the park includes extensive trails and paths for hiking,

BELOW: at play in Rock Creek Park.

a marked bike route, picnic areas, recreation fields, **tennis courts** (16th and Kennedy Streets, NW; tel: 202 722-5949), an 18-hole **golf course** (16th and Rittenhouse streets, NW; tel: 202-822-7332), a stable and riding center (Military and Glover roads, NW; tel: 202-362-0117) and more.

Historical sites in the park include **Peirce Mill**, a 19th-century gristmill waiting to be restored, and the nearby 1880s **log cabin of Joaquin Miller**, "Poet of the Sierras."

An open-air theater within the park is **Carter Barron Amphitheatre ❷** (16th Street and Colorado Avenue, NW; box office open noon–9pm on day of concert; free tickets distributed on concert day; fee for other events; tel: 202-426-0486 for concert information; www.nps.gov/rocr). It features a summer festival of pop, rock, and jazz. Of particular appeal to children is the **Rock Creek Park Nature Center ❸** (5200 Glover Road, NW; Wed–Sun, 9am–5pm; closed Jan 1, July 4, Thanksgiving, Dec 25; tel: 202-895-6070). Here, National Park Rangers lead guided nature walks and help children learn about the wildlife in the park. The hands-on Discovery Room is a favorite. So is the **Rock Creek Park Planetarium** (in the Nature Center; free shows at 1pm Sat and Sun for children 4 to 7 years and at 4 pm for children 7 and older).

The **tennis center** is the site of top tournaments, to which Washingtonians flock, especially in August. Despite the heat, it hosts the important Legg-Mason Tennis Classic.

For an old-fashioned motor tour, follow the 10-mile-long (16-km) **Beach Drive,** which winds its narrow way through the entire park. West of Rock Creek Park, the roadless **Glover-Archbold Park ❹** offers picnic areas and a 3-mile (5-km) nature trail. **Battery-Kemble Park ❺**, once a Civil War outpost, is an escape from the sounds of the

city. Narrow trails through this jungly park join the **C&O Canal towpath** *(see page 165).*

The main Upper Northwest thoroughfares – Massachusetts, Wisconsin, and Connecticut avenues – slice through the neighborhood on a northwest course into the Maryland suburbs. Just after you cross Rock Creek on Massachusetts from downtown is the **British Embassy ❻** (3100 Massachusetts Avenue, NW; tel: 202-588-6500) on the left.

There is a larger-than-life statue of Winston Churchill giving the "V for Victory" salute (some joke that he's hailing a cab). The base of the statue contains a time capsule to be opened in 2063, the centenary of the conferring of Churchill's honorary US citizenship by President John F. Kennedy.

The British chancery and residence, an adaptation of an English country house, was designed by the illustrious British architect Sir Edwin Lutyens in 1931. The embassy's celebration of the Queen's birthday – which takes the form of a garden party with strawberries and Devon-

Churchill gives his "V" sign at the British Embassy.

BELOW: braving the winter in Rock Creek Park.

Map on page 160

shire cream, plus a sprinkling of notables – is a highlight of Washington's spring social season.

Observation decks

Massachusetts Avenue then curves in a gentle arc around **Observatory Circle** to distance rumbling automobiles from the sensitive instruments housed in the **US Naval Observatory ❼** (free tours by reservation only on alternating Mondays, 8.30pm–10pm; tel: 202-762-1467 or www.usno.navy.mil). The Observatory charts the position and motion of the celestial bodies,

measures the earth's rotation, determines precise time and maintains the nation's master clock. Weather permitting, visitors may look through the 26-inch refractor telescope used to discover the Martian moons in 1877.

Also on the Observatory grounds is the Victorian-era **house of the Vice President of the United States** originally built for the superintendent of the Naval Observatory. This turreted, informal-looking building is a far cry from the White House, for it is little known, little publicized, and seen even less. The

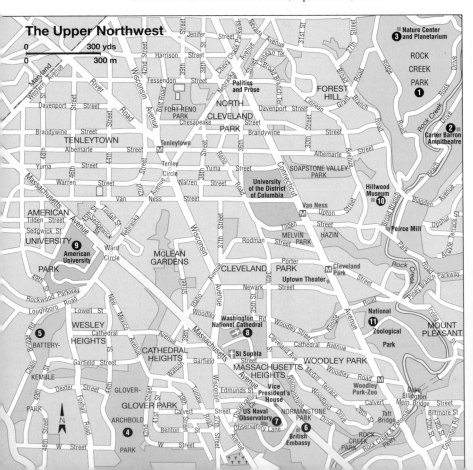

The Upper Northwest

Map on page 160

house was co-opted from the Navy in the 1970s, as it was felt that an official home located on the grounds of a military post would be easier – and less expensive – to protect than a private residence elsewhere in the city. Needless to say, the VP's home is not open to the public.

Dominating the city's skyline from the crown of Mount Saint Alban at Massachusetts and Wisconsin avenues is the towering **Cathedral Church of St Peter and Paul**, also known as the Washington Cathedral or **National Cathedral ⑧** (May–Sept, Mon–Fri, 10am–9pm; Oct–Apr, Mon–Fri, 10am–5pm, Sat all year 10am–4.30pm, Sun all year 8am–4.30pm; tel: 202-364-6616). President Theodore Roosevelt laid the corner stone of this magnificent Gothic-style cathedral in 1907. Eighty-three years and 300 million tons of Indiana limestone later, one of the world's largest ecclesiastical structures was officially completed.

The cathedral serves as the seat of the Episcopal Diocese of Washington, but it welcomes people of all faiths to its services, concerts, and annual festivals. This is truly a national cathedral – a fact made gloriously evident through the stunning, quite modern stained-glass windows that tell stories about American history and American heroes. The **Space Window** in the nave commemorates the scientists and astronauts of Apollo 11 and includes a piece of moon rock retrieved on that mission Other windows depict the home life of Martha and George Washington at Mount Vernon, Lewis and Clark's explorations of the American Northwest, the struggle for religious freedom in Maryland during the 17th century, and the events of World War II. Thomas Jefferson, Robert E. Lee, Abraham Lincoln as well as his mother and stepmother are glorified in other scenes.

Allow plenty of time not only to study these radiant windows, but to gaze at the nave's soaring vaulted ceiling, to explore the several small chapels, and to gaze at the kaleidoscopic **West Rose Window** as it glows in the setting sun. The best views of Washington and of the

National Cathedral took 83 years to build (1907–90), at a cost of $65 million, all raised privately. It welcomes nearly 700,000 visitors and worshipers a year.

BELOW: the house of the Vice-President of the United States.

cathedral's exterior carvings are from the 70 windows in the **Pilgrim's Observation Gallery**, the highest vantage point in the city. The crypt level includes the London Brass Rubbing Center, the Rare Book Library, and the gift shop. A stroll on the peaceful cathedral grounds will lead you through a 12th-century Norman arch into the medieval-style **Bishop's Garden**, to the Herb Cottage shop, and greenhouse.

The largest Greek Orthodox church in the United States graces the block just south of the National Cathedral. **Saint Sophia** (36th Street and Massachusetts Avenue, NW; tel: 202-333-4730) is famous for its stunning and intricate mosaics that decorate the edifice and interior dome of the church. The best time to visit the church, and to hear the a cappella choir singing from the circular balcony, is during Sunday morning services.

Farther north on Massachusetts at **Ward Circle**, is **American University** (4400 Massachusetts Avenue, NW, tel: 202-885-1000), an independent university chartered by Congress in 1893. The public is invited to attend on-campus lectures, concerts, movies and art exhibitions.

From Ward Circle, take Nebraska Avenue northeast to Connecticut Avenue, then head south a few blocks to **Politics and Prose** (5015 Connecticut Avenue, NW; tel: 202-364-1919; www.politics-prose.com), a bookstore specializing in literature and current events. Readings, book-signing parties, and wine-and-cheese receptions are held regularly here.

Continuing south leads you into **Cleveland Park**, a residential neighborhood recently designated an historic district. Named after President Grover Cleveland, who spent the summers in the area, Cleveland Park is dominated by grand, late 19th-century homes, mostly in Queen Anne or Georgian revival styles. Stroll down Newark Street to Highland Place, then onto Macomb Street to see a panoply of porches, turrets, Palladian windows, gabled roofs, balconies, and white picket fences.

At Connecticut and Ordway is the **Uptown Theater** (tel: 202-966-

BELOW: the National Cathedral was built from 300 tons of Indiana limestone.

5400, or check the *Washington Post* listings), an art-deco gem that features epic-size movies on a big screen. Traffic gets tangled in front of the theater when private premier shows lure stars and fans. There's a convenient strip of shops across the street with neighborhood restaurants.

Grand mansions

A bit farther north and off Connecticut Avenue is **Hillwood** ❿ (4155 Linnean Avenue, NW; $10 adults, $8 seniors, $5 students; by appointment only; admission fee; tel: 202-686-5807 or 1-877-HILLWOOD; www.hillwoodmuseum.org), the estate of the late Marjorie Merriweather Post, Washington socialite and heiress of the Post cereal fortune. Hillwood is a rather quirky place, comprising a 40-room Georgian mansion, a museum of decorative arts and wonderful gardens. The inside of the house can be visited only by joining the two-hour guided tour to view 18th-century French decorative objects and masterpieces of Russian Imperial Art, many pieces collected when Mrs Post and

her fourth husband served as the first American envoys to Moscow after the Russian Revolution.

If you prefer to go it alone, you can explore Hillwood's other buildings and 25 acres (10 hectares) of grounds. Here you'll find a *dacha* housing Russian folk art; an Adirondack-style cabin featuring American Indian artifacts; the greenhouse protecting thousands of orchids; and the pleasantly airy café building offering light fare and an afternoon tea with scones. The grounds also have formal Japanese and French gardens and a sweeping view over Rock Creek all the way to the Washington Monument. In the pet cemetery, Mrs Post's two dogs – Café au Lait and Crème de Cocoa – are buried amid dogtooth violets, weeping dogwoods and forget-me-nots.

Woodley Park, just south of Cleveland Park, was also a summer retreat for several US presidents. The neighborhood takes its name from Woodley Manor (now Maret School, at 3000 Cathedral Avenue), where US presidents Van Buren, Tyler, Buchanan, and Cleveland headed

Map on page 160

Marjorie Merriweather Post's Hillwood mansion.

LEFT AND BELOW: statuary at Hillwood.

Map
on page
160

*Marilyn Monroe
gazes down on
Connecticut
and Calvert.*

in summer. Woodley Park's most famous residents these days, however, are **Marilyn Monroe** (painted on a huge mural at Calvert and Connecticut) and two giant pandas.

At the zoo

The pandas live at the **National Zoological Park ⓫** (3001 Connecticut Avenue, NW; free admission; open daily May 1–Sept 15, grounds 6am–8pm and buildings 10am–6pm; open daily Sept 16–Apr 30, grounds 6am–6pm and buildings 10am–4.30pm; tel: 202-673-4717 or visit www.si.edu/natzoo).

Established in 1889 by the Smithsonian Institution to protect an acquired herd of buffalo, the zoo now accommodates some 4,000 animals living in semi-natural environments on 163 wooded acres (66 hectares). The zoo's main trails have been beautifully re-landscaped according to the original plans of architect Frederick Law Olmsted, Jr. These paths link together a dozen looping side paths that lead to outdoor and indoor caged habitats supporting rare blue-eyed white tigers,

lowland gorillas and a variety of other unusual animals.

Two recent additions to the zoo include the animal **Think Tank**, which shows how scientists investigate the process of thinking, and the **Pollinarium**, inside the greenhouse. Popular attractions for children include the **Panda House**, home of Tian Tian and Mei Xiang, a breeding pair of panda bears on loan from the People's Republic of China, and the **Reptile Discovery Center** which houses the world's largest lizard, the Komodo dragon.

For the "peaceable kingdom" experience of the zoo, visit the grounds in the morning well before the buildings open or in the evening hours after the buildings close. This way, you can enjoy the meandering pathways before crowds of homo sapiens and baby carriages create mile-long conga lines. Many of the animals are fed and are most active in the morning before 10am.

If you can't get to the zoo, you can visit the Smithsonian's website, www.si.edu, click on the zoo's page and watch the "Panda Cam." ❏

Restaurants

American

New Heights
2317 Calvert St., NW. Tel: 202-234-4110. Open: D, Tues–Sat; Sun brunch. $$$
Upscale inventive menu in a pleasant dining room overlooking Rock Creek Park.

Buck's Fishing and Camping
5031 Connecticut Ave., NW. Tel: 202-364-0777. Open: D only Tues–Sun. $$–$$$
Reminiscent of a Boy Scout menu but without the canned beans. Short, excellent menu includes steaks and fries, wood-grilled fish.

Asian

Neisha Thai
4445 Wisconsin Ave, NW. Tel: 202-966-7088. Open: L & D. $–$$
New and stylish, with patio and bar a wide menu of Thai classics.

Tono Sushi
2605 Connecticut Ave, NW. Tel: 202-332-7300. Open: L & D, daily. $
Good sushi bar plus a menu of other Asian favorites.

Yanyu
3435 Connecticut Ave., NW. Tel: 202-686-6968. Open: D daily. $$$–$$$$
Upscale pan-Asian in a beautifully outfitted dining room. Try the Peking duck.

French

Lavandou
3321 Connecticut Ave, NW. Tel: 202-966-3003. Open: L & D, Mon–Fri; D only Sat & Sun. $$
Neighborhood favorite newly renovated with excellent Provençal-style soups and stews, and desserts.

Middle Eastern

Café Ole
4000 Wisconsin Ave, NW. Tel: 202-244-1330. Open: L & D, daily. $
Appetizers known as mezze, plus sandwiches and salads and some good traditional stew entrées, plus a good wine list.

Tex-Mex

Cactus Cantina
3300 Wisconsin Ave., NW. Tel: 202-656-7222. Open: L & D, daily. $
Same excellent menu as its sister Lauriol Plaza in Adams Morgan featuring mesquite-grill favorites. Good and inexpensive. Near Washington Cathedral.

PRICE CATEGORIES

Prices for three-course dinner per person with a half-bottle of house wine, tax and tip:
$ = under $25
$$ = $25–$40
$$$ = $40–$50
$$$$ = more than $50

The C & O Canal

Slicing a narrow liquid strip through the northwest sections of Washington is a piece of Victorian-era true grit. The Chesapeake & Ohio Canal, which begins in affluent Georgetown and lopes its way alongside the Potomac River for 185 miles (300 km) until it reaches the Allegheny Mountain town of Cumberland, Maryland, is a relic from another time. An ambitious transportation scheme that went awry, it survives as a playground for outdoor-loving Washingtonians.

The Georgetown section of the canal is well-preserved and enjoyable. During warm weather months, restored canal boats are drawn by mules plodding their way along the towpaths, and guides in period costume entertain their audience with tales of the rise and demise of the canal system. (Hour-long rides depart from 1057 Thomas Jefferson Street and are offered April through mid-October; tel: 202-653-5190; www.nps.gov/choh).

The journey is slow, but not too slow. On board, the smells of dankness and fresh mint intermingle, and the mules vie for towpath space with joggers. Soon after, the vista opens up with views of the Potomac and, behind the river, high-rise suburban buildings. Here and there on the banks is a large cardboard box, which looks suspiciously as if it has been used as a temporary home.

About 10 miles (16 km) farther up the canal lies the wealthy commuter community of Great Falls. In this much more rural setting, passengers may catch a glimpse of a white-tailed deer or a raccoon. An abandoned goldmine, worked from the 1860s through the 1940s, is located nearby, and hastily dug graveyards in the hills pay tribute to those who labored to build this extensive waterway but succumbed to diseases.

The best times to view wildlife are either early or late in the day. The more exotic inhabitants include turkey vultures, the great horned owl, beaver and, rumor has it, bears.

Less than 10 miles (16 km) beyond Great Falls, the canal abruptly runs dry. It remains

so with the exception of a brief rewatered section near its terminus 150 miles (240 km) away in Cumberland. As originally conceived, the canal was to have stretched well beyond Cumberland all the way to the Ohio River, hence its name: the Chesapeake and Ohio Canal. There, the plan went, canal boats would load up with bulky raw materials and carry them eastward to the Chesapeake Bay and beyond. But it never happened.

The C&O Canal had its problems from the start. On July 4, 1828, President John Quincy Adams turned the first shovelful of dirt only to encounter roots and then rocks. Seventy-four lift locks later, in 1850, the canal reached Cumberland, but there it halted, having cost slightly more than $11 million.

Labor shortages and unrest and frequent flooding from the nearby Potomac plagued construction. Materials were difficult to come by, there were never enough funds, and there were constant legal battles with the upstart Baltimore and Ohio Railroad (the B&O).

The dawning of the railroads sealed the fate of the C&O Canal as a viable means of carrying goods. The B&O was inaugurated the very same Independence Day as the canal, rendering this languid mode of transportation obsolete before it had even fully begun. ❏

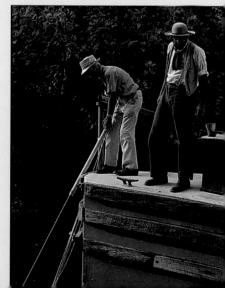

RIGHT: the canal is now a popular leisure spot.

LOGAN CIRCLE AND THE NORTHEAST

This fringe district outside the bounds of "tourist" Washington has several choice religious sites, two notable off-beat theaters, and, at the National Arboretum, a popular recreational expanse.

BELOW:
tasty food at a shelter
for the homeless.

Picture Logan Circle – that Victorian-ringed rotary intersected by Rhode Island and Vermont avenues – as the focal point for the vast, amorphous area north of downtown and Capitol Hill, and east of Dupont Circle, that extends through the northeast quadrant. Bounded on the west by 16th Street, it is raggedly defined on the south by Massachusetts Avenue. The Anacostia River forms its eastern border, with North Capitol Street, Florida Avenue and Benning Road the main thoroughfares. The Maryland border contains the rest.

The circle itself appeared originally on city architect Pierre L'Enfant's plan not as a circle, but as a triangle. The area sat neglected until the 1870s when what had been primarily a field for grazing cattle was transformed into a stylish Victorian neighborhood called Iowa Circle. In the 1930s, the circle was renamed for Illinois Senator John A. Logan *(see panel on opposite page)*. In the center of **Logan Circle ❶**, a statue by American sculpture Franklin Simmons commemorates him, the impassioned Union-general-turned-senator sitting astride his horse.

Gentrified and exclusively white, Logan Circle was one of the city's poshest neighborhoods in the 1930s and 1940s, remarkable for its concentration of three- and four-story Victorian mansions and townhouses. As the residents moved up and out, many to still larger mansions around Massachusetts Avenue, black Washingtonians made the neighborhood theirs and for a time Logan Circle was a center of black intellectual and social life. By the end of World War II, the neighborhood fell into decline and remains one of the city's more troubled areas, known for drug dealers, small-time pimps, and prostitutes.

It was near here that DC's inim-

Map on page 168

itable former mayor Marion Barry was arrested for crack cocaine possession at the Vista International Hotel on **Thomas Circle**. Of late, thanks to tighter controls and impressive restoration efforts, Logan Circle is being yuppified. Still, it's wise to confine your wanderings around here to daylight hours.

Housed in a pristine Victorian house one refurbished block off the circle at 1318 Vermont Avenue is the **Bethune Museum-Archives for Black Women's History ❷** (tel: 202-673-2402; Mon–Sat, 10am–4pm; free; guided tours every hour on the hour). It is named for the pioneering civil rights activist and educator Mary McLeod Bethune, who founded the National Council of Negro Women here in her one-time residence. Don't expect to see a "preserved" home or even a single personal article. This no-frills museum tells the history of black women, but its exhibits are surprisingly lean.

A choice of stages

West of the circle, scattered along the seedy stretch of 14th Street now trendily tagged the "Uptown Arts District" – a reference to the area's city-supported cultural revival – is DC's funkiest and most enterprising alternative theaters, along with a growing batch of unpretentious restaurants and cafés.

On the corner of 14th and P streets, the **Studio Theatre ❸** (tel: 202-332-3300; www.studiotheatre. org) occupies an old car warehouse – complete with an industrial-sized elevator capable of transferring fully assembled sets from studio to stage – which has been outfitted as a state-of-the-art theater. Studio productions range from classic to contemporary, and feature artists from around the country.

Farther up the street, the **Source Theatre Company ❹** (1835 14th Street, NW; tel: 202-462-1073; www.sourcetheatre.com) has a stark, black interior where the audience is never more than six rows away from the actors. The Source spotlights work by new playwrights, and you can sometimes catch a late-night comedy show here.

The ambience changes considerably when you get to 16th Street,

Bethune Museum.

BELOW:
cool kids on the block.

John A. Logan

Logan Circle is named after General John Alexander Logan (1826–86), who first rose to prominence as a Congressman from southern Illinois. Known as "Black Jack," he originally favored the South, but the outbreak of the Civil War convinced him that "the Union must prevail." After fighting as a civilian at Bull Run, he volunteered for the war, rising from colonel to major-general. He later stopped angry Union troops from burning Raleigh, North Carolina. After the war, he was energetic in both his support of Union veterans and his loathing of the South for what he regarded as its treachery. He became a US Senator in 1871 and campaigned for the vice-presidency in 1884.

House of the Temple.

two blocks to the west. Perfectly and impressively aligned with the White House, the wide, terraced boulevard was designed as *the* approach to the District by car. It also runs alongside the city's central meridian, surveyed in 1816 as a possible alternative to the prime meridian at Greenwich. The line's presence is recalled around **Meridian Hill**.

Once considered as the site for a new presidential residence, Congress instead purchased 12 hillside acres between Florida Avenue and Euclid Street for a public park. Not just a green space, **Meridian Hill Park** ❺, also known as Malcolm X Park, is reminiscent of the formal gardens of 17th-century France and Italy. Sadly, the park is ringed with crumbling and high-crime housing projects, making it a bad idea to visit, even by day.

Sacred places

Along 16th Street are many houses of worship, ranging from Baptist to Buddhist, Universalist to Unification, Swedenborgian to **Scottish Rite**. The latter – not a church, but nevertheless sacred – is between R and S streets and is without a doubt one of the most remarkable.

The Masons commissioned the capable John Russell Pope to design their **House of the Temple** ❻ (1733 16th Street, NW; tel: 202-232-3579; free admittance; guided tours offered Mon–Fri, 8am–2pm) in the image of the Tomb of Mausolus, one of the Seven Wonders of the ancient world. Every inch of this colossal, sphinx-flanked temple is masonically symbolic, down to its very proportions and the sequences of its front steps, which represent the sacred numbers of Pythagoras.

As you veer northeast, you will run into a hive of activity on Georgia Avenue around U Street, where the 150-acre (60-hectare), city-worn campus of **Howard University** ❼ (2400 6th Street, NW; tel: 202-806-

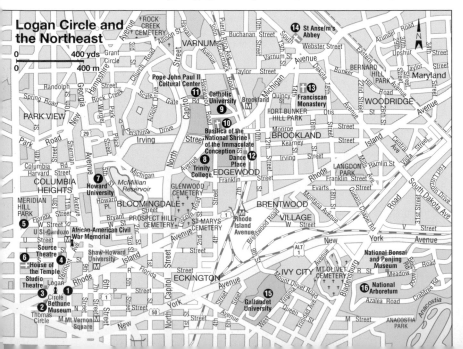

6100) begins. This prestigious and predominantly black institution, established in 1867 by civil rights champion Oliver O. Howard, has produced such high-caliber alumni as Andrew Young and Thurgood Marshall. If you can find it, the small **art gallery** in the **College of Fine Art** has a wonderful collection of African art and exhibits the work of major black American artists, as well as those by students, faculty, and alumni.

Brookland

Once you cross North Capitol Street, you're in the city's northeast quadrant in the up-and-coming neighborhood of **Brookland**. The Catholic Church has a decided presence along this stretch of Michigan Avenue. In fact, it has a monopoly on the neighborhood's attractions.

At **Trinity College** ❽ (125 Michigan Avenue NE; tel: 202-884-9000), a Catholic women's college founded in 1897, the prize-winning Byzantine **Chapel of Notre Dame** has a 67-ft (20-meter) dome, marvelously filled with a La Farge mosaic depicting a scene from Dante's *Divina Comedia.* You may have to hunt for someone to unlock the door, however.

Just beyond sprawls the gray-stone campus of **Catholic University** ❾ (620 Michigan Avenue, NE; tel: 202-319-5000). Founded in 1887, it is the only university established by American Roman Catholic bishops. The majority of its board members belong to the clergy. The university's **Hartke Theatre** (box office tel: 202-319-4000 during the academic year) is known not only for the quality and range of its productions, but for star alums like Jean Kerr, Jon Voight, and Susan Sarandon.

What commands attention here, with its mosaicked and gold-crowned dome, is the magnificent **Basilica of the National Shrine of the Immaculate Conception** ❿ (4th Street and Michigan Avenue, NE, on the campus of Catholic University; tel: 202-526-8300; Nov 1–Mar 31, daily 7am–6pm; Apr 1–Oct 31, daily 7am–7pm; guided tours Mon–Sat, 9am–11am and 1pm–3pm; Sun, 1.30pm to 4pm; www. nationalshrine.com). The largest

Map on page 168

BELOW:
Basilica of the
National Shrine
of the Immaculate
Conception.

Roman Catholic church in the hemisphere and the seventh-largest church in the world, this Byzantine-Romanesque monument consumes 3 acres (1.2 hectares) donated by Catholic University – a gift sanctioned by Pope Pius X, who sent $400 along with his blessings. Dedicated to the Virgin Mary, the Marian shrine was constructed in fits and starts between 1920 and 1959 with funds from American parishes.

The basilica's ground floor holds the original dark and clammy **Crypt Church**; the sarcophagus of Bishop Thomas J. Shahan – the only person buried here; a hall of donors; and the tiara of Pope Paul VI. It all pales, though, compared to the glittering **Great Upper Church**, whose mosaic-covered walls contain an entire Italian quarry. Not to be missed are the three oratories and 57 unique chapels.

On the edge of Catholic University is the **Pope John Paul II Cultural Center** ⓫ (3900 Harewood Road, NE; tel: 202-635-5400; open Tues–Sat, 10am–5pm; Sun noon–5pm; admission fee; www.jp2cc.org).

This three-story modern facility explores the Catholic faith in the modern world and highlights the life of Karol Joseph Wojtyla, the first non-Italian pope in 455 years. Several art treasures borrowed from the Vatican are on display and an interactive center covers a wide variety of topics, ranging from original sin to cloning.

You can take in a performance at the **Dance Place** ⓬ at 3225 8th Street (tel: 202-269-1600; visit www.danceplace.org for a schedule of events), the enterprising force behind DC's contemporary, avant-garde, and ethnic dance scene. It stages the best local, national, and international troupes each weekend, with special performances for Black History month in February and an annual African Dance Festival in June.

Place of pilgrimage

A pilgrimage to Brookland is incomplete without a visit to the **Franciscan Monastery** ⓭ at 1400 Quincy Street (tel: 202-526-6800; open Mon–Sat, 9am–4pm; Sun 1pm–4pm; guided tours on the hour except

BELOW: the National Arboretum.

at noon; www.gardenvisit.com). The Franciscans built this hilltop American headquarters and named it Mount Saint Sepulchre. A sort of monastic theme park modeled after Istanbul's Hagia Sophia, it contains replicas of holy shrines, grottoes, and Roman catacombs.

Byzantine in style with Renaissance touches, the blindingly opulent monastery church, completed in 1899, contains stained-glass windows from Bavaria and a 5-ton bronze altar canopy. In season the meticulous cloister garden is redolent with the scent of roses.

Much more modest in comparison is **St Anselm's Abbey ⑭**, the well-hidden Benedictine monastery at 4501 South Dakota Avenue and 14th Street (tel: 202-269-2300; www.stanselms.org). The monks annually host a spring flower show and sale on the grounds of the monastery.

South of Brookland at 800 Florida Avenue, **Gallaudet University ⑮** (tel: 202-651-5000), the world's only college for the deaf, holds its own against the surrounding mean streets. Still, you can safely tour within the walled grounds of the Gothic-style campus, which were designed by Frederick Law Olmsted, Jr, the architect of New York's Central Park.

National Arboretum

Not far to the east, by the banks of the Anacostia River, lies the **National Arboretum ⑯** (tel: 202-245-2726; open daily 8am–5pm, closed Dec 25; www.usna.usda.gov). Although established in 1927, it is so little known that you can feel as though you have the entire rolling refuge of 444 acres (180 hectares) of gardens and woods plus 3 miles (5 km) of walking paths all to yourself – except in spring when the 70,000 azaleas, the arboretum's most prolific planting, are in bloom and it's mobbed.

For an olfactory treat, be sure to smell the historic roses and specialty herbs opposite the bonsai exhibit, and then wander over to the surreal-looking stand of 22 Corinthian columns salvaged from the old portico of the US Capitol building. There are no concessions, so consider packing a picnic if you plan to spend time here. ❑

A resident of the Franciscan Monastery.

Restaurants

American

Ben's Chili Bowl
1213 U St., NW. Tel: 202-667-0909. Open: B, L, D, Mon–Sat; D only Sun. $, cash only
DC legend since 1958 serving real fries, shakes and burgers and the famous chili dog. Attracts all kinds.

Café Saint-Ex
1847 14th St., NW. Tel: 202-265-7839. Open: L & D, daily Sat & Sun brunch. $–$$
Vintage-airplane and travel theme combined with a classic bistro menu. Order cocktails at the "Gate 54" lounge.

Colonel Brooks Tavern
901 Monroe St., NE. Tel: 202-529-4002. Open: L & D, daily; Sun brunch; bar open until 1.30am weeknights, 2.30am weekends. $
Long-time, lively neighborhood pizza/burger/ fries hangout. Entertainment most nights.

Logan Tavern
1423 P St., NW. Tel: 202-332-3710. Open: L & D, daily, Sun brunch. $–$$
New neighborhood hang-out features the usual American favorites.

Asian

Sushi Taro
1503 17th St., NW. Tel: 202-462-8999. $–$$
All sushi. Fast service,
pleasant atmosphere. Good for a light meal.

Thai Tanic
1326 14th St., NW. Tel: 202-588-1186. Open: L & D, daily. $–$$
Good food, generous portions, goofy décor, long beer list.

Italian

Coppi's
1414 U St., NW. Tel: 202-319-7773. Open: D daily. $–$$
Sophisticated Italian fare, organic ingredients, excellent pizza.

Latin American

Julia's Empanadas
1410 U St., NW. Tel: 202-387-4100. Open: L & D. $
Nothing fancy, but the empanadas are generous and tasty with lots of sides on the menu.

Spanish

Mar de Plata
1401 14th St., NW. Tel: 202-234-2679. Open: D daily. $–$$
Fish, meat, paellas, but best for tapas. Near Studio Theatre.

PRICE CATEGORIES

Prices for three-course dinner per person with a half-bottle of house wine, tax and tip:
$ = under $25
$$ = $25–$40
$$$ = $40–$50
$$$$ = more than $50

SOUTHWEST WATERFRONT AND THE SOUTHEAST

The neighborhoods that stretch beyond official Washington's gleaming marble epicenter are some of its toughest, but they contain several important historic sites and a beautiful garden.

The waterfront is the heart of DC's Southwest and Southeast neighborhoods. At the **Maine Avenue Fish Market ❶** along the Washington Channel, dozens of vendors hawk fresh seafood from the Chesapeake Bay and the lower Potomac and Delaware rivers. Boatside stands are piled with everything from bluefish and rockfish, to oysters and soft-shell crabs.

The market is open daily, year round, but go on a summer weekend when vendors are shouting, families are hauling away bushels of still-snapping blue crabs, and cars are squeezing in and out of the parking lot. Even if you're not planning a feast, it's worth stopping by to savor the scene and enjoy a plate of freshly shucked clams or oysters.

This is one area of town where you're likely to find a cab driver who'll get you to your destination on time. If he stopped locally before picking you up, chances are the cabbie will have a crate of dripping seafood tucked away in the trunk of the car. It's in *both* your interests for him to step on the gas pedal pronto.

Mixed fortunes

Not all of this part of DC is this lively, however. When the Federal City was laid out in 1791–92, the Southeast and Southwest quadrants north of the Anacostia River were slated as mixed residential and commercial areas. The mismanaged City Canal, which once flowed along Constitution Avenue, was intended to bring some of Georgetown's trade to this area. But the stinking canal and the addition of a new railroad depot sent the wealthier residents packing and created a squalid neighborhood of substandard buildings and high crime.

Beginning in the 1930s, redevelopment plans were introduced, then

BELOW: tipping the scales at Maine Avenue Fish Market.

either abandoned or only partially realized. As a result, much of this area is dominated by a jumble of "innovative" architect-designed buildings of little interest to most visitors.

The rest of Southeast DC, separated from the city by the **Anacostia River**, developed slowly and independently from the nation's capital. The name Anacostia derives from the local tribe of Indians who originally settled the region before traders and tobacco farmers, and then freed blacks in the early 19th century claimed the area. Thanks to the middle-class flight into the suburbs and the 1968 riots, which destroyed many of the of the area's homes and businesses, Anacostia went into decline where, unfortunately, it remains.

Waterfront attractions

Both the **Washington Channel** ❷ and the riverfront are lined with private yacht clubs and boat yards. From the pier at 6th and Water streets you can take a scenic cruise on the Potomac on the 145-ft *Spirit of Washington* ❸ (tel: 202-554-8000 or www.spiritofwashington.com for schedules and ticket information). This line offers day and nighttime cruises along the river, plus daytime trips to George Washington's home, Mount Vernon.

The waterfront is also popular for dining. Several cavernous restaurants along Water Street specialize in seafood and panoramic views of the Washington Channel, marina, and downtown monuments, and offer a variety of entertainments such as happy hours, comedy acts, dancing, and live jazz.

One of the best places in DC for first-rate dramas by contemporary playwrights such as August Wilson is nearby **Arena Stage** ❹ at 6th and M streets (tel: 202-488-3300; www.arenastage.org for schedule and ticket sales). It also stages versions of Marx Brothers comedies and new

takes on classic Broadway musicals. From its humble beginnings in the old vat room of the former Heurich Brewery (where the Kennedy Center now stands), the company performs in a complex that includes the 800-seat **Arena Theater** (in the round), the 500-seat **Kreeger Theater**, and the 180-seat cabaret-style **Old Vat Room**. Arena was the first theater outside of New York to be awarded a Tony, this for the overall quality of its productions.

Southwest of the Arena, occupying the mile-long peninsula near the confluence of the Washington Channel and the Potomac and Anacostia rivers, is **Fort McNair** ❺ (not open to the public), originally an 18th-century fort and arsenal known variously as Turkey Buzzards Point, Greenleaf Point and Fort Humphreys. It is one of the oldest active military posts in the US. In 1865, four of John Wilkes Booth's fellow conspirators in Lincoln's assassination were imprisoned and hanged here. One of them, Mary Surratt, whose crime had been to rent rooms to Booth in the boarding house she operated, was the

Map on page 174

During heavy rains, Washington's sewage and flood waters flow into the Anacostia River at 17 discharge points, making it unsafe to swim in or to eat its fish. But improved water treatment systems, underground water storage facilities and the reintroduction of native plants and animals should help restore the river over the next 20 years.

BELOW:
riots devastated the area in 1968 after Martin Luther King's assassination.

first American woman executed by federal order. The fort was renamed in 1948 in honor of Lesley J. McNair, commander of the army's ground forces in Normandy in 1944. The fort is now home to the **National War College** and the **National Defense University**.

Naval traditions

Sailor from the Washington Navy Yard.

Farther up the Anacostia River in Southeast at 9th and M streets is the **Washington Navy Yard 6**. This historic precinct dates from 1799 and was the navy's first shore facility until the commandant ordered the yard burned to avoid it being captured by the British during the War of 1812. It was rebuilt and served as a naval gun factory during the 19th century and again during both world wars. The yard ceased operating in 1961 and now serves as an administrative center.

The precinct comprises the **Marine Corps Museum** (daily 10am–4.30pm; closed Jan 1, Thanksgiving, Dec 25; tel: 202-433-3840) and the **Navy Memorial Museum** (Apr–Aug, Mon–Fri, 9am–5pm; Sept–Mar, Mon–Fri, 9am–4pm; weekends and holidays all year, 10am–5pm; closed Jan 1, Thanksgiving, Dec 24–25; guided one-hour tours can be reserved; tel: 202-433-4882; www.historynavy.mil).

The Marine Corps Museum galleries include combat art, uniforms, weapons, and technology. Also on display is memorabilia of John Philip Sousa, master of the Marine Band from 1880 to 1892 and composer of about 140 military marches. The Navy Memorial Museum's 5,000 artifacts trace naval history from the Revolutionary War to the age of space exploration.

Anacostia

On the south side of the Anacostia River is **Anacostia 7**, one of the city's less affluent neighborhoods. It

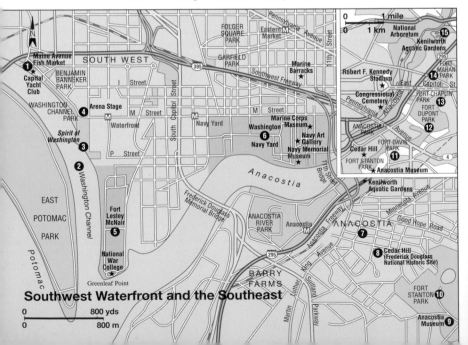

Southwest Waterfront and the Southeast

Map on page 174

is best visited by car, only during the day, never alone, and even then with a degree of caution.

Incorporated in 1854 as Union-town, one of Washington's earliest subdivisions, **Old Anacostia** retains a certain historical appeal as a result of several restored 19th-century churches and frame houses. But, as the home of Washington's poor and disenfranchised, it is neither the city's most beautiful section nor its safest. This is where much of the city's serious crime occurs.

About the only good reason to go there is **Cedar Hill** ❽ (visit by guided tour only, year round, 9am–4pm; must call ahead, tel: 202-426-5961 www.nps.gov/frdo; or arrange through Tourmobile tel: 202-554-5100, a sightseeing company, which offers tours in summer). Built on a tree-shaded hilltop at 14th and W streets, this is the stately home of Frederick Douglass, a self-educated former slave, presidential advisor, and writer *(see page 177)*. The 21-room house speaks volumes of the life and times of Douglass, who lived here with his family from 1877 to 1895.

During this period, he served as the US Marshal for DC, the Recorder of Deeds for DC, and Minister to the tiny nation of Santo Domingo, which shared a Caribbean island with Haiti and which, as a possible home for newly freed Southern blacks, had petitioned the US for admittance to the Union after the Civil War.

Many of Douglass's original possessions are on display, including his impressive personal library of 1,200 volumes and gifts from President Lincoln, Harriet Beecher Stowe, author of *Uncle Tom's Cabin* (1852), and the abolitionist leader William Lloyd Garrison (1805–79). Cedar Hill is not a sanitized period home, but a home that keeps Douglass's memory very alive.

At 1901 Fort Place, SE, is the **Anacostia Museum** ❾ (daily 10am–5pm; closed Dec 25; tel: 202-287-3369), one of the Smithsonian Institution's off-the-Mall museums. This innovative museum documents the history, culture, and contributions of notable African Americans. Created by the Smith-

Cedar Hill statuette.

BELOW:
run-down Anacostia.

Map on page 174

TIP

After 30-plus years without a team, baseball, the nation's so-called pastime, has returned to the nation's capital. The Nationals, formerly the Montreal Expos, begin play at RFK Stadium in 2005. Tickets range between $7 and $40. For details, tel: 202-675-6287. The Nationals will move into a new stadium in 2008. Located just west of the Navy Yard, the new stadium should boost lagging efforts to revitalize the area.

sonian in 1967, it serves as combination museum and cultural arts center, focusing on the history of Anacostia from its 16th-century Indian days to the present.

Civil War forts

Around Anacostia are five of the nearly 50 forts built in a ring around the city at the outbreak of the Civil War. **Forts Stanton** ⑩, **Davis** ⑪, **Dupont** ⑫, **Chaplin** ⑬, and **Mahan** ⑭ now form a chain of city parks where the forts' original earthworks are still visible. Fort Dupont, the best preserved, also includes recreational facilities, hiking and biking trails and a series of summer jazz concerts (details: www.nps.gov/nace/ftdupont.htm).

With just a little bit of imagination you can visit Monet's gardens at Giverny at **Kenilworth Aquatic Gardens** ⑮ (1900 Anacostia Drive, SE; daily 7am–4pm; closed Jan 1, Thanksgiving, Dec 25; admission free; tel: 202-426-6905). Just off the Anacostia Freeway and a short walk from Metro's Deanwood Station, this 12-acre (5-hectare) sanctuary,

founded in 1882 near the marshlands of the Anacostia River, has pond after pond of exotic water lilies, lotuses, and aquatic plants in a natural outdoor setting.

Summertime promises the most blooms, and early mornings are the best time to visit since you can see the night-blooming flowers before they close and day-bloomers as they open. This garden is a joy just to wander in, filtering color and light as if to please an Impressionist painter.

The gardens are also a treat for amateur naturalists. Behind the visitor center there are three ponds of labeled species where you can familiarize yourself with the tropical lilies and ancient lotuses (the rest of the gardens are label-free). The most extraordinary lilies are the Victoria *amazonica* from South America which have platter-like leaves up to 6 ft (1.8 meters) across.

The quieter you are on your visit, the better your chances for spotting the toads, turtles, muskrats, green herons, red-winged blackbirds, and migrating waterfowl who reside in this tranquil place. ❏

Restaurants

American

H20
800 Water St., SW. Tel: 202-484-6300. Open: L & D, daily; Sun brunch. $–$$
Former old-line food emporium with a water view, hence the name. Blow-out dance party Friday nights.

Phillip's Flagship
900 Water St., SW. Tel: 202-488-8515. Open: B, L & D, daily; Sun brunch. $–$$
Old-line, family-run seafood eatery. Pleasant, but nothing fancy.

Pier 7
In the Channel Inn Hotel, 650 Water St., SW. Tel: 202-554-2500. Open: B, L & D, daily; Sun brunch. $–$$
Caters mostly to bus tour groups. Order from the bar and enjoy the water view.

Asian

Café Mozu
Mandarin Oriental Hotel, 1330 Maryland Ave., SW. Tel: 202-787-6868. Open: B, L & D, daily. $$–$$$
Ambitious French, Italian, Asian menu wins praise and includes lobster, lamb, French toast, nori seaweed and a black-and-white martini shake. Near Arena Stage.

Jenny's Asian Fusion
1000 Water St., NW. Tel: 202-554-2202. Open: L & D, daily; also takeaway. $–$$
Former SW neighborhood favorite in new waterfront location with long menu including signature wontons and traditional seafood dishes.

Caribbean-Cajun

Zanzibar On the Waterfront
700 Water St., NW. Tel: 202-554-9100. Open: L & D, daily; Sun brunch; nightly entertainment. $–$$
Blackened or mango- and cilantro-flavored dishes with a good water view from the deck. Busy bar scene;

Afro-world beat music and dancing.

Tex-Mex

Cantina Marina
600 Water Street, SE. Tel: 202-554-8396. Open: L & D, daily. $–$$
Casual American Southwest. Order a Corona-with-lime and barbecue.

PRICE CATEGORIES

Prices for three-course dinner per person with a half-bottle of house wine, tax and tip:
$ = under $25
$$ = $25–$40
$$$ = $40–$50
$$$$ = more than $50

Frederick Douglass

Eloquent voice for the silenced and an unshakable force against the evil that was slavery, Frederick Douglass was not only a great orator but also the embodiment of the American ideal of freedom.

Born Frederick August Washington Bailey in Talbot County, Maryland, in 1818, he acquired an education, forbidden to slaves, by observing his white friends as they were tutored. "With play-mates for my teachers, fences and pavements for my copy books, and chalk for my pen and ink," he later wrote, "I learned the art of writing." From a volume of contemporary speeches, which he bought for 50 cents, the whole of his savings after having been hired out to perform the dirty job of caulking ships on the Baltimore docks, he learned the art of oration and made a life-changing discovery. Enlightened Americans not only opposed slavery, but in the North where blacks were free, they were actively speaking against it.

In 1837, Douglass escaped to New York with his wife Anna Murray, a freed slave whom he met in Baltimore, and then to Massachusetts where he changed his last name to Douglass to avoid capture by his Maryland owner. Educated and articulate, Douglass, whose "diploma was written on his back" as one abolitionist put it, was in demand as a public speaker before anti-slavery gatherings.

In 1845, he published the first volume of his autobiography, in part to document the horrors of slavery for disbelieving Americans, and three years later began writing and publishing *The North Star*, an influential abolitionist periodical that he produced from his home in Rochester, New York.

Douglass threw his support behind Abraham Lincoln and the newly-formed Republican Party which, during its early years, championed the cause of freedom, and helped raised a regiment of black soldiers. After the Civil War he cautioned freed slaves, though they were destitute, against accepting the government's post-war handouts of food, clothing and medicine, arguing that it would only enrage the embittered Southern whites and lead to paternalism and an unhealthy dependency. Despite lynchings, oppressive Jim Crow laws, and the rise of the Ku Klux Klan, which combined to drive many Southern blacks to the cities in the North, Douglass urged blacks to stay in the South and claim the land to which they were entitled. "His labor made him a slave," Douglass wrote of his fellow blacks, "and his labor can, if he will, make him free, comfortable, and independent."

Douglass remained committed to the Republican Party, even after it abandoned its promise of restoring civil order to the South, and moved to Washington to accept several political appointments. In 1882, his first wife died and two years later he married Helen Pitts, his white assistant.

Douglass also took on the cause of women's suffrage. In 1895, after completing an address to an audience of Washington women, he died of a heart attack.

Through the sheer force of his character, Frederick Douglass not only transformed himself but also, through the written and spoken word, changed what it means for all Americans, regardless of color or gender, to participate fully in democratic life. ❏

RIGHT: Frederick Douglass, champion of freedom.

AROUND WASHINGTON

Within easy reach of the city are majestic Arlington National Cemetery, quaint Old Town Alexandria, George Washington's beloved Mount Vernon, and the Potomac's dramatic Great Falls.

The Capital's rapidly expanding Virginia and Maryland suburbs offer almost as many attractions and distractions as the city itself. Surrounding the District on four sides, the suburbs hold dozens of residential neighborhoods, parks, museums, restaurants, and commuter traffic that are urban enough to be within DC's borders.

Southern perspective

This fact often makes the transition between the city and suburbs indistinguishable, especially inside the Beltway around the city. The most popular sights are Arlington County and the City of Alexandria, and parks in Montgomery County in Maryland and in Fairfax, Virginia. Since Arlington County and a section of Alexandria were part of Washington from the late 18th to the mid-19th centuries, the historic homes and museums here chronicle the history of the nation and of its developing capital city during this vital period, but with a slightly southern perspective. Beyond the Beltway, the suburbs become more rural and the influence of the federal government becomes less pronounced.

You can visit most of the nearby suburban attractions by public transportation, car or bike. Expect traffic congestion on most roads during the morning and evening rush hours. You can often beat the traffic by taking the **W&OD bike trail**, which runs 45 miles (72 km) from Alexandria west into Loudoun County, or on the **Mount Vernon Trail** which parallels the Potomac River from the Lincoln Memorial south to Mount Vernon.

Before leaving DC proper, it's worth stopping in the middle of the Potomac River on the 88-acre (36-hectare) **Theodore Roosevelt Island ❶**. Walking paths criss-cross this wooded wildlife haven and lead

Map on page 180

LEFT: Memorial Bridge statue.
BELOW: the Iwo Jima Memorial in Arlington.

Pausing for breath on Memorial Bridge

to a 23-ft-tall (7-meter) statue of President Theodore Roosevelt.

Just south on the Virginia side of the river is **Lady Bird Johnson Park ❷**, a 121-acre (49-hectare) man-made island planted with some 1,000 flowering dogwood trees and a million daffodils. Within this park is the **Lyndon Baines Johnson Memorial Grove** where white pines, dogwoods, rhododendrons, and azaleas surround a monolith of pink Texas granite.

As you cross **Memorial Bridge** into Arlington, **Arlington House** (Apr–Sept, 9.30am–6pm; Oct–Mar, 9.30am–4.30pm; closed Jan 1, Dec 25; tel: 703-557-0613; www.nps.gov/arho) dominates the hill before you. Arlington House was the home of Robert E. Lee and his wife Mary Anna Randolph Custis, great-granddaughter of Martha Washington. The couple lived in this gracious Greek Revival mansion with their seven children from 1831 until Lee resigned his commission in the US Army to defend his native Virginia in the Civil War. During the war, hundreds of Union Army soldiers occupied the property and cut most of the 200 acres (80 hectares) of virgin oak

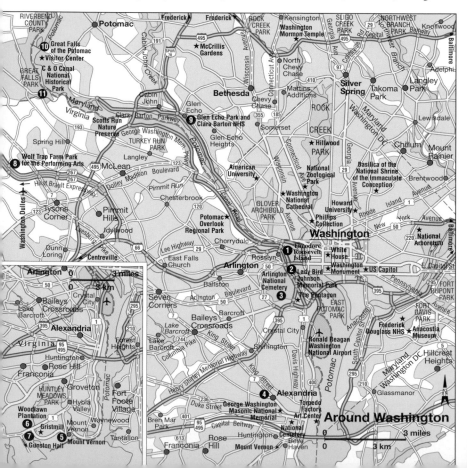

Around Washington

forest for fortifications and firewood. In 1864, after Mrs Lee refused to pay the property tax, the Federal government confiscated the estate and established what is now Arlington National Cemetery on the grounds. The house has been restored to its mid-19th-century appearance to offer a glimpse of pre-war Southern gentility. You can walk the scenic route to the house via 200 easy steps north of the main gate of the cemetery.

Soon after the Civil War broke out, it became apparent that a burial ground would be needed. The Quartermaster-General of the Union Army, Montgomery Meigs, chose Lee's former plantation as the site where the Union dead would be buried. Meigs considered Lee a traitor and, both in retribution and to discourage Lee's ever returning, made a point of burying the first war dead within easy sight of the house.

The rolling hills of **Arlington National Cemetery ❸** (daily Apr–Sept 8am–7pm, Oct–Mar, 8am–5pm; tel: 703-697-2131) stretch over 612 acres (248 hectares) and contain the graves of more than 240,000 mil-

itary personnel and other patriots, including the dead from every war or conflict in which America was a participant, beginning with the Revolutionary War. The simple white headstones, set in even rows, stretch as far as the eye can see.

Unless you are visiting the grave of a relative or friend, access is possible only by Tourmobile buses departing from the **Visitors Center ❹** or, even better, on your own two feet. Walking is preferable: lines for Tourmobiles can sometimes be long, and the narrated tour covers only the central cemetery.

The Tomb of the Unknown Dead of the Civil War ❸ on the former site of Mrs Lee's rose garden marks the grave of the 2,111 unidentified Union soldiers who died on nearby Virginia battlefields. The mast of the **battleship Maine** marks the grave of 229 men who died in the explosion preceding the Spanish-American War. **The Tomb of the Unknowns ❼** (formerly the Tomb of the Unknown Soldier), carved from a 50-ton block of Colorado marble, holds the remains of four US

Maps on page 180, 182

TIP

You can buy tickets for the 1½ to 2-hour bus tour of Arlington Cemetery only at the Visitors Center. Tours depart daily except Christmas Day, Apr–Aug 8.30am–6pm, Sept–Mar 9.30am–4.30pm. The last tour each day takes in the changing of the guard. Details: Tourmobile Sightseeing, tel: 202-554-5100, www.tourmobile.com

BELOW: a funeral procession in Arlington National Cemetery.

Tomb of the Unknown.

BELOW:
Arlington National Cemetery in winter.

servicemen, one each from World Wars I and II, and the Korean and Vietnam Wars.

The Changing of the Guard, which takes place here every half-hour in summer, every hour in winter and also throughout the night, is on many visitors' list of things to see while in Washington.

Others buried here include Pierre L'Enfant, Oliver Wendell Holmes, Rear Admirals Robert E. Peary and Richard E. Byrd, and presidents Taft and Kennedy. **John F. Kennedy's grave ❶**, with its simple, eternal flame glowing in all weathers, still attracts crowds. The tomb of Robert F. Kennedy is not far away in a grassy plot.

At the cemetery's north end stands the **Iwo Jima Memorial ❷**. The 100-ton bronze statue depicts the raising of the US flag on Iwo Jima, the World War II battle site where more than 5,000 marines died. On Tuesday evenings in sum-

mer, the Marine Silent Drill Team and Drum and Bugle Corps hold a sunset ceremony here.

Just south of Arlington Cemetery is one of the world's largest office buildings, the **Pentagon**, which is not open to the public. This five-sided headquarters of the Department of Defense is comprised of five concentric circles around a 5-acre (2-hectare) courtyard. It covers 6½ million sq ft (60 hectares) and provides offices, restaurants, and shops for more than 23,000 civilian and military employees.

West of the Pentagon, you'll find Arlington's high-rise office and apartment complexes of **Rosslyn** and **Crystal City**. The immigrant Asian population in Arlington's Clarendon section has created a wealth of Vietnamese, Cambodian, Korean and Thai restaurants, many located in what is called **Little Saigon** on Wilson Boulevard.

Back along the Potomac River is

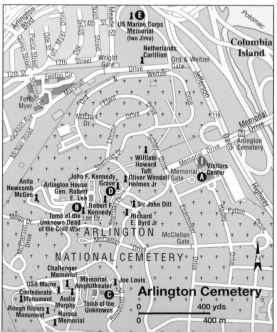

Maps
on page
180, 184

Washington Reagan National Airport, thc "Reagan" added in 1999 at the insistence of Congress and in honor of the former president, but to the locals it's still National. Just 3 miles (5 km) from downtown, this airport has been refurbished and expanded to ease the legendary congestion, both air and ground. Conveniently, there's a Metro station in the airport to make it easier to get in and out of the District.

For a close-up view of the planes taking off and landing, head south along the GW Parkway, named for George Washington, toward the **Washington Sailing Marina** (1 Marina Drive; tel: 703-548-9027). The marina offers lessons and rentals in sailing and windsurfing as well as renting out bicycles. The marina's **Potowmack Landing** (tel: 703-548-0001) restaurant has outdoor seating with great views of the river and DC.

Old Town Alexandria

The parkway, continuing south to **Alexandria ❹**, becomes Washington Street in **Old Town Alexandria**, a charming eight-square-block district of 18th- and 19th-century buildings with an invigorated and very modern town dock. Pleasure craft of all sorts tie up around a small barge with a red-roofed structure on it. That's the **Alexandria Seaport Foundation** (Mon– Fri, 9am–4pm; for additional hours and programs, tel: 703-549-7078). This is run mostly by volunteers who teach boat-building skills to kids at risk and offer several on-the-water programs to help locals and visitors alike get better acquainted with Alexandria's seaport past and the Potomac's marine and wildlife.

In 1699, the Scottish settler John Alexander bought the land that would eventually become Alexandria from an English ship captain for 6,000 pounds of tobacco. By the 18th century, the area was a thriving center for the export of that profitable crop. To facilitate shipping and put it on a par with the likes of New York and Boston, both important seaport centers, Scotsmen William Ramsay and John Carlyle successfully petitioned the Virginia General Assembly to establish a town. By 1749, Alexandria was born.

It's similar in many ways to Georgetown, but this Virginia port city is generally less crowded (though you're likely to be shoulder-to-shoulder if the weekend weather's good), and has managed to preserve more of its colonial heritage. Strict building codes are in force here, so the block upon block of restored Federal-style townhouses you'll see will give you a good indication of what the city looked like in centuries past.

A good place to begin is at the **Ramsay House Visitors Center ❹** on King Street (221 King Street; daily 9am–5pm; tel: 703-838-4200; www.FunSide.com), home of the Scottish merchant. You can pick up some maps and brochures here, and

Traditional Alexandria architecture.

BELOW: Alexandria.

Old-style service at Gadsby's Tavern.

BELOW:
Old Town Alexandria.

get advice from the helpful guides.

To get a background in Alexandria's history, stop by the local history exhibits at the **Lyceum** ❸ (201 South Washington Street, tel: 703-838-44994), a Greek Revival structure dating from 1839 where much of the city's history is told in photographs and other artifacts, or the **Carlyle House** ❸ (121 North Fairfax Street; Tues–Sat, 10am–4pm, Sun, noon–4pm; tel: 703-549-2997), a grand home in the Scottish-manor style on North Fairfax Street and one of the first homes built in Alexandria. Signs proclaiming "George Washington Slept Here" are common and questionable from New York to Georgia, but Alexandria's claims are bona fide.

In 1765 Washington built a townhouse here at 508 Cameron Street (a replica of the original home now stands in its place) and Washington celebrated his last two birthdays in the ballroom of what is now

Gadsby's Tavern Museum ❹ on North Royal Street (134 North Royal Street; open Mar–Oct, Tues–Sat 11am–4pm, Sun 1pm–4pm; Apr–Sept Tues–Sat 10am–5pm, Sun 1pm–5pm; closed Mon; tel: 703-838-4242). The museum preserves an original tavern (1770), and the City Hotel (1792) that was a center of political, business, and social life in early Alexandria. Next door, the 200-year-old **Gadsby's Tavern Restaurant** offers hearty 18th-century victuals served by waiters in period dress and character.

On weekends, you can ride an Alexandria city Dash bus from the King Street Metro station and hop on and off at any bus stop along King Street. The service is free and operates on a 15-minute schedule

Grand mansions and art

Among Alexandria's favorite native sons is Robert E. Lee, who lived in the red-brick house on Oronoco

Street, now a private residence, from 1812 until his West Point enrollment in 1825. Across the street, on the corner of Washington Street, is the white-frame **Lee-Fendall House ❺** (614 Oronoco Street; open Tues–Sat 10am–4pm; Sun noon-4pm; closed Mon; tel: 703-548-1789). It was built in 1785 by one of Robert E. Lee's ancestors and contains an inventory of Lee family furnishings. Cross Washington Street and stop at **Christ Church ❻** (Cameron and North Washington streets; tel: 703-549-1450) which dates from 1767. George Washington's pew is here and, surrounding the church, a pleasant garden.

Alexandria's art scene is as vital as its history, with more than 20 Old Town galleries and the **Torpedo Factory Art Center ❼** (105 North Union Street; open daily 10am–5pm; closed major holidays; tel: 703-838-4565; www.torpedofactory.org). A former munitions factory, the Torpedo Factory houses 165 artists who create, display, and sell their works on the premises.

The Torpedo Factory is also home to the **Alexandria Archaeology Museum** (open Tues–Sat, 10am–3pm, Sat 10am–5pm; closed Mon; tel: 703-838-4399). Here you can watch the urban archaeologists at work, putting together the city's history shard by shard.

Mount Vernon

Farther south, at the end of the GW Parkway, is **Mount Vernon ❺** (open daily including major holidays, Apr–Aug, 8am–5pm; Mar, Sept, Oct 9am–5pm; Nov–Feb 9am–4pm; entrance fee; tel: 703-780-2000; www.mountvernon.org), Martha and George Washington's estate from 1754 to 1799. Situated on a bluff above the Potomac River, the white Georgian mansion was bought by the Mount Vernon Ladies' Association in 1858 and has

been meticulously restored to its appearance during the last years of Washington's life. On first glance, the mansion seems to be constructed of stone, but it is actually made of boards that have been grooved and beveled to look like stone.

Washington, an innovative farmer, cultivated just under half of the 8,000-acre (3,200-hectare) estate. He experimented with various crops – tobacco, initially, then a less labor-intensive, more soil-friendly and highly profitable wheat crop. In 1771, he established a grist-mill 3 miles (5 km) east of the estate. This has been restored.

An introductory video is followed by a 20-minute tour, accompanied by docents who explain each of the rooms in turn. The stunningly ostentatious main **parlor** was designed with the deliberate intention of impressing the Washingtons' guests. The walls were finished in vertigis, the furniture is of the finest quality, and Washington's personality projects from six paintings reflecting his love of nature. It was in this room that he planned the Battle of

Maps on page 180, 184

Christ Church.

BELOW: in the Lyceum Museum.

Yorktown, received the news of his presidential election, and lay in state after he died on December 14, 1799.

Washington's personal **study** is furnished with interesting pieces, including his presidential chair and a peculiar but practical chair with pedals that drove an overhead fan. Another highlight is the second-floor **master bedroom**.

You can spend some time exploring the outbuildings (some contain exhibitions) and the two museums, and seeing the impressive coach that belonged to Philadelphia mayor Samuel Powel. The tomb, too, is interesting. Washington provided for its creation in his will, and he and Martha were entombed there in 1831. Other family memorials are outside, and nearby is a dignified memorial to the slaves, numbering 316 in 1799 compared to 50 in 1759.

Washington was knowledgeable about livestock. Reportedly, he introduced mules – harder working than horses and donkeys – to America. Animals present today include endangered black and white pigs, 2,000 of which once roamed the estate, and a breed of sheep whose fleece the slaves once spun into yarn for clothing.

About 10,000 tourists a day visit Mount Vernon during peak season – so an early start is recommended.

The **George Washington Pioneer Farmer Site** is also worth seeing. The highlight is a 1996 replica of the innovative 16-sided barn designed by Washington. Around the 12-ft (3.6-meter) wide wooden lane that surrounded a center section, cattle would tread the unthreshed wheat, separating the grain. The grain would then fall between purpose-designed gaps in the floor boards to the lower floor, there to be gathered for the gristmill. The brown Milking Devon cattle chosen for this chore are still bred here and are used in demonstrations at 11am, 12.30pm, and 3pm daily.

Three miles (5 km) south of the mansion is the refurbished **Gristmill** (tickets available at Mount Vernon). This is part of the original plantation and has a water-powered grinding wheel.

If driving, travel a mile or so to

TIP

Cruises to Mount Vernon on the *Miss Christin* leave from Alexandria's waterfront at 11am Apr–Oct and return at 4pm. The narrated trip takes 50 minutes each way and costs $27, including admission to Mount Vernon. Details: Potomac Riverboat Company, tel: 703-548-9000, www.potomacriverboatco.com

BELOW: Mount Vernon

Map on page 180

Woodlawn Plantation ❻ (9000 Richmond Highway; open daily 10–5; closed Jan, Feb, Thanksgiving, Dec 25, admission fee; tel: 703-780-4000). This is the estate George Washington gave his niece as a wedding present and which was designed by William Thornton, architect of the US Capitol. On these grounds is another interesting building: the **Pope-Leighey House**, designed by famous American architect Frank Lloyd Wright, has Wright's contemporary style and was moved here from its original location in a nearby suburb.

Drive another 8 miles (13 km) south along Route One to **Gunston Hall ❼** (10709 Gunston Hall Road, Mason Neck; daily 9.30am–5pm; closed Jan 1, Thanksgiving, Dec 25), home of founding father George Mason, who was responsible for adding the Bill or Rights to the US Constitution. The beautifully restored mansion has several outbuildings, including a schoolhouse, and a boxwood garden dating from the 1760s, all spread over several quiet acres above the Potomac. Although a bit off the beaten track, it's a gem of a house and is seldom crowded.

Fun in the park

An easy drive west of DC toward Vienna, Virginia, is **Wolf Trap Farm Park ❽** (1645 Trap Road; tel: 703-255-1860; www.wolftrap.org or check the *Washington Post* for schedules), America's only national park for the performing arts. The much-loved **Filene Center** stage draws some 6,800 picnic-toting patrons here in summer for concerts (opera, ballet, modern dance, jazz, stand-up comedians) in covered and lawn seating. The intimate **Barns at Wolf Trap** hosts a variety of performances in winter and spring.

To the west, near the Blue Ridge Mountains, is **Washington Dulles International Airport**, a graceful sweep of a building designed in 1962 by Eero Saarinen. Close by is the National Air and Space Museum's **Steven F. Udvar-Hazy Center** (tel: 202-357-1729; www.nasm.si.edu; open 10am–5.30pm; free). Its soaring halls house more than 300 flying

Part of a mural at the National Air and Space Museum's Steven F. Udvar-Hazy Center.

BELOW: the National Air and Space Museum's Steven F. Udvar-Hazy Center.

Map on page 180

The falls in Great Falls Park (9200 Old Dominion Drive, McLean, VA) are a 5- to 10-minute walk on a straight, level trail from the Visitor Center. Vehicles pay $5 to enter the park but are not allowed on the trails or in the picnic area (where picnic tables and small grills are provided). Three overlooks offer views of the falls and one is handicap-accessible. Details: tel: 703-285-2965, www.nps.gov/gwmp/grfa/

BELOW: fishing near Great Falls.

machines, including the *Enola Gay* and a Concorde (*see page 77 for more details*). An observation deck allows you to view traffic using the airport.

Between the Potomac River and MacArthur Boulevard in Maryland is **Glen Echo Park** ❾ (tel: 301-492-6229; www.nps.gov/glec; free admission into the park, charges for attractions). This is an arts and performance center remembered by generations of Washingtonians as a countryside amusement park at the terminus of DC's old trolley line. It almost closed in the 1960s, but community efforts have restored it and now, as a National Park, Glen Echo mixes applause from theater audiences, squeals from roller-coaster riders, and the plinking tunes of the merry-go-round.

Many of its buildings are now art studios and classrooms. Glen Echo offers lectures, craft workshops, dance classes and theatrical performances including puppet shows each year. On weekends you can dance in the ornately redecorated **Spanish Ballroom**, or ride the lovingly restored 1920s-era **Dentzel carousel**.

Nearby is the **Clara Barton National Historic Site** (by guided tour offered on the hour daily 10am–4pm; closed Jan 1, Thanksgiving, Dec 25; free admission; tel: 301-492-6245), the 36-room home of the woman who founded the American Red Cross in 1881.

The Great Falls

No visitor should leave the area without paying homage to the natural feature that determined the location of the capital city. The spectacular and turbulent **Great Falls** ❿ of the Potomac can be viewed from parks on both Maryland and Virginia shores. Here, the Potomac River makes its final plunge down rapids and cataracts en route to the Chesapeake Bay. *(See margin note.)*

On the Maryland side, off MacArthur Boulevard, the falls are part of the **C&O Canal National Historical Park** that includes the towpath, restored canal locks, and the 1828 **Old Angler's Inn** (10801 MacArthur Blvd.; tel 301-365-2425), known more for its atmosphere than for its food.

On the Virginia side, in Fairfax County off Georgetown Pike, **Great Falls Park** ⓫ (open daily 7am–dark; Visitors Center open summer weekdays 10am–5pm, weekends 10am–6pm; winter 10am–4pm; closed Dec 25; www.nps.gov/gwmp) offers dramatic views of the 76-ft (23-meter) falls from an observation area and from huge boulders above the river.

The best time to visit is during spring floods when the volume of water can exceed that of Niagara Falls. Swift currents and slippery rocks are responsible for several drownings each year; caution is strongly advised when venturing near the water. The park's extensive trails parallel the river, cut through woodland and marshy areas, and offer views of the Potomac River and the chasm of **Mather Gorge**. ❏

RESTAURANTS

Suburbs of DC

The Inn at Little Washington
Main and Middle Streets, Washington, Virginia. Tel: 540-675-3800. Open: D only Wed–Mon; jacket and tie requested; $$$$
Dinner in heaven and only 65 miles from DC; the chef is self-taught; the food is among the best in the US.

L'Auberge Chez Francois
332 Springvale Road (near Georgetown Pike), Great Falls, Virginia. Tel: 703-759-3800. Open: D only Tues–Sun. $$$$
Alsatian fare; among DC's favorites for special occasions; family-owned; country setting with romantic garden; reserve in advance.

Alexandria, Virginia

Blue Pont Grill & Oyster Bar
Franklin & S. Washington streets. Tel: 703-739-0404. Open: L & D, Mon–Sat. $$
Short menu of new-American entrées; good seafood; small bar; small patio; next door to a gourmet market.

Elysium
In the Morrison House, 116 S. Alfred St. Tel: 703-838-8000. Open: D Tues–Sat; Sun brunch. $$$$

PRICE CATEGORIES

Prices for three-course dinner per person with a half-bottle of house wine, tax and tip:
$ = under $25
$$ = $25–$40
$$$ = $40–$50
$$$$ = more than $50

High-end, French-inspired American; fine and one of Old Town's secrets.

Gadsby's
134 N. Royal St. Tel: 703-838-4242. Open: D daily. $$
Open since George Washington's days and where he and Martha enjoyed the social season; waitstaff in period costumes. Totally American fare.

La Madeleine
500 King St. Tel: 703-739-2854. Open: L & D, daily. $
Cafeteria-style French with excellent quiches, soups, pastries; the best coffee.

Le Bergerie
218 N. Lee St. Tel: 703-683-1007. Open: L & D, daily. $$
Elegant and long-time Old Town favorite features French and Basque specialties.

Le Gaulois
1106 King St. Tel: 703-739-9496. Open: L & D, Mon–Sat. $
Local favorite offers French comfort food; brick courtyard; order what's freshest and dessert.

Mount Vernon Inn
At Mount Vernon Estate. Tel: 703-780-0011. Open: L & D, daily. $$–$$$
Early American fare, plus seafood and beef. Tour the mansion, then stop here.

Southside 815
815 S. Washington St. Tel: 703-836-6222. Open: L & D, daily; Sun brunch. $
Strictly Southern; always busy because it's good; hopping bar scene.

219
219 King St. Tel: 703-549-1141. Open: L & D, daily; Sun brunch. $–$$
New Orleans-style fare; refined setting; small patio; good for brunch; jazz at the Basin Street Lounge.

Union Street Public House
121 S. Union St. Tel: 703-548-1785. Open: L & D. daily $–$$
Pub fare; good seafood and oyster bar; good seafood stew; busy bar; near the Torpedo Factory Art Center.

Vermilion
1120 King St. Tel: 703-684-9669. Open: L & D. daily $–$$
Modern but cozy setting; well done American standards. Near good shops and galleries.

Xando Cosi
700 King St. Tel: 703-299-9833. Open: L & D, daily. $
Modern American; excellent sandwiches, soups, salads, coffee; in the exact middle of Old Town.

Arlington, Virginia

Mexicali Blues
2933 Wilson Blvd. Tel: 703-812-9352. Open: L & D, daily; until 4am Sat & Sun. $
Converted storefront; small, excellent Mexican and Salvadoran menu.

Queen Bee
3181 Wilson Blvd. Tel: 703-527-3444. Open: L & D, daily. $
Among the first Asian restaurants to open after the arrival of the Vietnamese immigrants;

authentic, delicious, go early to avoid the line.

Tara Thai
4001 Fairfax Drive. Tel: 703-908-4999. Open: L & D, daily. $$
Upscale Thai with ocean decor and aquarium. Excellent seafood.

Maryland

Old Angler's Inn
10801 MacArthur Blvd. Potomac, Maryland. Tel: 301-365-2425. Open: L & D, Tues–Sun. $$$
Across from the C & O Canal and best for its view from the deck; entrées are simple, but good.

Inn at Glen Echo
6119 Tulane Ave. Glen Echo, Maryland. Tel: 301-229-2280. Open: L & D; Sun brunch. $$–$$$
A feel of the country without the long drive; American menu; grilled fish and pork roast.

RIGHT: formal dining can be found at many old inns.

DAY TRIPS: MARYLAND

Maryland's reach from mountains to shore offers railroad towns and 19th-century villages, big-city diversions in Baltimore, the Chesapeake Bay's famous blue crabs, and the Antietam National Battlefield.

To the north, east and west of Washington, DC lie ample opportunities for day trips. You can follow the path of the 17th-century pioneers through the Allegheny Mountains to the Cumberland Gap and Deep Creek Lake. There is a major Civil War site at Antietam, near the old town of Sharpsburg. For summer sun and swimming there are the beaches of the Chesapeake Bay and, if you don't mind the driving, more beaches in the state of Delaware. Along the way are the historic coastal towns of Annapolis and the Eastern Shore, and the port of Baltimore.

Baltimore

The city on the Chesapeake Bay is the site of the nation's oldest monument to **George Washington**, a 178-ft (24-meter) **column** whose spiral staircase you can climb for the best view in Baltimore (Mt. Vernon Place; Wed–Sun, 10am–4pm).

Baltimore's famous sons include **Edgar Allan Poe** (museum home at 203 North Amity Street; call for tour information; tel: 410-396-7932), the waspish man of letters H. L. Mencken, and the baseball hero **Babe Ruth** (museum home at 216 Emory Street; Apr–Sept 10am–5pm, Nov–Mar, 10am–4pm; closed Sun; admission fee; tel: 410-727-1539). As the

city is only an hour's drive from Washington, it can't be too many decades before it becomes a formalized extension of the capital, as the suburbs creep towards one another.

Baltimore ❶ is an elderly, distinguished city that has suffered some drastic revitalizing, particularly around the old run-down **Inner Harbor** area, now a throbbing tourist attraction. The wide pedestrian area that swings round the waterfront hums with action – jugglers, trick cyclists and magicians

Map on page 194

PRECEDING PAGES:
Maryland horse farm.
LEFT: bass fishing.
BELOW:
Baltimore harbor.

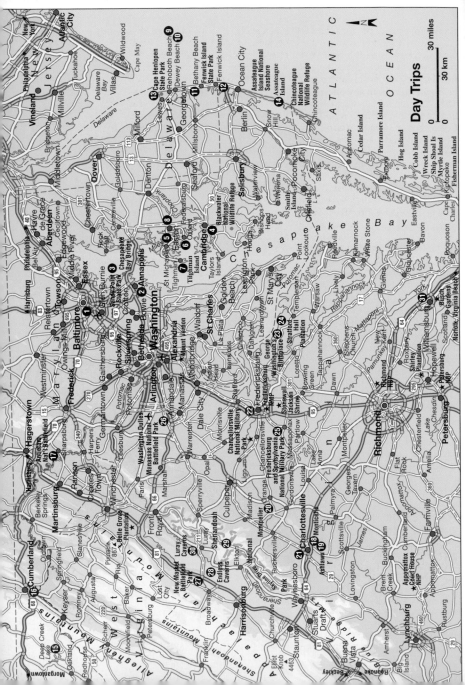

Day Trips

Map
on page
194

giving impromptu performances to the crowds that it draws from out of the vast shopping mall behind. You can cover the entire harbor area on foot, but it's more fun to catch one of the water taxis from any one of the 15 landing sites. Tied up in the harbor, and worth seeing, is the *USS Constellation* (daily 10am–5pm; admission fee; tel: 410-539-1797), a 22-gun three-masted sloop-of-war and the last surviving ship of the Civil War.

The **National Aquarium** (Pier 3, 501 East Pratt Street; open Sat–Thurs, 10am–5pm; Fri, 10am–8pm; tel: 410-576-3800), is expensive ($17.50 adults, $9.50 children) but a great introduction to the underwater world. You begin the visit on the top story of the pyramid-shaped building, and gently wind your way down the middle of a glass-fronted, 220,000-gallon **Open Ocean tank** that mirrors the marine life you would find at equivalent depths in the sea – brightly colored fish on the top floor, the sharks down in the murky depths on the ground. There is a **Hands-On pool** where children can touch starfish, anemones, shellfish and sea vegetation, as well as other tanks that present specific marine habitats.

Across the other side of the harbor is the Maryland **Science Center** (601 Light Street; open Mon–Fri, 10am–5pm; Sat, 10am–6pm, Sun, noon–5pm; admission fee; tel: 410-685-5225) and a planetarium. Although in summer there are lines to get into the aquarium, they are better managed than those at the Science Center, so be prepared for a disorderly wait.

But children generally find it worthwhile, particularly when they can watch – or volunteer for – live demonstrations that set their hair standing on end or show how they can emit electric sparks from their bodies. It is a predominantly hands-on experience, with excellent displays that explain many of modern science's inventions and discoveries in an easy-to-understand fashion. There are also permanent exhibits on the life of the Chesapeake Bay, geology and energy exhibits, plus thought-provoking temporary shows.

Also housed in the building and almost more fun than the scientific section is the awe-inspiring display of stars and planets in the night sky of the **Davis Planetarium**, as well as a cinema screen, five-stories high, showing IMAX theater movies that almost push you into the action.

Take in an **Orioles'** baseball game at **Camden Yards** (333 West Camden Street; tel: 410-685-9800), a new 46,000-seat park made to look old-fashioned. The star-shaped **Fort McHenry** (E. Fort Avenue; open daily in winter 8am–4.45pm; daily in summer 8am–7.45pm; $5 adult; children free; tel: 410-962-4290) is the site of the famous victory of the Americans over the British during the War of 1812 that inspired Francis Scott Key to pen *The Star Spangled Banner*.

Francis Scott Key, who wrote "The Star Spangled Banner."

BELOW: on parade at Fort McHenry.

Cross the harbor and stop at **Fell's Point**, a funky neighborhood of 18th-century row houses and warehouses mixed in with early 20th-century storefronts that has held on to its colorful Baltimore character. Yard sales spring up on the square on weekends. Amid it all is the stately **Admiral Fell Inn** (888 South Broadway; tel: 410-522-7377) with a pleasant dining room.

Nearby is **Little Italy**, chock full of terrific little Italian restaurants.

Annapolis

A water town only an hour from Washington, **Annapolis** is on the Chesapeake and some consider it the world's sailing capital. Start at the **Historic Annapolis Foundation Museum Store and Welcome Center** at 77 Main Street (tel: 410-268-5576) to pick up maps and brochures useful for a walking tour.

Little has changed in the 18th-century heart of the town, though Annapolis has grown enormously beyond the city center. It is a charming and easy place to cover on foot, particularly along the waterfront.

This still presents a soothing vista of masts and sails, since the harbor has always been too shallow to accept anything but small vessels. Unless you are a boat enthusiast, it can be a place to avoid on the last weekend in April and in October when the city hosts America's largest sail and power boat shows and all other movement grinds to a halt.

The **Maryland State House** (State Circle; Mon–Fri 8:30am–5pm, Sat–Sun 10-4pm, closed Sun, Jan 1, Thanksgiving, Dec 25; guided tours 11am and 3pm; tel: 410-974-3400), built in 1772, is the oldest state capitol building in continuous use in America. This is where George Washington resigned his commission as commander-in-chief of the Continental Army in 1783; where the Treaty of Paris that officially ended the Revolution was signed in 1784; and where Thomas Jefferson was appointed the first United States ambassador to France. Its cypress-beam dome is the largest wooden dome in the country. The elegant plasterwork in the central hall cost the life of Thomas Dance, the crafts-

TIP

Various boat trips around the Severn River and Chesapeake Bay from the City Dock, Annapolis, are offered during the summer by Watermark Cruises (tel: 410-268-7600; www.watermark cruises. com).

BELOW: City Harbor, Annapolis.

man who executed it, when he fell 90 ft (27 meters) from the scaffolding.

Other interesting sites include the **Old Senate Chamber**, where a bronze plaque marks the place where George Washington stood to deliver his farewell address, the **House of Delegates** and the **New Senate Chamber**, both with skylights designed by Tiffany.

Many of the city's Federal-style homes are original to the colonial era and there are three you can visit:

● The **house of William Paca** (18 Pinkney Street, mid-Mar–mid-Dec, Mon–Sat, 10am–5pm; Sun noon–5pm; intermittently the rest of the year, admission fee; tel: 410-267-7619) was built in 1765 and displays period furniture and paintings. In the restored terraced garden is a fish-shaped pool. Paca was a signatory of the Declaration of Independence and governor of Maryland.

● **Hammond-Harwood House** (19 Maryland Avenue; by reservation; admission fee; tel: 410-269-1714) was built in 1773–74 and has one of the most beautiful carved doors of the time.

● Opposite is the **Chase-Lloyd House** (22 Maryland Avenue; by reservation; tel: 410-263-2723), was begun in 1769 by Samuel Chase, later a justice on the new nation's Supreme Court. It was continued in 1771 by Edward Lloyd IV, a wealthy planter, when Chase ran out of funds. This house is on three floors with a formidable hall of Ionic pillars and a so-called "floating" staircase.

Main Street, which leads to the water, has restaurants, shops and small art galleries worth exploring.

If there's time, and security considerations allow, the **Naval Academy** is worth a tour. (Visitors' Center on King George Street open daily 9am–4pm; for tour availability, tel: 410-263-6933.) There's lots of naval memorabilia and John Paul Jones, Revolutionary War hero and father of the navy, is buried here.

Chesapeake Bay Area

For some reason, Washingtonians seem to truly believe they have been to the beach only if they have spent three hours – or more frequently,

Map on page 194

The house of William Paca, Annapolis.

BELOW:
dress parade at the US Naval Academy.

given traffic jams, five hours – getting there. But there are two alternatives to the Atlantic shore haul, where it is just as possible to get sunburnt without the stress of the drive. One is the Eastern Shore, with its small and evocative old colonial towns; the other is the beaches of the Bay.

There's a $2.50 toll to cross the **Chesapeake Bay Bridge**, but it's collected only once, heading east toward the Eastern Shore. No toll is collected on the westbound return.

On the Annapolis side of the bridge, the string of small beaches is less imposing than on the other side, with gentler waves and unthreatening currents. These beaches do attract jellyfish, however, and many have nets to keep them out of the swimming areas. But there is a generous supply of beach amenities, such as paddle-boat rentals, barbecue grills and picnic tables, and swings and playgrounds for children. Right by the Bay Bridge on the last Route 50 exit before the bridge is **Sandy Point State Park ❸** (mid-Sept– Nov, 6am–9pm; Mar–May 6am– 9pm; remainder of the year

All you can eat at a crab festival.

BELOW:
Eastern Shore.

8am–dusk; tel: 410-974-2149; www. dnr.state.md.us/publiclands/southern/ sandypoint.html), which is good for picnicking, fishing and swimming.

Cross the bridge and you'll be on Maryland's **Eastern Shore,** one of Washington's best kept secrets. While energetic young people tear across the Bay Bridge in their open jeeps, radios blaring, heading for the Atlantic coast resorts of Rehoboth and Ocean City, the relaxed and unassuming towns of the Eastern Shore lie closer to home and are for the most part ignored.

On the far side of the Chesapeake Bay from Baltimore and Annapolis, this is where the gentry of more gentle times came to take the sea air. It's an area of farms and marshlands, wild bird sanctuaries and road-side produce stands, seafood restaurants and small beaches dusted with shells.

Cambridge ❹, a small town of some 11,000 people, is characteristic of the Eastern Shore's watermen's way of life. Founded in the 1680s, this fishing village sits between the **Choptank River** and the **Blackwater National Wildlife**

Refuge, a stretch of tidal marshlands and woods favored in winter by tens of thousands of migrating ducks and Canada geese. For touring information, start at the Dorchester County Historical Society (902 McGrange Avenue; Tues–Sat, 10am–1pm; tel: 410-228-7953) in the **Meredith House**. This is a well restored 18th-century manor house beside the **Neild Museum** (Thur–Sat, 10am–4pm) with its smokehouse, antique doll collections, crafts and furniture.

You pass by **Annie Oakley's house** on Bellevue Avenue where the retired cowgirl, Cambridge's most celebrated transplant, kept up her sharpshooting skills by firing out the upstairs windows, much to the dismay of the neighbors.

St Michaels

Less than two hours from Washington is the old but still active village of **St Michaels ❺**, a center of boating activity located where the **Miles River** meets the Chesapeake Bay. Apart from the very attractive **harbor**, the main focus for visitors is the **Chesapeake Bay Maritime Mu-**

seum (Mill Street; open daily, hours vary by season, but usually 9am–5pm; admission fee; tel: 410-745-2916; www.cbmm.org). The waterfront campus has a screwpile lighthouse, which first saw service in the Bay in 1879 and which is restored and open for touring. There are also skipjacks, deadrises, dug-out canoes, and other traditional Bay vessels either undergoing restoration, tied up at the dock, or on display in the shed. It's possible to enrol in one-day classes to learn about building wooden boats.

Next door is the **Crab Claw**, a laid-back tourist-friendly place where you can watch the watermen unload their crab bushels on the dock, then order a dozen steamers for yourself. If you've never tried the Chesapeake Bay's specialty, blue crab, and aren't sure how to go about cracking one open, follow the directions on the paper placemat.

You can take two worthwhile trips from St Michaels – one to **Oxford ❻**, taking the **Oxford-Bellevue ferry** (tel: 410-745-9023), supposedly the oldest privately owned ferry in the US. In the town you can visit

The harbor at St Michaels.

LEFT:
Chesapeake blue crab.

Chesapeake's Blue Crabs

A particular Maryland delicacy is *Callinectes sapidus*. The first word means "beautiful swimmer" – a reference to the paddle-shaped pair of hind legs that gracefully propel these blue crabs, members of the crustacean family, up and down the Chesapeake from the salty mouth, which they prefer when young, to the fresh water at the top of the Bay. *Sapidus* means "tasty," which they are when boiled and served up with plenty of Old Bay seasoning.

There's an art to "picking" crab. Pull off the claws first and set aside, then open the apron on the underside, scrape away the organs and the "dead man," or the gills, and dig out the meat; now crack open the claws and pull the meat off with your teeth.

Although crabs are found all along the Atlantic coast, they're most plentiful in the Chesapeake, shallow and grassy and a perfect home, and which, in a good year, can yield a harvest of 100 million lbs (45 million kg). In its three-year life span, a crab will molt several times, shedding its old shell for a bigger model. Between shells it's known as "soft-shell" crab, best breaded and fried, and easy to handle with a knife and fork.

Tilghman Island.

BELOW:
parental concern on
Assateague Island.

the historic **Robert Morris Inn** (tel: 410-226-5111), a restaurant and B&B and the former home of wealthy merchant Robert Morris whose son is often called the "financier of the Revolution."

Tilghman Island

The second trip is to **Tilghman Island ❼**, 10 miles (16 km) farther on the only road out of St Michaels. Once there, you may notice a lighthouse askance and sticking out of the Bay. This is Sharp's Island Lighthouse, abandoned and slowly sinking. The local watermen will be happy to tell you the story as they work on their boats and nets.

St Michaels is not far from **Easton ❽**, an old colonial bay-side town full of antique shops and old bookstores. This is an area with a strong religious background. In 1777, the Eastern Shore Quakers vowed to "disunite" any member of the congregation who still employed slaves. In Easton, William Penn, the Quaker who founded Pennsylvania, preached at the **Third Haven Meeting House** (405 South Washington Street; tel: 410-822-0293), built in 1682 and possibly the oldest frame house of worship still in use.

There are numerous historical manor houses and dwellings around Easton, but most of them are scattered outside the town itself. Contact the Historical Society of Talbot County at the courthouse on Washington Street (tel: 410-770-8000) for information, guides and maps.

Atlantic Ocean Beaches

Washingtonians head for **Ocean City** in Maryland, and quieter **Rehoboth ❾**, **Dewey Beach ❿**, **Bethany Beach ⓫** and **Fenwick Island ⓬** in Delaware to avoid the heavy humidity of summer. Just 3½ hours from Washington, on the southern Atlantic shore, Rehoboth in summer is a jumping hot bed of noise, music, T-shirt emporia, beach beauties and Adonises.

Along the boardwalk is a run of stores selling saltwater taffy, hot dogs and souvenirs and a small fun fair with airplane rides and dodgem cars. On Saturdays there are band concerts and talent opportunities for summer visitors. As well as the usual fast foods, there are a number of up-market restaurants just behind the main drag, not necessarily charging up-market prices, and striving to serve original and pleasantly presented dishes.

If you prefer your seaside experience a little less brash, the beach at **Cape Henlopen State Park ⓭** (tel: 302-645-8983) is in a protected nature reserve near Lewes, Delaware, and simply offers you hundreds of yards of open beach and empty sand dunes. Those with small children should be aware that the surf along all of this coast is sometimes quite strong and the current can be vigorous. However, all of the beaches are well manned by efficient-looking lifeguards.

For a more peaceful experience,

head for **Chincoteague Island**, just inboard of **Assateague Island** , a national seashore and barrier island, uninhabited except for birds and the famous ponies that live here (some will remember from their childhood Marguerite Henry's *Misty of Chincoteague*). Chincoteague, actually in Virginia, has the usual tourist joints, but Assateague (National Seashore Visitors Center, daily 9am–5pm; tel: 410-641-1441), which is split between Virginia and Maryland, is pristine, with a wildlife preserve and miles of untouched beaches.

Deep Creek Lake Area

Washington's other water sports center, 4 hours west from the capital and turning itself into a skiing resort in winter, is **Deep Creek Lake** in the heart of the Appalachian Mountains. Built in 1925 as a reservoir, it encompasses 3,900 acres (1,580 hecrares) of fresh water that draws fishermen and watersports enthusiasts. It's a bit of a drive and more than you can reasonably expect to cover in a day, so call ahead (Deep Creek, McHenry,

Garrett County, Maryland, tel: 301-387-4386 or visit www.garrettchamber.com) and line up one of the several rental homes or check into an inn (try Lake Pointe Inn; tel: 1-800-523-5253; www.deepcreekinns.com), and rent a boat.

Sailboats, power boats and canoes can be rented at the several marinas around the lake. There are regular weekend sailboat races and water skiing events, including the Barefoot Skiing Championships. From May to October sponsored fishing contests award prizes for the biggest largemouth bass, bluegill, chain pickerel, walleye and more. The woods that reach down to the lake offer cool and quiet trail walks.

East of Deep Creek Lake is the town of **Cumberland** , which began as Fort Cumberland, a crucial frontier outpost during the French and Indian War. George Washington defended the town and you can visit his one-room log cabin headquarters – the only remains of the fort – in **Riverside Park**.

A handsome town of fine buildings, parks and gardens, Cumberland

Map on page 194

Chincoteague National Wildlife Refuge is part of two Atlantic barrier islands and on the flyway for many species of migrating birds. In spring many shorebirds, including the endangered piping plover, nest alongside the beach of adjacent Assateague Island. In autumn you can see peregrine falcons, bald eagles, herons, egrets and pelicans. Refuge contacts: tel: 757-336-6122; www.chincoteague.com/

BELOW: steaming through Cumberland.

is full of antique and curio shops. **Washington Street** is where the rich coal and rail barons lived, in mansions ornately executed in all styles from Federal to Georgian Revival.

The **History House** (218 Washington Street; Tues–Sat, 11am–4pm; tel: 301-777-8678) is full of household gadgets, technical machinery and toys of the 19th century. Nineteen fully furnished rooms illustrate life in 1867, while another room depicts an early 1900s schoolroom. In the basement is the old servants' quarters, with kitchen and pantry. Elsewhere in the house rooms display 19th-century costumes, veterinary, medical and dental equipment. One of the oldest buildings on the street is the **First Church of Christ Scientist**.

But the railway station, with its displays of memorabilia, is where you should start. The **Western Maryland Scenic Railroad** (13 Canal Street; reservations necessary; call for hours of departure; $19 adults, $13 children; tel: 1-800-872-4650 or visit www.wmsr.com) offers three-hour excursions. A 1916 Baldwin steam engine hauls you through the Allegheny Mountain's scenic railroad passes, gorgeous in the fall, over an iron truss bridge and through a 900-ft (270-meter) tunnel to Frostburg where you can take a lap around historic Main Street before hoping on board and chugging back to Cumberland.

Antietam National Battlefield

The battle of Antietam, when the South's General Lee tried to follow up his victory at Manassas by invading the northern states, was the scene of the greatest and bloodiest carnage of the entire Civil War. It all took place in a single day, September 17, 1862. More than 23,000 men were killed and "lay in rows precisely as they had stood in their ranks a few moments before," according to Union General Joseph Hooker.

Clara Barton, founder of the American Red Cross, was among those who tended the wounded. After the Manassas battle in Virginia, Lee sent Stonewall Jackson to seize the vital river crossing and arsenal of

Antietam National Battlefield.

BELOW: violent knight life at the Maryland Renaissance Fair.

Map on page 194

Harper's Ferry, and lead his soldiers into Maryland in the hope of forcing the evacuation of Washington and swinging the slave-owning state of Maryland to the Southern cause. Unfortunately, his battle plan fell into the hands of Union General George McClellan. When the Confederates marched into the little town of Sharpsburg they walked straight into 87,000 Union soldiers. Although the resulting carnage left both sides wondering who had won, and whether the cost was worth the victory, the battle was a crucial turning point in the Civil War.

After the South's defeat, it lost its very real hope of winning diplomatic recognition and the support of European countries. President Lincoln took the battle as an apposite moment to denounce slavery officially. One week after the battle, on September 23, 1862, a draft of Lincoln's Emancipation Proclamation was published in the press.

The 26-minute film at the **Visitor Center of Antietam National Battlefield** ⓱ (1 mile north of Sharpsburg on Route 65, open Jun–Aug, 8:30am–6pm, Sept–May, 8.30am–5pm admission fee; tel: 301-432-5124; www.civilwar-va.com/ maryland), set in the rolling Maryland pastureland where the battle occurred, gives the best orientation to start your tour. It takes you from **Dunker Church**, where fighting commenced, to the cornfield which saw most of the military action, and to **Bloody Lane** where, in four hours, 5,000 soldiers died. Unless you are a sturdy hiker (the Visitor Center provides maps if you are), you will need to tour by car as the site is large and enclosed inside a network of minor roads.

Perhaps the most dramatic spot is **Burnside's Bridge**, where a handful of Georgian sharpshooters held off Burnside's infantry division, shooting them down as they tried to cross a narrow stone bridge. Burnside's scouts did not find a ford across the river until it was too late. You can still see the Georgians' foxholes on the hill above the bridge. A map and brochure detail the events at the 11 stops along the 8½-mile (14-km) drive. ❏

Abraham Lincoln reviews the latest war situation at Antietam, 1862.

Restaurants

Baltimore

Chiapparelli's
237 High St. Tel: 410-837-0309. Open: L & D, Mon–Fri; D only Sat–Sun. $$–$$$
One of the best known places in Little Italy. Generous salads trimmed out with Italian delicacies; good veal. Pasta is home-made.

Della Notte Ristorante
801 Eastern Ave. Tel: 410-837-5500. Open: L & D, Mon–Fri; D only Sat & Sun. $$–$$$
All-Italian award-winning menu in Roman-style setting. Try the rockfish or crab, straight from the Chesapeake, or the grilled lamb. Piano-playing duo nightly.

Obrycki's Crab House
1727 E. Pratt St. Tel: 410-732-6399. Open: L & D, daily; closed in winter. $$$
Order Chesapeake Bay crabs here; no need for a follow-up.

Paolo's
310 Light St. Harborplace. Tel: 410-539-7060. Open: L & D, daily. $
Creative pastas and salads in this trattoria with a view of the harbor; busy, good.

Annapolis

Café Normandie
185 Main St. Tel: 410-263-3382. Open: L & D, daily. $
Cozy bistro with fireplace offers excellent stews, soups, crepes; in the center of town.

Treaty of Paris
At the Maryland Inn, 16 Church Circle. Open: L & D, Mon–Fri; Sun brunch. $$
Here's where the American Revolution was signed into peace; elegant seafood; white tablecloth service; near the dock.

Eastern Shore

The Crab Claw
156 Mill St. St. Michaels, Maryland. Tel: 410-745-2900. Open: L & D, daily. $$
Watermen unload their catch on the dock, so you know it's fresh; tackle steamed crabs on paper-cover picnic tables on the deck.

Robert Morris Inn
314 N. Morris St. Oxford, Maryland. Tel: 410-226-5111. Open: L & D, daily. $$
Original 18th-century inn still serving crab cakes to perfection; near ferry dock to St. Michaels in quaint Oxford.

PRICE CATEGORIES

Prices for three-course dinner per person with a half-bottle of house wine, tax and tip:
$ = under $25
$$ = $25–$40
$$$ = $40–$50
$$$$ = more than $50

DAY TRIPS: VIRGINIA

Beyond the Beltway, Virginia's suburban sprawl gives way to a gentle countryside filled with some of the nation's most historic homes and attractions, including Monticello and colonial Williamsburg.

Washington was founded as a geographical compromise midway between the Northern and Southern states. And, as a result, it is wonderfully placed for day trips that bring the visitor very different flavors of the surrounding countryside, its turbulent history and cultural progress.

Ninety minutes to the west of the city lie the Blue Ridge Mountains of Virginia. Its Shenandoah Valley is perfect for fall drives to admire autumn leaves the equal of any leaf-

BELOW: Monticello.

color view in New England. To the south and west are the poignantly moving battlefields of the Civil War, each with detailed on-the-spot explanations and diagrams; near Charlottesville, about 120 miles (190 km) southwest of Washington, are monuments to America's more peaceful development: Monticello (Thomas Jefferson's house) and the University of Virginia, two of the most civilized establishments to be found on any continent.

Presidential Trio

Located on the top of a foothill of the Blue Ridge Mountains close to the town of Charlottesville, **Monticello ⑱** (Route 53, two miles southeast of Charlottesville; open Mar–Oct, 8am–5pm; Nov–Feb, 9am–4.30pm; $13 admission; tel: 434-984-9822; www.monticello.org) is perhaps the only historical house in America that entirely expresses the character of its owner.

It's also the only American house on the United Nations' list of World Heritage sites. Jefferson's "essay in architecture," as he thought of his home, is a classical tribute to the architects of ancient Greece and Rome. For this citizen president, it was also a haven after the burdens of life in the White House.

Jefferson built the home and con-

tinued to expand it between 1769 and 1809. There are 43 rooms altogether, not counting the wings and outbuildings, outfitted with eight fireplaces and fine timeless furnishing, about 60 percent of them original.

Monticello also incorporates many of Jefferson's own innovative ideas: in his study is a desk-cum-chaise he designed that allowed him to write while lying down; on the long windows are sliding double glass doors to keep in the heat, and nearby are silent "dumb waiters" that travel between floors to carry light parcels upstairs or down. When he died, Jefferson was more than $107,000 in debt and his heirs were forced to sell the house. It passed among a few private owners until, after the Civil War erupted, the Confederate government seized and sold it. It went back into private ownership, fell into serious disrepair, and was then, in 1923, given to the Thomas Jefferson Foundation and beautifully restored.

Jefferson's garden, restored according to his detailed gardening notes, expresses the civilized nature of the man, laid out in a perfect balance of shape and showing where he practiced his experimental gardening and cultivation techniques. Here the president grew 20 varieties of his favorite English pea, and more than 250 kinds of vegetables. Save time to explore the grounds, especially Mulberry Row, the 1,000-ft (300-meter) long road where about half of Jefferson's 135 slaves lived.

It may not be as well known, but **Ashlawn** (1000 James Monroe Parkway; 11am–5pm daily; extended hours in summer; closed Jan 1, Thanksgiving, Dec 25; admission fee; tel: 434-293-9539; or visit www.avenue.org/ashlawn), home of the country's fifth president, James Monroe, is cozier. The furnishings

are 18th-century elegant, and you can tour the original smokehouse, overseer's cottage, and the reconstructed slave quarters.

Next, stop at **Montpelier** (11407 Constitution Highway near Orange, VA; Apr–Oct, 9.30am–5.30pm; Nov–Mar, 9.30am–4.30pm; admission fee; tel: 540-672-2728; www.montpelier.org), home of president James Madison and a curious mix of old and new. The Dupont family, of Delaware chemical fame, bought the house in 1901 and made extensive renovations, doubling its size. Here, colonial-era trappings nudge modern artifacts.

Charlottesville

For brochures and maps, start at the **Charlottesville Visitors Center** at the intersection of Route 64 and 20 South (daily 9am–5pm; closed Jan 1, Thanksgiving, Dec 25; tel: 434-293-6789), or head straight for the **University of Virginia** (free guided tours of the Rotunda and Lawn are offered year round by the University Guide Service; tel: 434-924-7969; www.virginia.edu).

Map on page 194

TIP

Virginia's Festival of the Book is held in late March every year on the University of Virginia campus and in surrounding bookstores, hotel ballrooms and cafes in Charlottesville. It draws some of the best authors. Details: www.vabook.org

BELOW: Charlottesville.

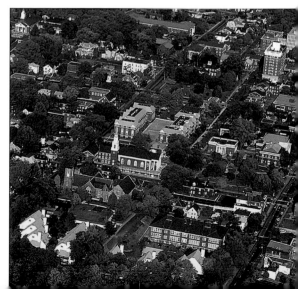

Rural Virginia is horse country.

BELOW: Jefferson's Rotunda at the University of Virginia.

Charlottesville ㉑ is the graceful Virginia town, set against a backdrop of rolling foothills, where, in 1817, along with James Madison and James Monroe, Jefferson laid the cornerstone for the university. The former president was 75 years old when he drew up the blueprints for these elegant grounds with their classical buildings united by a covered colonnade of lyrical arches and pillars. You can see the influence of ancient Roman architecture – particularly in the **Rotunda**, modeled after the Roman Pantheon – and the designs of the Italian Renaissance architect, Andrea Palladio.

A block from the Rotunda is the **University of Virginia Art Museum** (155 Rugby Road; Tues–Sun, 1pm–5pm; free; tel: 434-924-3592; www.virginia.edu/artmuseum), small but impressive with Old Masters, Chinese porcelains, Native American artifacts, and Roman statuary.

Next, head downtown to the **mall** on Main Street between First and Fifth streets, a blocked-off city thoroughfare for pedestrians only. There are lots of little cafes, and antique and specialty shops including the **New Dominion Book Shop** (404 East Main Street; tel: 434-295-2552).

Fredericksburg

This peaceful town is famous not only as the place where George Washington grew up, but also for the devastating Civil War battles fought around it. Over 750,000 troops clashed in the fields near here, but the town of Washington's boyhood is a tranquil, civilized place where more than 350 buildings were erected before 1870. It is here, rather than at Mount Vernon, where he was supposed to have thrown a dollar – not across the mile-wide Potomac, but the 300-ft (90-meter) Rappahannock River. What's more, the future president threw not a dollar, but a Spanish doubloon.

Fredericksburg ㉒ is full of history. The best place for a pre-tour briefing is the **Visitors Center** on Caroline Street (706 Caroline Street; daily 9am–5pm; closed Jan 1, Thanksgiving, Dec 25; tel: 540-373-1776; www.fredericksburgvirginia.net), which has a film show and maps.

On **Charles Street** is the house of the president's mother, **Mary Washington** (1200 Charles Street; call for tour information; tel: 540-373-1569), in which she lived for the last 17 years of her life. It is furnished with period pieces, and the garden restored to its original 18th-century form. Costumed guides show visitors both. Look out for the ornamental plasterwork in the **Great Room** and Mary Washington's needlepoint. Tea and gingerbread prepared according to Mary Washington's own recipe are served in the kitchen building by folks in period dress.

The **James Monroe Law Office** at 908 Charles Street (Mar–Nov, daily 9am–5pm; Dec–Feb, 10am–4pm; admission fee; tel: 540-654-1043) displays the correspondence

between Monroe and Jefferson, Washington and Benjamin Franklin; White House china and cutlery from the period; and pieces of furniture President Monroe acquired for the White House, some of them from France and said to have belonged to Marie Antoinette.

Kenmore (1201 Washington Avenue; Mon–Sat, 9am–5pm; Sun, noon–5pm; admission fee; tel: 540-373-3381) is the home of another of Washington's relatives, his sister Betty. This lovely Georgian mansion, once situated on a 1,200-acre (480-hectare) plantation, is now surrounded by more modern residences. The wealth of Betty's husband, Fielding Lewis, is reflected in the lavishly festooned plaster ceilings and mantelpieces. A brick-pathed and boxwood-lined garden is out back.

The Rising Sun (1304 Caroline Street; Mar–Nov, 9am–5pm; Dec–Feb, 10am– 4pm; admission fee; tel: 540-371-1494) was Fredericksburg's first tavern and formerly the home of George Washington's brother Charles. It doesn't offer food or drink but does provide a taste of the 18th century's tavern-centered life.

Slavery remembered

By 2007, the city should have opened the new **National Slavery Museum**, destined to be a major international research center staffed by scholars and historians whose work will spur exhibits and academic courses. In a town full of historic homes and other relics of early American and antebellum life, the museum, designed by Chien Chung Pei, son of the famed architect I.M. Pei, promises to be a more fitting acknowledgement of the divisive and cruel institution of slavery than the small brass plaque in front of an Italian restaurant that marks the spot where the city's slave auction block used to be.

Historians and activists have argued over the location of the museum, lobbying for a spot on the Mall in Washington, or at least in Richmond, Virginia, the one-time capital of the Confederacy, but Fredericksburg has come out on top in the debate, winning the $200 million project that Pei has said will be something "forward-looking – not something just looking back."

Washington's birthplace

For more history, head about 40 miles (64 km) east of Fredericksburg to **Westmoreland County** in Virginia's so-called **Northern Neck**, a peninsula formed by the Rappahannock and Potomac rivers. This rural jut of land includes the site of **George Washington's birthplace ㉓** at Popes Creek Plantation (daily 9am–5pm; closed Jan 1, Thanksgiving, Dec 25; admission fee; tel: 804-493-0130; www.nps.gov/gewa/), a restored brick home and former tobacco farm manor house on 500 peaceful acres (200 hectares). This is the site of the famous "cherry tree incident" – though Washington, born in 1732, lived here only until he was

George Washington's Memorial House was built in 1932 despite the arguments of Frederick Law Olmstead, renowned as designer of New York's Central Park, that many visitors would assume it was the first president's authentic birthplace. The scheme's supporters said that the reconstruction captured the spirit of the great man.

BELOW: costumed docents lead tours at some Virginia plantations.

Thomas Jonathan Jackson (1824–63), the most famous Confederate leader, earned his nickname on the battlefield at First Manassas when General Bernard Bee is said to have shouted: "Look, men, there is Jackson standing like a stone wall." Two years later, while reconnoitering at night, Jackson was mistakenly shot by some of his own troops and died of complications.

BELOW:
recreating the second battle of Manassas.

three and at that age was probably incapable of wielding an ax, much less felling a tree.

Stratford Hall Plantation  (daily 9:30–4pm; closed Jan 1, Thanksgiving, Dec 25, admission fee; tel: 804-493-8038; www.stratfordhall.org) was home to several generations of Lees, including Richard Henry Lee and Francis Lightfoot Lee, both signers of the Declaration of Independence. Francis Lightfoot was a Revolutionary War hero and father of Robert E. Lee, who was born here. The plantation has a restaurant.

Civil War sites

Enthusiasts of the War Between the States will find no shortage of sites to visit within an easy day's trip from Washington. One of the bloodiest battles was at Antietam in Maryland (*see page 202*) but 60 percent of the engagements were fought on Virginia soil. Between December 1862 and May 1864, more than 100,000 soldiers in Confederate and Union forces were found dead or wounded on the fields of what is now the **Fredericksburg and Spotsylvania National Military Park** (daily, sunrise to sunset, battlefield visitors centers 9am–5pm with extended summer hours; admission fee, www.civilwar-va.com).

Four devastating major battles of the Civil War were fought on an area that stretches beyond the 6,000 acres (2,500 hectares) of woods and meadows that make up the military park: the Battle of Fredericksburg, December 11–13, 1862; the Battle of Chancellorsville, April 27–May 6, 1863; the Battle of the Wilderness, May 5–6, 1864; and the Battle of Spotsylvania Court House, May 8–21, 1864, the first confrontation between General Robert E. Lee and General Ulysses S. Grant.

This is an area punctuated with trenches and gunpits. It makes for an immensely moving experience when viewed while listening to the taped narrative available from the Visitors Centers. It is hard to imagine that this gentle countryside was once the scene of the most appalling carnage; it is difficult to tell which is more sobering, the closely-wooded country around **Chancellorsville** where the enemy got frighteningly close before being seen, or the open killing field of Fredericksburg itself. General Robert E. Lee's troops, sheltered almost invulnerably behind a country wall, mowed down line after line of advancing Union soldiers – almost 10,000 men in a matter of hours.

At Chancellorsville is the small building in which General Stonewall Jackson died after being mortally wounded by his own troops as he reconnoitered Union troop movements. It is now the **Stonewall Jackson Memorial Shrine** (9am–5pm in summer; Fri–Tues in spring and fall; Sat–Mon in winter; closed Jan 1, Dec 25) and commemorates his life and military career.

A mapped driving tour follows a loop that includes most of the major

Map on page 194

battles, while there are also maps for a 7-mile (11-km) hiking trail, both available at the park Visitors Center.

Manassas (Bull Run)

Twenty-five miles (40 km) west of Washington lies **Manassas (Bull Run) National Battlefield Park 26** (grounds open daily dawn to dusk, Henry Hill Visitors Center daily 8.30am–5pm, closed Jan 1, Thanksgiving, Dec 25; admission fee; tel: 703-361-1339; www.civilwar-va.com), the site of two of the largest and bloodiest battles of the war. Both forces sought control over a strategic railroad junction. Known by the Confederates as Manassas after the nearby town and by the Unionists as Bull Run for the local stream, this is where the first major land battle was fought on July 21, 1861.

Expecting something akin to a sporting event, Washingtonians totted picnic hampers onto the battlefield only to watch the Union forces go down in quick defeat. Well supplied and with plenty of reinforcements, the Confederates trounced their unprepared foes. What followed was "the great skedaddle" as the remaining Union army and the spectators high-tailed it back to Washington, though not everyone arrived. New York Congressman Albert Ely, "down for the fun" according to one rebel, was caught hiding behind a tree and jailed.

The Henry Hill Visitors Center is an evocative spot from which to picture the nearly 30,000 soldiers killed or wounded in 1861 and 1862, when the opposing forces met on this same spot a second time. Take the driving or walking tour, following the markers which begin at the Visitors Center. There are quite a number of edifices that were part of the battle still to be seen: the **Stone Bridge** over Bull Run stream where the Union soldiers opened fire to launch the first battle; the raised railroad where General Jackson's troops maintained ground during the second battle; and the **Stone House tavern** that was used as a field hospital.

It was to **New Market Battlefield Park 27** (open daily 9am–5pm; closed Jan 1, Thanksgiving, Dec 25, Dec. 31; admission fee; tel: 540-740-3102; or visit www.civilwar-va.com) on May 15, 1864, that 247 young cadets, all under 20 years old, were summoned in desperation from the Virginia Military Institute in Lexington. They were needed to give vital support to Confederate General Breckinridge, whose men were being decimated by the forces of Union leader General Sigel. The young cadets fought with such courage that they helped the Confederates vanquish the more experienced and larger opposition force. A walking tour takes you round the parkland, following the development of both sides of this important battle.

The battlefield park is smaller than the other two, only 280 acres (113 hectares). Right in the middle of the field is the **Hall of Valor**, in memory of the cadets, a museum that gives

Monument at New Market Battlefield.

BELOW: train trestles guarded by troops at Manassas in 1863.

Luray Caverns.

BELOW: Virginia Beach, at the southeast corner of the state, is the Atlantic coast's longest resort beach.

both sides of the Civil War story in film, dioramas, and exhibits. Outside in the park are replicas of cannons, plus a farmhouse from the period whose outbuildings have been restored to display a 19-century working farm with garden and black-smith's. This is where, in May, a re-enactment of the battle is staged in full costume by nearly 1,000 players.

For the battle-weary there are the **Endless Caverns** ㉘ (open daily 9am–4pm with extended summer hours; admission fee; tel: 540-896-2283 or 1-800-544-2283), whose extraordinary caves deep inside Mas-sanutten Mountain are dramatically lit to display the different caves' intri-cate and colorful formations.

The Skyline Drive

Between the towns of Front Royal and Waynesboro lie 105 twisting miles (170 km) through the tree- and flower-covered summits of the **Blue Ridge Mountains**. There are dozens of overlooks along **Skyline Drive** from which to gaze upon the **Virginia Piedmont** and the **Shenandoah Valley**, to take pho-tographs. There are more than 500 miles (800 km) of trails, all accessi-ble from the Drive. (Enter Skyline Drive at Fort Royal or Luray; open 24 hours year round; enter Shenan-doah National Park through the Drive; admission fee; tel: 540-999-3500; www.nps.gov). The speed limit is a leisurely 35 mph (56 km/h); even that can seem a bit fast.

In summer, these are soft green in a bluish haze, punctuated by flowers. But Skyline Drive really comes into its own in the fall when the colors of the changing leaves are spectacular. This is a relatively recent bonus. Though originally this land had been covered in thick forest, by 1935 when the **Shenandoah National Park** ㉙ was created, the trees had been cleared, the streams fished out and the wild game decimated by the local set-tlers. In 1976, the efforts of the park's conservationists to reforest and regen-erate natural growth were so success-ful that Congress declared roughly 40 percent of the park an official wilder-ness. Under the protection of the National Park System, the forest has been reclaimed and returned to its natural state.

The Park Services offer several good restaurants, accommodations in overnight log cabins, camp-grounds and lodges, as well as many ranger-conducted activities, such as hikes, talks and campfire get-togeth-ers. The **Dickey Ridge Visitors Center** (mid-Apr–late Nov, 9am–5pm; tel: 540-999-3500) can pro-vide information and tips on camp-ing in the Shenandoah Valley. The name Shenandoah, by the way, is an Indian word which means "Daugh-ter of the Stars." Ancient native peo-ples believed that the valley used to be a lake and that once every 1,000 years the stars would sing around it.

Nine miles west (14 km) of the Luray entrance to Skyline Drive are **Luray Caverns** ㉚ (daily 9am; closing times vary with season;

admission fee; tel: 540-743-6551), the largest underground caverns in Virginia. The tour covers 1¼ miles (2 km) of some of the weirdest and most impressive icicle-shaped limestone stalagmites (extending up from the cave's floor) and stalactites (hanging from the ceiling), formed over thousands of years by the erosive action of underground streams. As you tour the caves, you'll be treated to a concert by a guide armed with a rubber mallet who'll bang out a tune on a portion of the cave's stalactites that the guides humorously refer to as the Stalacpipe Organ. This is a perfect outing for one of Virginia's typical scorching summer days, since the temperature underground can be 20°F (11°C) degrees cooler.

Williamsburg

It's a bit of a drive for one day – 3½ hours south of Washington, if the traffic cooperates – but if you have the time, plan a trip to **Williamsburg ㉛**, the restored colonial-era capital of Virginia. (Grounds open 24 hours; buildings daily 9.30am–

4.30pm; admission $37 adult, $18.50 children; for information and reservations, tel: 1-800-HISTORY, or visit www.history.org; lodging at the Williamsburg Inn and reservations for dinner at one of the four colonial-style taverns must be made in advance and can all be made by telephoning 1-800-TAVERNS or 757-229-2141; for information on nearby motels, check the website).

From 1699 until just before the end of the Revolutionary War, this quaint town was the essential gathering spot for American notables. Thomas Jefferson, George Washington, George Mason and Patrick Henry (of "Give me liberty or give me death" fame) all either served here in the Virginia legislature, or debated the merits of and plotted the course of the war of independence here. By the time the capital moved to Richmond in 1780, the town was headed for serious decline.

As is the case with so many of Virginia's treasured historic sites, the state refused to involve itself in the restoration and upkeep. (George Washington's Mt Vernon is run by a

Map on page 194

The Governor's Palace, Williamsburg.

LEFT: Williamsburg demonstration of the 18th-century techniques of wig-making.

Napa East

Thomas Jefferson, first in so many things, persuaded an Italian vintner to assess the potential for growing grapes in Virginia. Initial progress was slow, but today the state has become one of the country's notable wine regions. In 1985 there were maybe two dozen wineries here; today there are 80. The Virginia Wine Marketing office (tel: 1-800-828-4637; www.virginiawines.org) provides a list of vineyards and details about touring. Remember that many wineries are small, family-owned operations, so phone ahead.

If you're near Charlottesville, stop at the Barboursville Vineyard (tel: 540-832-3824), credited with reinvigorating the Virginia wine industry when it opened in the late 1970s. Jefferson Vineyards (tel: 434-977-3042) is within easy striking distance of Monticello. Minutes away is the Kluge Estate Winery and Vineyard (tel: 434-977-3895).

If you're swinging through Williamsburg, stop at the Williamsburg Winery (tel: 757-229-0999) whose slightly sweet Governor's White has helped put them on the wine map. And if you're passing through Virginia's Northern Neck, look out for Ingleside Plantation Vineyards (tel: 1-800-747-4645 or 804-244-8687).

TIP

Families with children may wish to stop at Busch Gardens (tel: 1-800-343-7946, or visit www.4adventure.com/buschgardens), a theme park 3 miles (5 km) east of town. As theme parks go, it's one of the nicer ones and has something of a European flavor.

RIGHT:
traditional shopping at Williamsburg.

group of dedicated women, Bill of Rights author George Mason's Gunston Hall was saved by volunteers, most Civil War battlefields are the province of the federal government if they aren't in private ownership).

Fortunately, Williamsburg hung on just long enough for Rockefeller money to rescue it early in the 20th century. "That the future may learn from the past," is how John D. Rockefeller put it when he committed millions to the restoration effort that has turned this former rubble into one of the grand examples of American life in the colonial past.

Tours start at the **Governor's Palace**, three floors of Georgian grandeur that, during the years that the succession of royal governors (the king's representatives in Virginia) lived here, took 25 servants and slaves to maintain. The complex includes a stable, carriage house, scullery, and other outbuildings, plus a wine cellar large enough to hold 3,000 bottles.

Duke of Gloucester Street is Williamsburg's main avenue, with red-bricked shops and residences lining both sides. Tradespeople in period costumes work in the shops, spinning and weaving, dipping candles, making furniture, forging, and practicing all the other the crafts of 18th-century life. They'll stop in the midst of their work to give impromptu talks and to answer any questions. One of the nicest things you can do for yourself is to stop in your travels and pause at **Bruton Parish Church**, which dates from 1715 (though it was completely renovated in 1939–40). The usual suspects (Jefferson, Washington, Henry, and Mason) all worshiped here, assigned to their respective and enclosed boxed pews, designed for privacy and to keep out winter drafts.

The town has two good art museums, the **Abby Aldrich Rockefeller Folk Art Museum** (daily 11am–5pm) and the **DeWitt Wallace Decorative Arts Museum** (daily 11am–5pm), both offering wonderful collections of American folk art, furniture, paintings, Chinese porcelains, and more. ❑

Restaurants

Flint Hill

Four and Twenty Blackbirds
650 Zachary Taylor Highway, Tel: 540-675-1111. Open: D only Wed-–Sat; Sun brunch $$–$$$
The chef's inventiveness, especially with pork tenderloin, draws an upscale horse-country crowd. Small and quirkily decorated.

Fredericksburg

Kenmore Inn
1200 Princes Anne St. Tel: 540-371-7622. Open: L & D, daily. $$
Colonial fare in elegant period setting; menu of

Southern classics; have lunch on the porch.

Charlottesville

C & O Restaurant
515 East Water St. Tel: 434-971-7044. Open: L & D, Mon–Fri; D only, Sat & Sun. $$$
French, Cajun and Thai-inspired entrées. Rustic setting; upstairs dining room more formal.

Ivy Inn
2244 Old Ivy Road, Tel: 434-977-1222. Open: D only, Mon-Sat. $$–$$$
Grand former home just off the UVA campus. French inspired menu is short, but top-notch.

Kluge Estate Farm Shop
100 Grand Cru Drive, Tel: 434-977-3893. Open: Tues-Sun, 9am-6pm $$–$$$

Full meals or light takeaway. Pastries are divine. Emphasis is on local produce and, thanks to adjacent vineyard, fine wine.

Washington

Ashby Inn
692 Federal St., Paris, VA. Tel: 540-592-3900. Open: D only Wed–Sat; Sun brunch $$$.
Small country inn, and one of the very best, with short menu that changes daily according to the season. Paris is small (49 residents), quaint and historic.

Williamsburg

Christiana Campbell's Tavern
Waller St. Tel: 757-229-

2141. Open: L & D, Tues–Sat. Reserve in advance $$$
Restored colonial-era tavern features seafood, early American fare, strolling musicians.

Trellis
403 Duke of Gloucester St., Merchants' Square. Tel: 757-229-8610. Open: D, daily. $$$$
Regional American dishes with French influence; each of the dining rooms with a different décor. Order Death by Chocolate for dessert; reserve in advance.

• • • • • • • • • • • • • • • • • • •
Prices for three-course meal for one, with half-bottle of house wine, tax and tip.
$ under $25. $$ $25–40.
$$$ $40–50. $$$$ $50-plus.

TRANSPORT

GETTING THERE AND GETTING AROUND

GETTING THERE

By Air

Washington, DC is served by three regional airports: Ronald Reagan Washington National Airport (or simply National, as it's often still called by locals) is closest to the city, just 4 miles (6.4 km) across the Potomac in Virginia; Dulles Airport is also in Virginia, 26 miles (42 km) from DC; and Baltimore-Washington International Airport (or BWI), 40 miles (64 km) north in the city of Baltimore in Maryland and about an hour by car. Reagan National offers mostly domestic service and also flights to and from some Canadian cities. Dulles and BWI are both international airports.

Airports

Dulles International Airport and **Reagan Washington National Airport** are physically located in Virginia and are operated together by the Metropolitan Washington Airports Authority.
Tel: 703-417-8600
www.mwaa.com
Baltimore-Washington International Airport (BWI)
Toll free: 1-800-I-FLY-BWI
www.bwiairport.com

Ground Transportation

There are several options for getting directly into DC.
From National: There's a Metro subway station here, easily accessible from the airport terminal with quick and inexpensive (about $6) service into DC with stops at all the convenient city locations. You can also take a taxi, available curbside when you pick up your bags, with fares that range from $10 to $20, depending on your destination. There is also limousine and SuperShuttle mini-van service from the airport (see opposite page).
From Dulles: Take a Washington Flyer Taxi directly into the city, which will cost about $50, or take the Washington Flyer Coach to the West Falls Church Metro station in Virginia. (Washington Flyer Taxi and Coach, toll free 1-888-WASHFLY or visit www.wash-

fly.com). Bus service runs about every 30 minutes and costs $8. Buy your bus ticket at the kiosk on the airport Arrivals level. From the West Falls Church Metro station you can take the subway into the city for a cost of about $7, depending on the time of day. There is also limousine and SuperShuttle mini-van service from the airport (see opposite page).
From BWI: A taxi from this airport, which you can hail at the curb near the baggage claim, will cost about $60 into DC. You can also take the free shuttle bus to the nearby Amtrak rail station (toll free: 1-800-USA-RAIL or 1-800-872-7245, or visit www.amtrak.com) and take the train into DC's Union Station for about $30, but you may have a wait, depending on the train schedule. There is also Metro

AIRLINES

Air Canada
US toll free 1-888-247-2262
American Airlines
US toll free: 1-800-433-7300
Continental
US toll free: 1-800-525-0280
Delta Airlines
US toll free: 1-800-221-1212
Northwest Airlines
US toll free: 1-800-225-2525

US Airways
US toll free: 1-800-428-4322
International service to BWI and Dulles only:
British Airways
US toll free: 1-800-247-9297
UK: Tel: 0870 850 9850
Virgin Arlantic
US toll-free:1-800-862-8621
UK: Tel: 0870-380 2007

TRANSPORT

bus service between the airport and the Greenbelt, Maryland, Metro station. The bus, the 30B, runs every day, every 40 minutes, and costs $3.50. From the Greenbelt Metro station, you can then take the subway into DC for about $5.

GROUND TRANSPORTATION
SERVICING ALL THREE AIRPORTS:
SuperShuttle: You can pick up one of these blue mini-vans at any of the airports and share a ride into the city. Service is friendly and dependable and you'll see them all over town. Cost from Dulles and BWI into DC is about $50; from National about $10. When you're ready to fly home, schedule a pick up from your hotel to the airport by phoning toll free: 1-800-BLUE VAN or 1-800-258-3826 or contacting your hotel's concierge.
Limousine Service: International Limousine is one of the city's oldest limo services and is available 24 hours. Tel: 202-388-6800 or visit www.internationallimo.com. You can also contact Fleet Transportation at 703-933-2600, or toll free at 1-866-933-2600 or visit www.fleettransportation .com. Check the kiosks at the airports.

Car Rental

Unless you're planning to make an excursion well beyond the city limits, you probably won't need a car. In fact, given the congestion and the scarcity of parking, it's advisable to avoid driving in DC if you can. *(See Driving, page 217).* If, however, you do decide you need a car, the agencies listed below serve all three airports.

You'll need a credit card to secure the car as well as a valid driver's license to operate it. Some companies don't like to rent to anyone under 25. If you already have auto insurance that will cover you in the case of an accident, there's no need to buy the additional insurance, which the agency will offer and which is usually expensive.

The tax on car rental varies

ABOVE: rush-hour by the Potomac.

from 8 to 11.5 percent, depending on the location.
Avis
Toll free: 1-800-331-1212 (US)
Budget
Toll free: 1-800-527-0700 (US)
Dollar
Toll free: 1-800-800-4000 (US)
Hertz
Toll free: 1-800-654-3131 (US)
National
Toll free: 1-800-328-4567 (US)

Hotel Shuttle Service

Don't overlook the free shuttle service that many hotels offer their guests. Ask when you make your reservations or, when you've landed, look for the marked vans that pull up curbside, usually near the baggage claim.

By Train

Amtrak, the national railway system, offers direct service between Washington and New York. Trains arrive and depart several times each weekday, and there is also service on weekends. Train service is also available to and from Philadelphia, New York and Boston to the north, Richmond, Virginia, to the south, and several other destina-

tions across the country. Union Station, only a few blocks from Capitol Hill, is one of the city's architectural gems, fully restored with several restaurants and shops. There are always plenty of taxis out front for a quick ride to any hotel or other destination in the city.
Amtrak fare and schedule information:
Toll free: 1-800-872-7245 (US)
www.amtrak.com

By Bus

If you're not fussy and are willing to sacrifice some comforts, service in and out of DC can be inexpensive if somewhat unreliable. For fares and scheduling information, contact:
Greyhound Bus Lines
1005 1st Street, NE
Toll free: 1-800-231-2222
www.greyhound.com

By Car

Washington is circled by a highway system known as the Capital Beltway (hence the phrase "inside the beltway," referencing the powerbrokers' turf) which is formed by two interstate highways, I-495 on the west, and I-95 on the east. Several major highways also intersect the beltway and lead in and out of the city. These include Route 50, which runs east and west between DC and Annapolis and the Chesapeake Bay region to the east, and Route 66, which links the city to the Virginia mountains to the west. Interstate 95, which forms the eastern half of the beltway, runs north and south along the US coast, from Florida to Maine. Once you've arrived by car, it's best to park it and rely on public transportation, which is good, or taxis, which are plentiful. You can also simply walk. *(See Driving, page 217.)*

ACCOMMODATION

ACTIVITIES

A – Z

GETTING AROUND

Street Plan

Washington is really the nation's first "planned city", a city deliberately intended rather than one that evolved. This diamond-shaped metropolis is laid out in four basic sections: Northwest, Northeast, Southwest and Southeast. Each quadrant runs in a compass direction from the US Capitol. You'll notice East, North, and South Capitol streets, but no West Capitol Street, when you consult the map. What happened to West Capitol Street? It's actually the Mall, where many of the Smithsonian museums are located and which runs from the Capitol to the Potomac.

Within the quadrants the numbered streets run north to south; lettered streets, east to west. All of this sounds sensible until you realize that – surprise! – DC has four 1st streets, four G streets, and so on, thanks to those pesky quadrants. That's why it's important to recognize and attach the quadrant designation – NW, NE, SW, SE – to all street addresses. As a visitor, though, you'll most likely spend much of your time in the northwest (NW) quadrant, where many of the sites are located, except, of course, for Capitol Hill itself.

As for the avenues, they're named for each of the states. They cut diagonally across the street grid and intersect at the various circles and squares such as Dupont Circle, Washington Circle, Mt. Vernon Square and Lafayette Square.

Public Transport

Using Metro

The best way to get around Washington is to use Metro, the city's

ESCALATOR ETIQUETTE

Every Metro station has an escalator; in fact, one of the world's longest is at the Dupont Circle station. Escalator etiquette requires that when riding a Metro escalator you stay to the right. Besides marking you as a tourist, when you stand to the left you block the way of those behind you, usually harried commuters rushing to make connections home or to their offices. Stay to the right, unless you're "walking" the escalator, too.

modern, color-coded, clean, safe and reasonably efficient subway system. There's a station near almost every attraction, or at least within easy walking distance, and considering that driving is challenging and parking scarce and expensive, there's no reason not to use Metro. The base fare is $1.35, one way, but don't expect that's all you'll pay. That will get you past the turnstile, but not much beyond the station platform.

Fares are calculated both on your destination and the time of day you travel, rush hour being more expensive, and they go up sharply from the base fare. Calculating the rate can be confusing, but if you look for the Chinese restaurant-like menu of fares posted on and near each

BELOW: bus routes are confusing.

stationmaster's kiosk you'll be able to figure out your costs, which you should double for your return trip.

Access into any of Metro's stations requires a farecard, a paper ticket about the size of a credit card equipped with a magnetic strip, which you can purchase from the machines in the station. Everyone, even children, must have a farecard.

To avoid the lines, buy a roundtrip card. You'll need the card to enter and then exit the system, so once you enter a station, hang on to your card. When you reach your destination you'll pass your card through the turnstile again and the card will automatically deduct your fare.

An easier and probably cheaper alternative is to buy a one-day pass for $6 that lets you make unlimited trips on Metro beginning after morning rush hour (9.30 am) until closing on weekdays and all day on weekends and holidays.

If you're thinking of hopping a city bus, best to avoid it if you can. Metro also operates a bus line, but the routes and schedules are confusing, you'll need exact change to board, and the buses are subject to the same surface traffic jams that delay every other DC motorist.

Of all the major attractions, only Georgetown is without a Metro stop. Fearing tourists and rowdy locals, residents of this historic neighborhood drew together to successfully block subway construction. The closest Metro stop is Foggy Bottom, a brisk but pleasant ten-minute walk. Like all the rest of DC, Georgetown is notoriously difficult to navigate and there's never any parking, so a car isn't a wise choice.

There is, however, a shuttle bus that you can take, the Georgetown Metro Connection, which runs a jitney every ten minutes from the Foggy Bottom Metro.

TRANSPORT

Washington Metropolitan Area Transit Authority (or Metro):
Tel: 202-637-7000
www.wmata.com
● *See the Metro system map on page 257.*

On Foot

DC is a walking city, safe in most sections where visitors are likely to go, with clean streets and wide sidewalks in good repair. To see most of the sites, such as the museums on the Mall, you can count on doing a lot of walking, so be sure to bring comfortable shoes. For handicapped visitors, all sidewalks feature curb cuts to make for easy street crossing, and in accordance with federal law all public buildings have handicap-accessible entrances.

Taxis

Taxis are plentiful, hailed easily in most sections of town, and operate on a zone system which helps to keep fares reasonable. You may be expected to share, though, so don't be surprised if while you're on board the driver stops to pick up another fare. Most drivers are courteous, though many are foreign and are still learning their way around English. More problematic is that many are also learning their way around the city, so leave time in your schedule and carry a map. To reserve a taxi, allow at least an hour. There are many taxi services in the city. Three of the most reliable are.
Yellow Cab: Tel: 202-544-1212
Diamond Cab Tel: 202-387-6200
Capitol Cab: Tel: 202-546-2400

Driving

This is best avoided. DC has the country's second worst traffic congestion, behind Los Angles. Though the layout of the streets may appear sensible, it can be a bewildering place to navigate, especially for the uninitiated. Roads regularly merge into tangles, highway exits are not always adequately marked, and

traffic lanes can and suddenly do switch direction, this to accommodate morning and evening rush hour traffic, which in DC is legendary. Parking is scarce and usually expensive ($20 or more per day). And if that wasn't enough, DC has one more added problem: diplomats. Unlike most American cities, DC is home to many foreign dignitaries whose driving habits can be sometimes less than civil and who bear little or no responsibility for their recklessness, thanks to diplomatic immunity. Get into an accident with one of them and you're likely to carry the full load of expenses, along with enduring any injuries. To give fair warning, diplomats sport special red, white and blue license plates on their cars.

Turning right at a red light is permitted in DC, providing there is no oncoming traffic.

If you do decide to brave it behind the wheel, remember that we keep to the right here, that you'll need a valid driver's license, and that parking tickets and clamps (boots) are distributed liberally and with impunity.

Sightseeing Tours

Lost in Washington? One of the best ways to get your bearings and see the sites is to sign on with a tour group for a day or even a half day. Some services even offer moonlight tours of the monuments, more relaxing since you'll miss much of the daytime traffic. The tour guides here are experienced, equipped to answer just about any question, and can impart a sense of history embellished with anecdotes and personal observations that can make the city come alive.

ACCOMMODATION

SIGHTSEEING TOURS

All About Town
Tel: 301-856-5556
www.allabouttowntours.webatonce.com
Both group and individual tours
DC Ducks
Tel: 202-966-3825
www.dcducks.com
Amphibious carrier tours the Mall, then splashes into the Potomac
Gray Line Tours
Tel: 202-289-1995
www.grayline.com
Bus and trolley tours starting at Union Station
Old Town Trolley Tours
Tel: 202-832-9800
www.historictours.com
Travels a 17-stop loop that takes about two hours, though you can get on and off at each attraction.
Tourmobile Sightseeing
Tel: 202-554-5100
www.tourmobile.com
Narrated sightseeing shuttle tours with stops across the city that allow you to get on and off at each attraction.

Zohery Tours
Tel: 202-554-4200
www.zohery.com
Insiders' tours offered by experts in the city's history.

Water Cruises

Spirit Cruises
Pier 4, 6th and Water streets SW
Tel: 202-554-8000.
www.spiritofwashington.com
Board for a narrated round-trip cruise between DC and George Washington's Mt. Vernon. Lunch and dinner cruises.
Dandy Restaurant Cruise Ship
City dock, Old Town Alexandria
Tel: 703-683-6076
www.dandydinnerboat.com
Dinner and dancing aboard a climate-controlled vessel, viewing monuments from the river.
Potomac Riverboat Company
Tel: 703-548-9000
www.potomacriverboatco.com
Cruise between Georgetown and Old Town on opposite shores of the Potomac, then stop to shop or dine. Cruises also available to Mt. Vernon.

ACTIVITIES

A–Z

ACCOMMODATIONS

HOTELS, YOUTH HOSTELS, BED & BREAKFASTS

Choosing a Hotel

DC has lots of hotel rooms, concentrated in the sections of the city of most interest to tourists and business travelers. Spring and summer are peak seasons for tourists, and weekdays are heaviest for those here on business. During autumn and winter the weather is moderate and the tourist crowds have diminished, so it's a good time to plan a trip. Hotels often offer reduced rates on weekends and off-peak seasons.

Occasionally you can negotiate a lower room rate by calling the individual hotel directly as opposed to making arrangements through the chain's main reservation line. Check the

ABOVE: the Willard Hotel's lobby.

hotel's website, too, or one of the travel and hotel booking sites where you'll often find lower rates and special promotions. Reservations are essential, so make them before you leave home. You'll need a credit card to secure your room.

Hotels are listed by neighborhood in the same order as the areas in the Places section, and from most to least expensive.

Bed & Breakfasts

To book a room in one of the many smaller guest houses and bed-and-breakfasts across the city and in Virginia, call either of the following organizations. They can help you make a reservation for an inn close to where you want to be.

Bed and Breakfast Accommodations, Ltd.
Tel: 202-328-3510
toll free 1-877-893-3233
www.bedandbreakfast.com

Alexandria and Arlington Bed & Breakfast Network
Tel: 703-549-3415
www.aabbn.com

Bridgestreet Corporate Housing
Tel: 703-208-9110
www.bridgestreet.com
Offers one to three-bedroom properties by the week or month.

AIRPORT HOTELS

These moderately priced hotels adjacent to Reagan Washington National Airport are an easy walk to the Metro into DC.
Holiday Inn National Airport Crystal City
2650 Jefferson Davis Highway
Tel: 703-684-7200
toll free: 1-800-465-4329
www.holiday-inn.com
Standard chain hotel, but comfortable and popular with business and military travelers. Rate includes breakfast buffet. 280 rooms.
Sheraton Crystal City Hotel
1800 Jefferson Davis Highway
Tel: 703-486-1111
toll free 1-800-325-3535
www.sheraton.com
Newly renovated chain hotel near a residential neighborhood with good restaurants. Shopping nearby. 210 rooms.

THE MALL AND CAPITOL HILL

HOTELS

Expensive

Best Western Capitol Skyline
South Capitol and I streets, SW
Tel: 202-488-7500
toll free 1-800-458-7500
www.bestwestern.com
Within sight of the Capitol with seasonal dining beside the outdoor pool, Chippendale outfitted lobby, and big screen TVs in the rooms. Walk to the Mall. 200 rooms

Capitol Hill Suites
200 C Street, SE
Tel: 202-543-6000
toll free 1-800-424-9165
www.capitolhillsuites.com
Converted apartment building near the Library of Congress on the House side of the Capitol outfitted in 18th century style with kitchens.

Walk to the Mall and other attractions; good for families. 152 suites.

Holiday Inn on the Hill
415 New Jersey Ave, NW
Tel: 202-638-1616
toll free:1-800-465-4329
www.holiday-inn.com
Contemporary-style rooms are newly upgraded and feature lots of wood and glass. There's a fully equipped fitness center besides all the usual ammenities. 343 rooms.

Loew's L'Enfant Plaza Hotel
480 L'Enfant Plaza, SW
Tel: 202-484-1000
toll free 1-800-23LOEWS
www.loewshotels.com
Top-notch and within easy walking distance of the Mall. Good dining room, health club and rooftop swimming pool. 392 rooms.

Washington Court Hotel
525 New Jersey Ave, NW
Tel: 202-628-2100

toll free: 1-800-321-3010
www.washingtoncourthotel.com
Full service hotel near Union Station, and the Mall, with health club. Good for business travelers. Many rooms sport views of the Capitol. 264 rooms and suites.

Moderate

Bull Moose B & B on Capitol Hill
101 5th Street, NE
Tel: 202-547-1050
www.bullmoose-b-and-b.com
Three-story Victorian townhouse converted to a city inn. Offers complimentary continental breakfast and access to a fitness room and indoor pool. Ten rooms, each with bath.

Doolittle Guest House
506 East Capitol Street, NE
Tel: 202-546-6622
www.doolittlehouse.com
Lovely refurbished Capi-

tol Hill townhouse offers peace and quiet. Library, dining room where breakfast features local produce. Three guest rooms, each with private bath.

Hyatt Regency Washington
400 New Jersey Ave, NW
Tel:202-737-1234
toll free: 1-800-233-1234
www.hyatt.com
Nicely appointed, spacious rooms; indoor pool and sauna. Walk to all major attractions, including Union Station. 834 rooms

Phoenix Park
520 North Capitol Street, NW
Tel: 202-638-6900
www.phoenixparkhotel.com
Irish hospitality at this hotel outfitted with 18th century period furnishings including Irish linens. Easy walk to the Capitol, Union Station. Irish entertainment in the bar. 149 rooms.

DOWNTOWN

HOTELS

Deluxe

Hay Adams
One Lafayette Square
Tel: 202-638-6600
toll free: 1-800-424-5054
www.hayadams.com
A block from the White House across Lafayette Square, this is where diplomats check in. Luxurious English country style, with fine art and silk. 136 rooms.

Hotel Monaco
700 F Street, NW

Tel: 202-628-7177
toll free 1-877-202-5411
www.monaco-dc.com
The city's old post office converted to a hotel in all its marble glory complete with luxury extras, modern art in the lobby, courtyard dining. 184 rooms.

The Jefferson
1200 16th Street NW
Tel 202-347-2200
toll free 1-800-368-5966
www.loewshotel.com
A small top-notch hotel with fine service, antiques everywhere, and canopied beds. The hotel has a good restau-

rant and there's access to the nearby University Club fitness center. 100 rooms.

Renaissance Mayflower
1127 Connecticut Ave. NW
Tel: 202-347-3000
toll free 1-800 HOTELS-1
www. renaissancehotels.com/WASSH
This 10-story hotel is on the National Register of Historic Places. Presidential inaugural balls are held here, and politicians and lobbyist make the bar and restaurant a regular gathering spot. Rooms are spacious, tastefully

outfitted in mahogany and decorated with fine art. 565 rooms.

St. Regis Washington
923 16th Street, NW
Tel 202-638-2626
toll free 1-800-325-3535
www.starwood.com
Located three blocks from the White House.

PRICE CATEGORIES

Price categories are for a double room without breakfast:

Deluxe	over $300
Expensive	$175–$300
Moderate	$125–$175
Budget	under $125

Elegantly decorated hotel, all amenities including free shuttle service within a five mile radius. 193 rooms.

Willard Intercontinental Hotel
1401 Pennsylvania Ave, NW
Tel: 202-628-9100
toll free 1-800-327-0200
www.hotels.washington.interconti
.com
This is the grandest of the capital's grand hotels, with sumptuous rooms and scrupulous service. Abraham Lincoln stayed here. The rooms are generously sized and decorated in 19th-century style, but with modern comforts. Amenities include two restaurants, bar, health club. 341 rooms.

Expensive

Capital Hilton
1001 16th Street, NW
Tel: 202-393-1000
toll free: 1-800 HILTONS
www.hilton.com
An easy walk to the White House and many of the monuments. Spacious, conveniently laid-out rooms; fitness center; two restaurants. 543 rooms

Governor's House
1615 Rhode Island Ave
Tel: 202-296-2100
toll free 1-800-821-4367
www.governorshousehotewdc.com
Small, elegant hotel near all the attractions but in a quiet neighborhood. Health club avail-

PRICE CATEGORIES

Price categories are for a double room without breakfast:
Deluxe   over $300
Expensive $175–$300
Moderate $125–$175
Budget   under $125

able. 149 rooms, 24 with kitchens.

Grand Hyatt
1000 H St
Tel: 202-582-1234
toll free 1-800-233-1234
www.grandwashington.hyatt.com
A busy central meeting place, this hotel's lobby features a 7,000 sq. ft. lagoon, plus underground access to the Metro. Outdoor pool, lounge, and laundromat. 900 rooms

Henley Park
926 Massachusetts Ave, NW
Tel: 202-638-5200
toll free 1-800-222-8474
www.henleypark.com
Tudor-style apartment building now a comfortable, clubby hotel with lots of period antiques. Afternoon tea, and a pleasant restaurant. Health club facility nearby. 96 rooms.

Hotel Washington
515 15th Street, NW
Tel: 202-638-5900
toll free 1-800-424-9540
www.hotelwashington.com
This National Historic Landmark dates from 1918. Caters to families and features a health club and a top-floor terrace café with a fine view, especially at night. 344 rooms.

JW Marriott Hotel
1331 Pennsylvania Ave, NW
Tel: 202-393-2000
toll free 1-800-228-9290
www.marriott.com
Caters to families and to business travelers. Rooms are modern with office amenities, and there's a pool, fitness center, and four restaurants. 755 rooms.

Morrison-Clark Inn
1015 L Street, NW
Tel: 202-898-1200
toll free 1-800-332-7898
www.morrisonclark.com
Lovely Victorian inn with

lace curtains and carved armoires and a 19th-century flavor. Listed in the National Register of Historic Places. Some rooms have porches, others overlook a lovely courtyard. Exercise facilities. 54 rooms.

Hotel Sofitel Lafayette Square
806 15th Street, NW
Tel: 202-730-8800
toll free: 1-800-SOFITEL
www.sofitel.com
Close to the White House, this French-style gem has a fitness center and a good restaurant. 237 rooms.

Moderate

Courtyard Marriott Convention Center
900 F Street, NW
Tel: 202-638-4600
toll free: 1-800-321-2211
www.marriott.com
This new downtown, hotel has comfortable rooms, a hot tub, fitness center and a lounge. 150 rooms.

Club Quarters
839 17th Street, NW
Tel: 202-463-6400
www.clubquarters.com
Overlooks Farragut Square near the White House and within easy walk of many restaurants, although it has its own casual French Café Soleil. 160 rooms.

Hamilton Crowne Plaza
14th and K streets, NW
Tel: 202-682-0111
toll free: 1-800-2CROWNE
www.sixcontinentshotels.com
Right in the heart of downtown and overlooking Franklin Square, this hotel's nice-sized rooms are done up in earth-tone florals, some with a view of the Washington Monument. 318 rooms.

Washington Plaza
10 Thomas Circle, NW
Tel: 202-842-1300
toll free: 1-800-424-1140
www.washingtonplaza.com
Once disreputable, this neighborhood's gone upscale with the help of the nicely appointed and kept Plaza. Landscaped outdoor pool is the focal point. Pets allowed. 340 rooms.

Budget

Red Roof Inn
500 H Street, NW
Tel: 202-289-5959
toll free 1-800-THE-ROOF
In the heart of Chinatown. The renovated rooms are comfortable. There's an exercise room, coin-operated laundry facility, and a small cafe. 195 rooms.

Hotel Harrington
11th and E streets, NW
Tel: 202-628-8140
toll free: 1-800-424-8532
www.hotel-harrington.com
A favorite with tour groups and families. Basic, comfortable, and centrally located. 245 rooms, 26 family suites.

Super 8 Motel
501 New York Avenue, NE
Tel: 202-543-7400
toll free: 1-800-800-8000
www.super8motel.com
Bare-bones, but clean and with an outdoor pool. Near bus stop.

YOUTH HOSTEL

Washington International Youth Hostel
1009 11th Street, NW
Tel: 202-737-2333
www.hiwashingtondc.org
There are 125 beds here. Accommodations are spartan, but it's clean and comfortable.

FOGGY BOTTOM AND GEORGETOWN

HOTELS

Deluxe

Four Seasons
2800 Pennsylvania Ave, NW
Tel: 202-342-0444
toll free 1-800-332-3442
www.fourseasons.com/washington
Extravagance with first-class service – and right on the edge of Georgetown. Tastefully decorated rooms with lots of overstuffed furniture; down comforters and bathrobes. 196 rooms

Park Hyatt
1201 24th Street, NW
Tel: 202-789-1234
toll free 1-800-922- PARK
www.parkwashington.hyatt.com
One block from Rock Creek Park, a quiet spot between downtown attractions and all the shopping and restaurants of Georgetown. The rooms are subtly decorated, and have sofa beds. 223 rooms.

Swissotel Watergate
2650 Virginia Ave, NW
Tel: 202-965-2300
toll free 1-888-737-9477
www.swissotel.com
Not the site of the infamous break in–that was the apartment building next door. Rooms are large, and outfitted with French Provincial furnishings. There's a lap pool and a health club, and the Kennedy Center is next door. 250 rooms.

Washington Fairmont
2401 M Street, NW
Tel: 202-429-2400
toll free 1-800-441-1414
www.fairmont.com
Small but elegant rooms overlook a nicely landscaped courtyard. Lower level houses an impressive fitness center. 415 rooms.

Expensive

Georgetown Inn
1310 Wisconsin Ave.
Tel: 202-333-8900
www.georgetowninn.com
One of the neighborhood's first hotels still offering friendly service with comfortable rooms and a popular lounge. Good location. 96 rooms.

The Latham
3000 M Street, NW
Tel: 202-726-5000
toll free 1-800-295-2003
www.thelatham.com
Small, comfortable and with an excellent view of the river and an outdoor pool. Right in the heart of Georgetown and home to the acclaimed Citronelle restaurant. 97 rooms.

One Washington Circle Hotel
One Washington Circle, NW
Tel: 202-872-1680
toll free: 1-800-424-9671
www.thecirclehotel.com
All suites with fully equipped kitchens, a health club and outdoor pool. Near the Kennedy Center and the Metro. Has an excellent café. 151 suites.

Savoy Suites
2505 Wisconsin Ave.
Tel: 202-337-9700
toll free 1-800-944-5377
Quiet upper Georgetown neighbourhood. Large rooms, some with jacuzzis; some with kitchenettes. Complimentary parking, shuttle service to the Metro. 152 rooms.

St. Gregory
2033 M Street
Tel: 202-223-0200
toll free 1-800-829-5034
www.stgregoryhotelwdc.com
This new hotel offers suites with fully equipped and stocked kitchens. Good coffee bar and all the usual business amenities. 154 rooms, some of them suites.

St. James Suites
950 24th St, NW
Tel: 202-457-0500
toll free 1-800-852-8512
www.stjamessuiteswdc.com
Generously sized suites tastefully decorated, with fully equipped kitchens. There's a fitness center and an outdoor pool. 74 suites.

Washington Marriott
1221 22nd Street, NW
Tel: 202-872-1500
toll free 1-800-228-9290
www.marriott.com
Comfortable rooms outfitted with modern-style furnishings. Pool, fitness room, sauna, good restaurant. 400 rooms.

Moderate

Doubletree Hotel Guest Suites
801 New Hampshire
Tel: 202-785-2000
toll free 1-800-222-8733
www.doubletree.com
One-bedroom suites with full kitchens, on a quiet residential neighborhood with easy access to the Kennedy Center. 105 suites.

Embassy Suites
1250 22nd Street, NW
Tel: 202-857-3388
toll free 1-800-EMBASSY
www.embassysuites.com
This chain caters mostly to business travelers who enjoy comfortably outfitted rooms and all the usual business amenities including breakfast. 318 suites.

Georgetown Suites
1000 29th Street, NW and 1111 30th Street, NW
Tel: 202-298-7800
toll free: 1-800-348-7203
www.georgetownsuites.com
One- and two-bedroom suites and two-level townhouses, each with kitchen, though there's complimentary continental breakfast in the lobby. Health club; adjacent to Georgetown's center. 186 suites.

George Washington University Inn
824 New Hampshire Ave, NW
Tel: 202-337-6620
toll free: 1-800-426-4455
www.gwuinn.com
Comfortably outfitted rooms include mini-fridge, microwave, access to the university's fitness center. Quiet residential neighborhood, near Metro and easy access to all sites. 95 rooms.

Holiday Inn Georgetown
2101 Wisconsin Ave.
Tel: 202-338-4600
toll free 1-800-HOLIDAY
www.hightown.com
It's a short downhill walk to Georgetown from this well-kept chain hotel with views of the Potomac and Washington Monument from the top floors. 296 rooms.

Hotel Lombardy
2019 Pennsylvania Ave, NW
Tel: 202-828-2600
toll free 1-800-424-5486
www.hotellombardy.com
Small hotel features spacious rooms outfitted with Italian-style decor. There's a beauti-

ful garden. Easy walk to Georgetown. 80 rooms and 50 suites.

Hotel Monticello
1075 Thomas Jefferson Street, NW
Tel: 202-337-0900
toll free 1-800-388-2410
www.monticellohotel.com
One- and two-bedroom suites; caters mostly to diplomats. Enjoy use of nearby health club; complimentary continental breakfast. 47 suites.

Melrose Hotel
2430 Pennsylvania Ave, NW
Tel: 202-955-6400
toll free 1-800-955-6400
www.melrosehotel.com
Comfortable rooms with a sitting area. On the edge of Georgetown and attracts an interna-

tional clientele. Restaurant, outdoor bar. Pets allowed. 240 rooms.

The Remington
601 24th Street, NW
Tel: 202-233-4512
toll free: 1-800-225-3847
Kitchen, washer/dryer, some units with fireplaces, accepts pets; good alternative to the traditional hotel. Near the Metro and an easy walk into Georgetown. 40 suites.

River Inn
924 25th Street, NW
Tel: 202-337-7600
toll free: 1-800-424-2741
www.theriverinn.com
Elegant Georgetown location offers full kitchen in each suite, breakfast buffet. Many suites have good city

views. Small, excellent restaurant. 126 suites.

Washington Suites Georgetown
2500 Pennsylvania Ave, NW
Tel: 202-333-8060
toll free 1-877-736-2500
There are 124 comfortable suites complete with kitchens, and the hotel also features a health club. Walk to the Kennedy Center.

Budget

Brickskeller Inn
1523 22nd St
Tel: 202-293-1885
Modest, no-nonsense, but right on the edge of Georgetown, and good if budget is a consideration. A b&b without one of the b's: breakfast.

44 rooms, 2 with private bath.

State Plaza Hotel
2117 E Street, NW
Tel: 202-861-8200
toll free: 1-800-424-2859
www.stateplaza.com
Comfortable suites feature fully equipped kitchens. There's also a dining room, a sundeck and a fitness center. Near the State Department; easy walk to Metro. 225 suites.

PRICE CATEGORIES

Price categories are for a double room without breakfast:

Deluxe   over $300
Expensive $175–$300
Moderate $125–$175
Budget   under $125

DUPONT CIRCLE AND ADAMS MORGAN

HOTELS

Deluxe

Churchill Hotel
1914 Connecticut Ave, NW
Tel: 202-797-2999
toll free 1-800-424-2464
www.thechurchillhotel.com
One of the so-called boutique hotels, classy and comfortable. Near the embassies and close to Dupont Circle. 144 rooms.

Washington Hilton and Towers
1919 Connecticut Ave.
Tel: 202-483-3000
toll free 1-800-445-8667
www.washington-hilton.com
A huge curving structure situated on a hillside, this is the site of the Reagan assassination attempt. Lots of amenities and hotel ser-

vices that business travelers expect, including a large fitness center, but also good for families. 1100 rooms.

Expensive

Hilton Embassy Row
2015 Massachusetts Ave, NW
Tel: 202-265-1600
toll free 1-800-445-8667
www.hilton.com
Just off popular Dupont Circle, but in a quiet neighborhood, with nicely appointed rooms, good views of the city, rooftop pool and lounge, and you-name-it service. 193 rooms

Hotel Rouge
1315 16th Street, NW
Tel: 202-939-6400
toll free: 1-800-368-5689
"High energy" is how they bill themselves; no beige-and-tan décor here. Outfitted with

modern furnishings and flat-screen tvs. Near Embassy Row; busy bar scene. 137 rooms.

Omni Shoreham
2500 Calvert Street, NW
Tel: 202-234-0700
toll free 1-800-228-2121
www.omnihotels.com
Built in the 1930s, this has been one of the settings for the inaugural balls. Near Rock Creek Park; upgraded facility with traditional furnishings, modern office amenities, new fitness center. Ask about Room 800G if you believe in ghosts. 800 rooms

Westin Embassy Row
2100 Massachusetts Ave.
Tel: 202-293-2100
toll free 1-800-WESTIN1
www.westin.com
This stately hotel along Embassy Row was once the boyhood home of Al Gore. Rooms are sump-

tuously outfitted with rich fabrics and marble baths. All the usual office amenities, and excellent service from the staff. Rooms on the higher floors overlook Georgetown.

Washington Terrace Hotel
1515 Rhode Island Ave, NW
Tel: 202-232-7000
toll free: 1-866-984-6835
www.washingtonterracehotel.com
Accessible to most sites, newly outfitted rooms are spacious and decorated with vivid colors. Home of one of the city's best restaurants. 220 rooms.

Wyndham City Center
1143 New Hampshire Ave, NW
Tel: 202-775-0800
toll free: 1-800-996-3426
www.wyndham.com
Upscale chain hotel near Metro offers the standard amenities plus

fitness center; good restaurant and busy bar. 352 rooms.

Wyndham Washington
1400 M Street
Tel: 202-429-1700
toll free: 1-800-996-3426
www.wyndham.com

Another branch of the quality national chain, this one built around a 14-story atrium with views of one of the city's main streets. Comfortable and newly renovated with fitness center, sauna, lounge. Walk to most sites. 400 rooms.

Moderate

Braxton Hotel
1440 Rhode Island Ave, NW
Tel: 202-232-7800
toll free: 1-800-350-5759
www.braxtonhotel.com

Comfortable Old World service with fridge and microwave in most rooms; free breakfast; tour bus pick-up point; easy walk to Dupont Circle. 62 rooms.

Carlyle Suites
1731 New Hampshire Ave.
Tel: 202-234-3200
toll free 1-800-964-5377
www.carlylesuites.com

Art Deco style hotel at prime location features comfortable suites; good for families and accepts pets. Fitness facility and a good restaurant. 176 suites.

Courtyard by Marriott
1900 Connecticut Ave.
Tel: 202-332-9300
toll free: 1-800-321-2211
www.marriott.com

A bit north of city central, but in a pleasant neighborhood and offering all the comforts and quality you'd expect from this chain, headquartered here. Near enough to some of the best

restaurants; walk to the Metro. 148 rooms.

Embassy Inn/ Windsor Inn
1627 and 1842 16th St. NW
Tel: Embassy 202-234-7800
Tel: Windsor 202-667-0300
toll free 1-800-423-9111
www.virtualcities.com

These twins are on the edge of Dupont Circle and offer small but nicely appointed rooms. Rate includes continental breakfast. Combined, there are 85 rooms.

Helix Hotel
1430 Rhode Island Ave, NW
Tel: 202-462-1202
toll free:1-800-706-1202
www.hotelhelix.com

Way cool, ultra-modern rooms colorfully furnished; flat-screen tvs; so cool they accept pets; swingin' lounge; near everything. 178 rooms.

Hotel Madera
1310 New Hampshire Ave, NW
Tel: 202-296-7600
www.hotelmadera.com

Small, quiet hotel, comfortable rooms, independently owned, centrally located. Near Dupont Circle and Metro. 82 rooms..

Radisson Barcelo Hotel Washington
2121 P Street, NW
Tel: 202-293-3100
toll free 1-800-333-3333
www.radisson.com

Large rooms recently renovated, each with a fridge. Near Rock Creek Park. There's a courtyard pool, fitness center and a restaurant with an emphasis on Latin cuisine. 301 rooms.

Tabard Inn
1739 N Street, NW
Tel: 202-785-1277
www.tabardinn.com

A 19th-century townhouse turned into a

quaint and quirky inn on a quiet street. Rooms have lots of personality. Good restaurant, great location. 40 rooms.

Topaz Hotel
1733 N Street, NW
Tel: 202-393-3000
toll free 1-800-424-2950
www.topazhotel.com

Small hotel on quiet side street in prime location. Some rooms have kitchenettes. Good bar; easy walk to downtown. 99 rooms.

Windsor Park Hotel
2116 Kalarama Road, NW
Tel: 202-483-7700
toll free 1-800-243-3064
www.windsarparkhotel.com

Comfortable, Queen Anne-style boutique hotel near Woodley Park and the zoo. All the basic amenities, plus continental breakfast included. 45 rooms.

Budget

Kalorama Guest House
1854 Mintwood Place, NW
Tel: 202-667-6369
Also, 2700 Cathedral Ave.
Tel: 202-328-0860
www.inntravels.com

Four eclectically furnished houses form this quirky and inexpensive B & B popular with young travelers. Half of the 30 rooms have private baths. Rate includes continental breakfast.

SOUTHWEST WATERFRONT

Expensive

Mandarin Oriental Hotel
1330 Maryland Ave, SW
Tel: 202-554-8588
www.mandarinorientalhotel.com

Asian elegance on the waterfront. Spa, gym, two good restaurants. 347 rooms, 53 suites.

Moderate

Channel Inn
650 Water St
Tel: 202-554-2400
toll free 1-800-368-5668
www.channelinn.com

On the waterfront. Popular with tour groups. Outdoor pool, restaurant. 100 rooms.

BELOW: Adams Morgan is a lively neighborhood.

VIRGINIA AND MARYLAND

VIRGINIA

Expensive

Boar's Head Inn
200 Ednam Drive
Charlottesville, Virginia
Tel: 434-296-2181
toll free 1-800-476-1988
www.boarsheadinn.com
Romantic 172-room
hotel with a historic
gristmill that serves as
the restaurant. Near the
wine country.

Embassy Suites
1900 Diagonal Road
Alexandria, Virginia
Tel: 703-684-5900
toll free: 1-800-EMBASSY
www.embassysuites.com
New, one of a national
chain with lovely indoor
courtyard; across the
street from the King
Street Metro station.
Classy rooms with all
amenities; two good
restaurants next door.
268 rooms.

Hilton Alexandria Old Town
1767 King Street
Alexandria, Virginia
Tel: 703-837-0440
toll free 1-800-445-8667
www.hilton.com
One of Alexandria's
newest hotels, right
next door to the King
Street Metro station
and an easy trip into
DC. Well-appointed; din-
ing room; easy walk into
Old Town. 241 rooms.

Holiday Inn of Old Town
480 King Street
Alexandria, Virginia
Tel: 703-549-6080
toll free 1-800-HOLIDAY
www.oldtownhis.com
Right on King Street,
Alexandria's main
street, and close to all

Old Town attractions.
Ten-minute walk to
Metro into DC. Comfy
rooms, good restau-
rant. 227 rooms.

Keswick Hall
701 Club Drive
Keswick, Virginia
Tel: 434-979-3440
toll free 1-800-174-5391
www.keswick.com
Romantic country inn
outfitted in the English
country style with Laura
Ashly prints and a golf
course designed by
Arnold Palmer.

Morrison House
116 Alfred Street
Alexandria, Virginia
Tel: 703-838-8000
toll free 1-800-367-0800
www.morrisonhouse.com
Nicely done inn with a
good restaurant on a
side street, but still
near the heart of Old
Town Alexandria. 45
rooms.

Ritz-Carlton Pentagon City
1250 South Hayes Street
Alexandria, Virginia
Tel: 703-415-5000
toll free: 1-800-241-3333
www.ritzcarlton.com
Charming 18-story hotel
in an upscale shopping
mall and on the Penta-
gon City Metro stop for
convenience into DC. All
the usual amenities,
first-class service,
health club and lap
pool, and tea in the ele-
gant dining room. 366
rooms.

Williamsburg Inn
136 Francis Street
Williamsburg, Virginia
Tel: 757-229-1000
toll free 1-800-HISTORY
www.colonialwilliamsburg.com
A romantic inn with the
feel of a country estate
and excellent dining.

There are 180 rooms
either in the main inn or
in the adjacent colonial
houses.

Moderate

Four Points by Sheraton
351 York Street
Williamsburg, Virginia
Tel: 757-229-4100
toll free 1-800-962-4743
www.fourpoints.com
Adjacent to Colonial
Williamsburg, and close
to Bush Gardens. There
are 199 rooms and
suites with kitchens
and an indoor pool.

Island Motor Resort
Main Street
Chincoteague, Virginia
Tel: 757-336-3141
Small, immaculate fam-
ily-run hotel with com-
fortable rooms, all with
small balconies facing
Chincoteague Bay and
the mainland. Health
club, pool, restaurant.

Key Bridge Marriott
1401 Lee Highway
Arlington, Virginia
Tel: 703-524-6400
toll free 1-800-228-9290
www.marriott.com
At the foot of Key Bridge
in Arlington, directly
across from George-
town. Pool, fitness
room, excellent rooftop
view. 588 rooms

Sheraton Suites Alexandria
801 North St. Asaph Street
Tel: 703-836-4700
toll free 1-800-325-3535
www.sheraton.com
Located on the north
end of Old Town, not far
from Reagan National
Airport. Modern two-
room suites with com-
plimentary breakfast
and lots of office ameni-
ties. 247 rooms.

MARYLAND

Expensive

Admiral Fell Inn
888 South Broadway
Tel: 410-522-7377
toll free 1-800-292-4667
This 80-room inn is a
restored sailors' lodg-
ing and is right on Baltimore's harbor at Fell's
Point.

Harbor Court Hotel
550 Light Street
Tel: 410-234-0550
toll free 1-800-824-0076
www.harborcourt.com
At the revitalized inner
harbor with 204 rooms
decorated with repro-
duction furniture.

Lake Pointe Inn
174 Lake Pointe Drive
Deep Creek Lake, Maryland
Tel: 1-800-523-5253
www.deepcreekinn.com
Fifteen rooms in a refur-
bished 19th-century
country lodge near ski-
ing and golf and deco-
rated in the Arts and
Crafts style. Rate
includes breakfast.

Campsite

Capitol KAO Camp-ground
768 Cecil Avenue
Millersville, Maryland 21108
Tel: 410-923-2771
toll free 1-800-KOA-0248
www.koakampgrounds.com

PRICE CATEGORIES

Price categories are for
a double room without
breakfast:
Deluxe over $300
Expensive $175–$300
Moderate $125–$175
Budget under $125

TRANSPORT

A CTIVITIES

FESTIVALS, THE ARTS, NIGHTLIFE, SHOPPING AND SPECTATOR SPORTS

CALENDAR OF EVENTS

January

Presidential Inauguration Day. Every four years the city turns out for the swearing in of the president followed by the parade along Pennsylvania Avenue and the inaugural balls.

Robert E. Lee's Birthday Celebration. Held at the Confederate General's former home, Arlington House, in Arlington National Cemetery. Open house features 19th-century music, samples of period food and exhibitions of restoration work.

Martin Luther King Jr's Birthday Observance. Wreath-laying ceremony at the Lincoln Memorial, accompanied by the presentation of King's "I Have a Dream" speech, local choirs and guest speakers.

February

Chinese New Year Parade. Firecrackers, lions, drums and dragon dancers make their way through Chinatown.

George Washington's Birthday Parade. Parade through Old Town Alexandria, plus special activities at George Washington's home, Mount Vernon.

March

St Patrick's Day Parades. Parades through Old Town Alexandria, and downtown along Constitution Avenue: dancers, bands, bagpipes and floats.

April

National Cherry Blossom Festival. The Cherry Blossom Festival Parade celebrates the blooming of 6,000 Japanese cherry trees, with princesses, floats and VIPs. Events include fireworks, free concerts in downtown parks, the Japanese Lantern Lighting Ceremony, the Cherry Blossom Ball and an annual Marathon Race.

Easter. Children, each accompanied by an adult, gather on the White House South Lawn for an Easter Egg Roll. For tickets and details, tel: 202-208-1631.

May

Cathedral Flower Mart. Washington National Cathedral holds it annual flower mart and crafts show.

Memorial Day Weekend. Ceremonies at Arlington Cemetery include a wreath laying at the Tomb of the Unknowns, the Kennedy gravesite, and services at the Memorial Amphitheater with military bands and a presidential keynote address. Also, a wreath laying at the Vietnam Veterans' Memorial. The National Symphony Orchestra performs on the West Lawn of the US Capitol.

June

Alexandria Red Cross Waterfront Festival. Tour ships tied up at the dock in Alexandria. Food, crafts, exhibits, games, and fun.

Smithsonian Festival of American Folklife. Annual celebration of folk culture takes place on the Mall and features concerts, craft demonstrations, food and more.

July

National Independence Day Celebration. Parade along Constitution Avenue, plus day-long concert event on the Mall and evening fireworks display over the Washington Monument.

September

Labor Day Weekend Concert. National Symphony Orchestra in concert on the West Lawn of the US Capitol.

Adams Morgan Day. Lively street festival with music, crafts and cooking, along 18th Street, Columbia Road and Florida Avenue NW.

November

Veterans' Day Ceremonies. Service in the Memorial Amphitheater

ACCOMMODATION

ACTIVITIES

A – Z

at Arlington National Cemetery and wreath laying at the Tomb of the Unknown Soldier.

December

Holidays at Mount Vernon. The recreation of an authentic 18th-century holiday season, with a tour of the mansion.

National Christmas Tree Lighting and Pageant of Peace Ceremony. Holiday celebration marked with seasonal music performed by military bands and the lighting by the president of the National Christmas Tree on the Ellipse.

US Botanic Gardens' Christmas Poinsettia Show. Massive display of red, white and pink plants amid Christmas wreaths and trees.

THE ARTS

Museums & Galleries

Besides the National Gallery of Art (open Mon–Sat 10am–5pm; Sun 11am–6pm; tel: 202-737-4215 or visit www. nga.gov) and the Smithsonian museums (open daily 10am–5.30 pm; tel: 202-357-2700 or visit www.si.edu) on the Mall and elsewhere around the city, there are a number of other smaller museums worth exploring. For details about special exhibits and openings at any of the museums, check the "Weekend" section of the *Washington Post* on Fridays for the latest events.

Bead Museum
400 7th Street, NW
Tel: 202-624-4500
Wed–Sat, 11am–4pm; Sun, 1–5pm
One room packed with displays of beads used for traditional and ceremonial jewelry. Good selection of beads for sale.

B'nai B'rith Klutznick Museum
2020 K Street, NW
Tel: 202-857-6583
Mon-Thur, noon–3pm, by advance reservation only.
Features Jewish folk and ceremonial art.

Kreeger Museum
2401 Foxhall Road, NW
Tel: 202-338-3552
Mon–Fri, 10am–5pm; $5 admission.
19th- and 20th-century European paintings and sculptures of the private collection of insurance tycoon David Kreeger.

National Museum of Health and Medicine
16th Street and Georgia Avenue, NW, on the grounds of Walter Reed Army Medical Center
Tel: 202-782-2200
Daily, 10am–5pm; free
Fascinating exhibits on the human body, including malformations, organs, skeletons and various tissues. Exhibits on medicine in the Civil War

The Octagon
1799 New York Avenue
Tel: 202-638-3105
Tues–Fri, 10am–4pm; Sat and Sun, noon–4pm
Elegant Federal-style home designed by William Thornton, architect of the Capitol, and now headquarters for the American Association of Architects.

Dupont Circle

Many of the galleries in this area coordinate their openings and showings on "First Fridays" between 6pm and 8pm, on the first Friday of every month except during August and September. Galleries are generally open Tuesday through Saturday, and all are within an easy stroll of the Dupont Circle Metro station. You'll find contemporary paintings and sculptures; work by emerging artists; African, Eskimo, American and other traditional folk works; silkscreen prints; paper and fabric works; ceramics, and vintage photographs in the galleries here. Many serve wine and cheese or other light fare, and most can ship your purchases home for you. For details and a complete list of participating galleries, visit www.artrgalleriesdc.com or check Friday's *Washington Post*.

Music

Washington is home to several exceptional musical groups, listings for which you can find in the Washington Post, especially the "Weekend" section on Fridays. The more prominent groups perform at the Kennedy Center and elsewhere in DC, such as DAR Constitution Hall, but you can find performances all over town.

Air Force, Army, Navy, and Marine Bands
Tel: 202-433-4011
The military bands perform concerts on the steps of the US Capitol, at Sylvan Theater near the Washington Monument, and at DAR Constitution Hall throughout the year. Concerts are free,

BELOW: Kennedy Center for the Performing Arts, by the Potomac River.

but tickets are required. Call for an up-to-date schedule and for ticket information.

Folger Consort
201 East Capitol Street, SE
Tel: 202-544-7077
Early music ensemble in residence at the Folger Shakespeare Library on Capitol Hill.

National Gallery Orchestra
National Gallery of Art
Tel: 202-842-6941
www.nga.gov
The Sunday evening concert series has been a favorite in Washington for over 60 years; free tickets on a first-come-first-served basic beginning at 6pm; concerts begin at 7pm.

National Symphony Orchestra
The Kennedy Center Concert Hall
Tel: 202-467-4600
The world-class National Symphony under the direction of Leonard Slatkin is in residence at the Kennedy Center, but also offers a summer series at Wolf Trap, an outdoor stage set in a park in the Virginia suburbs. You can also hear them perform for free on the grounds of the US Capitol on Memorial Day in May, on the Fourth of July, and on Labor Day in September, but it can get crowded.

Washington Opera
The Kennedy Center Opera House
Tel: 202-295-2400
www.dc-opera.org
"The National Opera", as Congress has designated it, is now under the direction of tenor Placido Domingo whose reputation and showmanship has boosted this company to international status. The Opera House has recently undergone an extensive renovation that included an acoustical upgrade.

Outdoor Concerts

Washingtonians enjoy summer concerts at these nearby parks where you can catch just about everything from a Broadway musical to a rock band.

Wolf Trap for the Performing Arts
1624 Trap Road
Vienna, Virginia

Tel: 703-255-1800
www.wolftrap.org
Musical acts including symphony orchestras, rock and jazz bands and folk singers, plus ballet, folk and modern dance troupes, theatrical companies, and comedy acts perform on stage in a pristine outdoor park setting efficiently operated by the National Park Service. Spread a blanket on the lawn, or buy a seat under cover. Bring your own picnic, or order one of theirs. There's also a small restaurant on site. You can ride Metro, and then take a short ride on a shuttle bus from the West Falls Church station.

Nissan Pavilion
Stone Ridge, Virginia
Tel: 202-432-7328; for concert information tel: 703-754-1288
www.nissanpavilion.com
A more utilitarian version of Wolf Trap known more for rock concerts with lots of concrete and a parking lot that can be a challenge in a crowd. Lawn or covered seating, but no fancy picnic food – wine, beer and hot dogs.

Merriweather Post Pavilion
10475 Little Patuxent Parkway
Columbia, Maryland
Tel: 1-410-715-5550
www.merriweathermusic.com
Performance schedule features current pop music favorites and usually draws a young crowd to this wooded park, about an hour's drive from DC. More attention is given to the music than to the setting or to the food, so bring your own.

Theater

Washington has several resident theater companies that stage everything from Broadway musicals to Shakespeare to new works by established and new playwrights. DC is also a regular stop for theatrical touring companies, comedy acts, and solo performers. Check the daily listings in the *Washington Post*.

Arena Stage
6th Street and Maine Avenue, SW
Tel: 202-488-3300
www.arenastage.org
American classics, Broadway musicals, new works, near the waterfront.

Church Street Theater
1742 Church Street, NW
Tel: 202-265-3748
www.churchstreettheater.com
Former private school gymnasium converted to a 125-seat theater and now home to a pair of theater companies who share the space and whose offerings tend to be experimental, sometimes uneven, always interesting.

Discovery Theater
Smithsonian Arts & Industry Building
900 Jefferson Drive SW
Tel: 202-357-1500
www.si.edu
Geared especially for children.

BELOW: a performance of *A Wonderful Life* at the Arena Stage.

Eisenhower Theater
The Kennedy Center
Tel: 202-467-4600
www.kennedy-center.org
Touring companies bring musicals and the classics here. Always top-notch performances in an excellent venue but sometimes the seats aren't the best (behind a post), so choose carefully.

Folger Theatre
201 East Capitol Street, SE
Tel: 202-544-7077
www.folger.edu
Elizabethan-era plays staged in a period theater on Capitol Hill. Part of the Folger Library, which houses the world's most extensive collection of Shakespeare.

Ford's Theatre
511 10th Street, NW
Tel: 202-347-4833
www.fordstheatre.org
Comedies, musicals, one-man shows and seasonal favorites, such as *A Christmas Carol*, in the theater that Lincoln made famous.

The National Theater
1321 Pennsylvania Avenue, NW
Tel: 202-628-6161
Touring companies, musicals and comedies; usually lighter performances by nationally recognized actors.

Shakespeare Theatre
450 7th Street, NW
Tel: 202-547-1122
www.shakespearetheatre.org
World-class resident Shakespeare company performs in this small but exquisite theater.

Signature Theatre
3806 South Four Mile Run Drive
Arlington, Virginia
Tel: 703-218-6500
New plays, musicals, comedies presented by an award-winning company associated with American musical theater great Stephen Sondheim.

Studio Theatre
14th and P streets, NW
Tel: 202-332-3300
www.studiotheatre.org
Experimental and always worth the ticket price. It's a fixture in this neighborhood, once blighted

but now up-and-coming.

Warner Theater
13th and E Streets, NW
Tel: 202-783-4000
Touring companies, comedy and solo performers in an old-line downtown theater.

Buying Tickets

To buy tickets by phone, you may call the theater directly or call Ticketmaster tel: 202-432-7328, or visit www.ticketmaster.com. You can also purchase half-price tickets on the day of the show from Ticket Place, located at 407 7th Street, NW, open Tues–Sat, 11am–6pm; Tel: 202-842-5387

Dance

Besides the permanent dance companies listed below, several national and internationally acclaimed dance troupes make Washington a regular stop on their tours. They perform mainly at the Kennedy Center, but also at venues across the city. Check the *Washington Post* for listings and ticket information.

The Dance Place
3225 8th Street, NE
Tel: 202-269-1600
Modern, African and other ethnic dance performances.

The Washington Ballet
Tel: 202-432-SEAT
www.washingtonballet.org
Washington's permanent ballet company performs at the Kennedy Center and elsewhere in the city.

Cinema

DC has several commercial theaters located around town that show showing first-run feature films. For a current listing see the daily movie listings in the *Washington Post*. The Friday "Weekend" section of the *Post* offers more detailed listings and reviews of new movie releases. Washington is also home to the American Film Institute, which offers a regular schedule of film classics. They have two locations, one at the Kennedy Center

near the Foggy Bottom Metro stop, and the other, newer theater, AFI Silver, in nearby Silver Spring, Maryland, also near a Metro stop. For a just-like-you're-there experience, take in one of the science and exploration documentaries on the giant screens at the Smithsonian's IMAX theaters.

American Film Institute (AFI) Theater
The Kennedy Center
Tel: 202-833-2348
AFI Silver, Silver Spring
Tel: 301-495-6720
www.afi.com

Smithsonian Theaters
Tel: 202-633-4629
Johnson IMAX Theater in the National Museum of Natural History, Lockheed Martin IMAX Theater in the National Air and Space Museum, Einstein Planetarium in the National Air and Space Museum
www.si.edu

NIGHTLIFE

Once a stodgy government town where the nightlife consisted mostly of private dinner parties held in the homes of Georgetown's elite, Washington has begun to let its hair down. Between the hip college crowd and the go-getting twenty-somethings, DC's nightspots have expanded from the more sedate old-line Capitol Hill bars to new high-energy dance spots and so-called hunting grounds, scene of aggressive romantic pursuits. There are still plenty of lower-key spots, though even these have evolved towards the swanky, attracting the martini-drinking set to unwind and talk world events.

Music is always a draw and, besides the dance floors presided over by DJs, you can take in a live performance of rock, hip-hop, jazz, blues, world beat, or just about anything else in a setting more intimate than a concert hall.

In a throwback to an earlier age, there's also a new interest in hotel bars. Once they were strictly the province of guests; now locals have discovered them as perfect after-work gathering spots. As for the city's most popular places, the list here – from dance and concert spots to cigar bars – will provide something for most people.

Night spots

88
1910 18th St., NW
Tel: 202-588-5288
Pleasant, friendly, piano bar (hence the name) with a good menu and brunch.

9:30 Club
815 V St., NW
Tel: 202-393-0930
www.930.com
Well-knowns and near-knowns stop at this club, long a local favorite for rock and alternative bands.

Bedrock Billiards
1841 Columbia Rd., NW
Tel: 202-667-7655
Billiards, beer, friendly crowd.

Black Cat
1811 14th St., NW
Tel: 202-667-7960
www.blackcatdc.com
Rock and alternative scene, reasonably priced tickets, complete with bar and a full and primarily vegetarian menu.

Blue Room Lounge
2321 18th St., NW
Tel: 202-332-0800
New, swanky, smoky, popular and with a dance floor

Blues Alley
1073 Wisconsin Ave.
Tel: 202-337-4141
www.bluesalley.com
DC's oldest jazz supper club and venue for jazz stars; Creole food.

Bohemian Caverns
2001 11th St., NW
Tel: 202-299-0800
www.bohemiancaverns.com
Strictly blues and jazz, bar and food.

Café Toulouse
2341 18th St., NW
Tel: 202-238-9018
Rooftop patio bar; quiet, at least for this neighborhood.

Chi-Cha Lounge
1624 U St., NW
Tel: 202-234-8400
Cozy, popular neighbhood spot with good drinks, appetizers; Latin jazz and dancing.

Crush
2323 18th St., NW
Tel: 202-319-1111
Loud; non-stop dancing; popular with younger crowd.

Dragonfly
1215 Connecticut Ave., NW
Tel: 202-331-1775
Modern cool, with sushi.

Eighteenth Street Lounge
1212 18th St., NW
Tel: 202-466-3922
Three bars on three floors with a hip DJ.

Felix and the Spy Lounge
2406 18th St., NW
Tel: 202-483-3549
French/Asian menu, full bar, hot spot for dancing.

Gazuza
1629 Connecticut Ave., NW
Tel: 202-667-5500
Modern glass-and-metal décor; for the hip.

Habana Village
1834 Columbia Rd., NW
Tel: 202-462-6310
Busy bar scene and some serious Latin dancing.

The Improv
1140 Connecticut Avenue

BELOW: jazz in Blues Alley.

Tel: 202-296-7008
www.dcimprov.com
The city's comedy club since 1963 draws nationally-ranked performers. They even have a comedy school, open to all.

Madam's Organ
2461 18th St., NW
Tel: 202-667-5370
Lively club in the heart of Adams Morgan. Look for the huge wall mural of the redhead.

MCCXXIII (1223)
1223 Connecticut Ave., NW
Tel: 202-822-1800
Classy, with sofas and a dance floor.

Ozio Martini and Cigar Lounge
1813 M St., NW
Tel: 202-822-6000
Swanky, smoky, with a dance floor.

Town & Country Lounge
In the Renaissance Mayflower Hotel, 1127 Connecticut Ave.
Tel: 202-347-3000
Classic DC powerbrokers' bar; legendary martinis.

Virginia

Birchmere
3701 Mount Vernon Avenue
Alexandria, Virginia
Tel: 703-549-7500
www.birchmere.com
Folk, blue grass and faded rock stars in a restaurant setting with full menu. Tables and chairs surround the stage in this small, intimate theater so you can't get a bad seat.

Iota Club and Café
2832 Wilson Blvd.
Arlington, Virginia
Tel: 703-522-8340
Cool, serious young crowd; there for the alternative music.

State Theater
220 North Washington Street
Falls Church, Virginia
Tel: 703-237-0300
www.thestatetheater.com
Serious rock, blues and jazz performers, big names and lesser-knowns perform in this converted old-style movie theater about 30 minutes from DC and accessible by Metro from the East Falls Church station.

SHOPPING

Like big cities everywhere, you can find anything you can imagine in DC, and some things that you wish you hadn't. There are, of course, the usual souvenir shops, but for the best array of finer goods you'll need to focus on DC's choicest neighborhoods. Two of Washington's best shopping districts are on opposite sides of the Potomac, in Georgetown on the DC side and Old Town in Alexandria on the Virginia side. Both were busy commercial ports well into the 19th century, with warehouses of tobacco, cotton and other agricultural stuffs lining the waterfront. You'll still see architectural evidence of that earlier age, but the streets on both shores have gone decidedly upscale, the weathered red-brick and once utilitarian structures converted into trendy clothing and home furnishing shops, with lots of art galleries, antique shops, cafes and more.

Downtown

When it comes to fashion, Washingtonians stand accused of the stodginess that the trendier world at large has always judged it as. The blue-suit-and-red-power-tie set has always preferred classic to stylish and in this part of town, crammed with government office workers and those doing business with the government, you'll find in the way of shops mostly the old reliables such as **Brooks Brothers** (1201 Connecticut Avenue); **J. Press** (1801 L Street, NW), originally a custom outfitter for men at Yale which then followed its customers after graduation to DC; **Burberry** (1155 Connecticut Avenue, NW), with it's famous beige plaid; and **Rizik's** (1100 Connecticut Avenue), an elegant dress shop staffed with a discrete and knowledgeable team of saleswomen who have been dressing first ladies and congressmen's wives for decades.

DC has only one real department store and it's **Hecht's**, (12th and G streets, NW) the last of the city's old-line emporiums, completely updated and stocked with everything from high-fashion to housewares. Downtown isn't all blue serge, though. Some of its best specialty shops include the **Tiny Jewel Box** (1147 Connecticut Avenue), which handles antique and estate jewelry, and the **Music Box Center** (1920 I Street, NW), which carries more than 1500 of the little musical gizmos.

Bedazzled (1507 Connecticut Avenue, NW) is all beads, beautiful semi-precious stones from all over the world and ready for stringing. Lastly, you must visit **Fahrney's** (1317 F Street, NW), once an ink stand and pen-repair shop for government workers and now purveyors of a select line of quality writing instruments and a DC institution.

Georgetown

The big characterless shopping malls that serve as focal points for so much of American life are absent here – which is not to say that the city lacks malls, only that they tend to be comparatively human-scaled and architecturally much more interesting.

One of the city's best, **Georgetown Park**, is right at the very heart of Georgetown, at M Street and Wisconsin Avenue, and an excellent place to start a shopping excursion. Quaintly Victorian, with lots of dark woods and wrought iron, park benches, parlor palms, and a bubbling fountain in the center, the mall has all the usual upscale favorite clothiers, such as **J. Crew**, **Abercrombie and Finch**, and **Ralph Lauren**, plus some local offerings including **Taxco**, which stocks distinctive silver jewelry, and **Bertram's Inkwell**, which carries fine writing instruments and leather accessories. There's a food court here, too, and a Japanese restaurant, **Benihana**, where you dine at communal tables, the center of each outfitted with a grill where the chef, in a series of acrobatic moves involving large knives, prepares your meal.

From the mall, join the mob on M street – Georgetown is nothing if not popular – of young trendsetters and professionals, tourists, college students, families, and, oh, yes, a few local residents, and browse the shops. There are chi-chi boutiques including all the usual chains, home furnishings emporiums, day spas, coffee shops and antique stores that front Georgetown's main street. In the true spirit of American egalitarianism, don't be surprised to find a priceless Tiffany lamp for sale in a shop right next door to a tasteless t-shirt stall.

If it's time for a pick-me-up, go to **Dean and Deluca** (3276 M St., NW), cruise the aisles of this gourmet shop, nosh on a few samples, come out with a bag of something delicious. Or stop in a

GETTING TO GEORGETOWN AND ALEXANDRIA

Georgetown has no Metro stop, but you can take the subway to Foggy Bottom/GWU, then pick up the shuttle bus, the Georgetown Metro Connection, if you'd rather not walk the 10 minutes or so. Old Town Alexandria does have a Metro stop, King Street, where you can pick up a Dash shuttle bus or stroll the length of King Street to the river, a little more than a mile. Best, though, is to combine shopping and sightseeing and cruise between the two. The Potomac Riverboat Company (31st and K Street, NW; Tel: 703-548-9000) docks at both ports so you can shop, dine and take in the sights on both sides. Call for fare and boarding information.

La Madeleine (3000 M St., NW) for a single-sized quiche, or a pastry and a cup of coffee (theirs is the best). Refreshed, it's time to hit the street again, this time Wisconsin Avenue, Georgetown's other main street.

Georgetown has some of the best antique stores anywhere. Good taste doesn't come cheap, of course, but you'll come away with a quality souvenir of your Washington experience.

These are some of Georgetown's best shops and boutiques:

Antiques
Alla Rogers Gallery
1054 31st St., NW, Canal Square; Tues-Sat, noon-6pm. Eastern European, Russian paintings, sculpture, photographs.
Cherub
2918 M St., NW, Mon-Sat, 11am-6pm; Sun, noon–5pm. Art nouveau metal ware, glass, accessories
The Old Print Gallery
1220 31st St., NW; Mon-Sat, 10am–5.30pm. Antique prints, maps, botanicals, city views, good range of Washingtoniana.
Susquehanna
3216 O Street; Mon–Fri, 10am–6pm; Sat, 10.30am–6pm. 17th–19th-century period American and English furniture, paintings, garden ornaments; the city's largest antique store.

Boutiques
Appalachian Spring
1415 Wisconsin Ave, NW; Mon-Sat, 10am–6pm; Sun, 11am–5pm. Jewelry, other artisan works.
Commander Salamanders
1420 Wisconsin Avenue, NW; Mon–Fri, 10am–6pm; Sat, 10am–9pm; Sun, 11am–5pm Trendy Georgetown fashion emporium and a long-time favorite with Washington's hip.
The Phoenix
1514 Wisconsin Avenue, NW; Mon–Sat, 10am–6pm; Sun, noon–5pm. Eileen Fisher, natural fiber clothing, silver jewelry, folk art.
Relish
3312 Cady's Alley; Mon–Sat,

ABOVE: interest in Americana has surged in recent years.

10am–6pm; Sun, noon–5pm. Forwardly stylish, name designers, accessories.

Dupont Circle, Adams Morgan, U Street

Here's where the really funky stuff is. Some of the best art galleries, including **Affrica** (2010½ R Street, NW), **America, Oh Yes!** (1350 Connecticut Avenue) and the **Marsha Mateyka Gallery** (2012 R Street, NW), are located in the Dupont Circle area and have joined together for "First Fridays", a casual, collective exhibit among all the galleries held on the first Friday of every month. (Check the "Weekend" section of the *Washington Post* for details.) There are more than a few trendy boutiques here, too, among the trendiest, **Betsy Fisher** (1224 Connecticut Avenue) with an eye toward pretty suits and dresses. Try **Secondi** (1702 Connecticut Avenue) if you like high-fashion on a budget. It's one of the city's best consignment shops.

Adams Morgan is where much of DC's immigrant population lives. Along with bringing their native foods and opening some of the city's most inventive ethnic

restaurants, these locals also operate some of its more interesting shops. Trouble is, shops open and close routinely, and regular hours are only a dream. Still, stroll its main streets, Columbia Road and 18th Street, NW, just for fun.

Once blighted, the U Street neighborhood is slowly making a comeback and offers some unique finds, including **Mccps Fashlonette** (1520 U Street, NW), a vintage clothier; **Trade Secrets** (1515 U Street, NW), which stocks African-inspired wearables; and **Nana** (1534 U Street, NW), mostly new clothes and lots of accessories.

Mall Shopping

Besides Georgetown Park, there are other malls in the city and in the surrounding suburbs. Here are a few of the best, all reachable by Metro except one.
Mazza Gallerie and Chevy Chase Pavilion
These two adjacent upscale malls on Wisconsin Avenue above Georgetown feature Neiman Marcus, Saks Fifth Avenue, and Lord and Taylor. Friendship Heights Metro stop.

TRANSPORT   ACCOMMODATION   ACTIVITIES   A – Z

Union Station
50 Massachusetts Avenue, NW
One hundred-plus small shops,
restaurants, and a nine-screen
movie theater in the city's beautifully restored Beaux Arts train station on Capitol Hill. Several
smaller vendors sell unique ethnic
clothing, jewelry and decorative
art. Union Station Metro stop.

Old Post Office Pavilion
1100 Pennsylvania Avenue, NW
Downtown mall with plenty of gift
and souvenir shops. The food
court is a convenient place to
stop when you need a break.
There's often live entertainment,
and the top of the clock tower
offers a great view of the city.

Shops at National Place
13th and F Streets, NW
Three-story mall with souvenir
and gift shops, several boutiques, and a food court in the
heart of downtown.

Fashion Centre at Pentagon City
1100 South Hayes Street, Arlington, Virginia
Four-story upscale mall includes
Macy's and Nordstrom's. Pentagon City Metro stop.

Potomac Mills
2700 Potomac Mills Circle,
Woodbridge, Virginia
Thirty minutes south by car, this
mile-long discount mall has over
200 stores.

Museum Shops

In a city full of museums, naturally you'll have museum shops,
and some of them offer some of
the best merchandise. In the
museum shops along the Mall
you'll find distinctive jewelry, silk
scarves, stationery, ceramics,
prints and sculptures, unique
toys for children, and a good
selection of books, plus the
usual array of postcards and
other souvenirs. The **National
Museum of American History** gift
shop is the largest of the Smithsonian's shops and carries a
good selection of American
crafts, art reproductions, books
and recordings. Try the **National
Gallery of Art**'s two shops for art

ABOVE: Georgetown Park Mall.

reproductions, stationery, and
art and photography books.
There are two off-the-Mall shops
that are among the best of the
city's museums shops. The
Indian Craft Shop is inside the
Department of the Interior Building (18th and C streets, NW) and
carries crafts from over 45 tribal
areas including Alaskan Native
crafts. Besides pottery, bead-
work, baskets and sand paintings, there is also an extensive
collection of books for sale. Try
the **Decatur House Museum**

DC's Original Mall

Tucked behind the Capitol
building at 7th and C streets,
SE you'll find a long, low, red-
brick building. This is **Eastern
Market**, the city's oldest and
continually operating "food
court" where you can find
fresh produce and meats. It's
old, it's a little on the funky
side, but there's a walk-up
lunch counter where you can
order an excellent crabcake. In
good weather on weekends,
there's a combination farmers'/flea market outside operated mostly by characters
who'll offer you all sorts of
small treasures.

Shop (1600 H Street, NW, on
Lafayette Square), which sells
fine 19th-century Americana rem-
iniscent of the naval hero and
White House aspirant, Stephen
Decatur, who once lived here.

Bookstores

Washingtonians are serious readers – serious enough that they
easily support several quality,
independent book stores when in
other cities in America the big
chains have all but closed them
down. The big chains are here, of
course, but so are a healthy number of independents.

Barnes and Noble
3040 M St, NW.
Three stories of books and music
in a former warehouse.

Borders
1801 K St., NW.
Books, magazines, music, cafe,
occasional jazz sessions.

Chapters
445 11th Street, NW
A literary book store with a regular schedule of readings.

Idle Time Books
2410 18th Street, NW
Good stock of used titles.

Kramerbooks and Afterwords
1517 Connecticut Avenue, NW
Small but important inventory
and a good café.

Lambda Rising
1625 Connecticut Avenue, NW
Specializes in books for gays and
lesbians.

Olsson's Books and Music
1307 19th Street, NW
Also at: 418 7th Street, NW
Washington's best local chain
with an excellent selection of
music and literary titles and a
knowledgeable staff.

Politics and Prose
5015 Connecticut Avenue, NW
Excellent for literature and current events; has a regular schedule of readings and other events.

Second Story Books
2000 P Street, NW
Good selection of used books in
the Dupont Circle area.

Trover Books
221 Pennsylvania Avenue, SE

Quality paperbacks and a good selection of newspapers; on Capitol Hill.

Old Town, Alexandria

Old Town, which bills itself as "The Fun Side of the Potomac" really is, with lots of shops and restaurants, mostly along King Street, Old Town's main avenue. Don't miss the **Torpedo Factory** at the foot of King and the corner of Union Street, near the river. At one time an actual torpedo factory, this hulking, thick-walled building sat neglected after World War II until the city teamed up in the 1970s with local artists looking for studio space and transformed it into Old Town's prime attraction. Painters, potters, weavers, printmakers, goldsmiths and more, 165 artists in all, set to work while you roam the three floors and stop to watch them produce some of the most distinctive, and often affordable, artworks you'll find. The city also houses its **Archaeology Museum** here *(see page 185)* and you can chat with the docents and examine the artifacts.

To its credit, Old Town has managed to retain more of its original 18th-century charm, even in its retail quarters, so you'll find it a little less "touristy" than Georgetown, though there are still plenty of good shops and galleries. Head up King Street, away from the river, and stop at **Artcraft Collections** (132 King Street), where furniture craftsmen, jewelry makers, potters and other artisans with a decidedly whimsical bent have consigned their work for sale. The **Principle Gallery** (208 King Street) is best for its showings of oils and lithographs by up-and-comers. There's a **La Madeleine** (500 King Street) on this side of the Potomac, too, if you're feeling in need of another cup of coffee and some pastry.

Where King Street meets Washington Street, Old Town's prime intersection, you'll see the

Gap, **Banana Republic**, **Ann Taylor**, and **Marshall's**, a chain discount department store, none of which offer anything you probably haven't already seen. Keep walking along King and you'll come to **Ten Thousand Villages** (824 King Street), which offers crafts and jewelry from Third World artisans. You'll come away with something interesting and at the same time do your bit to help support a distant cottage industry.

If you're looking for home furnishings, there are several good shops at this end of town, especially **Quimper Faience** (1121 King Street), best for hand painted French pottery and table linens, and **Banana Tree** (1223 King Street), owned by a former Foreign Service officer with a taste for Dutch and British colonial furniture.

Hungry? Stop at cozy **Vermilion** (1120 King Street) for something hearty and American, or at **Le Gaulois** (1106 King Street) for some French comfort food. Then head on to **Imagine** (1124 King Street), a shop full of wearable art crafted by some of the most inventive weavers and sewers; pricey, gorgeous, and definitely one-of-a-kind. Cross the street for more unusual crafts, much of it glass, at **Arts Afire** (1117 King Street), which has so many unusual pieces for sale that they've opened an annex around the corner on North Fayette Street.

SPORT

Spectator Sports

Football (Soccer)

Washington hosts both professional and college team sports, including baseball, basketball, football and soccer. As for football, tickets to the ever popular Washington Redskins are impossible to buy, the wait list extending past 10 years. If you want to see a game, best to watch it on TV. The home games are played at the 86,000-seat FedEx Field in nearby Laurel, MD.

Baseball

Washington Baseball Club
600 New Hampshire Avenue
Tel: 202-266-6610
Baseball is the newest addition to the professional sports line-up. The Nationals, formerly the Montreal Expos, moved to DC in late 2004 and will play its games at RFK, which used to be a football stadium, until the new baseball stadium can be built.

Basketball

Washington's two professional basketball teams play in the MCI Center (601 F Street, NW; tel: 202-628-3200), near the Gallery Place-Metro station.
The Washington Wizards
Men's professional NBA team.
www.washingtonwizards.com

BELOW: the Washington Wizards in action.

The Washington Mystics
Women's professional WNBA team.
www.washingtonmystics.com

Hockey

Hockey's gaining in popularity and this NHL winning team is part of the reason. Games played at the MCI Center, near the Gallery Place-Metro station.
Washington Capitals
MCI Center
601 F Street, NW
Tel: 202-628-3200

Soccer

Major league team with some outstanding players, including Freddy Adu, and a following among the locals. Games played at the old football stadium. Use the Stadium-Armory Metro station.
DC United
RFK Stadium
22nd and East Capitol streets
Tel: 703-478-6600

Tennis

Every August the Baltimore investment firm of Legg Mason hosts a tennis tournament that draws many of the top-ranked players and some of the sport's rising stars.
Legg Mason Tennis Classic
Fitzgerald Tennis Center, Rock Creek Park
16th and Kennedy streets, NW
Tel: 202-721-9500
www.leggmasontennisclassic.com

Participant Sports

Bicycling

For information about touring by bicycle, contact the Washington Area Bicyclist Association (tel: 202-628-2500). Bikes may be rented at these locations:
Big Wheel Bikes
1034 33rd Street, NW
Tel: 202-337-0254
City Bikes
2501-Champlain Street, NW
Tel: 202-265-1564
Fletcher's Boathouse
4940 Canal Road, NW

Tel: 202-244-0461
Thompson's Boathouse
2900 Virginia Avenue, NW
Tel: 202-333-9543

Boating and Sailing

Atlantic Canoe and Kayak
1201 North Royal Street
Alexandria, Virginia
Tel: 703-838-9072
Canoe and kayak rentals with river guides.
Fletcher's Boathouse
4940 Canal Road, NW
Tel: 202-244-0461
Canoe, rowboat, kayak rentals.
Swain's Lock
River Road
Potomac, Maryland
Tel: 301-299-9006
On the C&O Canal. Canoe or kayak rentals.
Thompson's Boathouse
2900 Virginia Avenue, NW
Tel: 202-333-4861
Canoes, rowboats, kayaks, rowing sculls rentals.
Tidal Basin
near the Jefferson Memorial
Tel: 202-479-2426
Paddleboat rentals.
Washington Sailing Marina
One Marina Drive
Alexandria, Virginia
Tel: 703-548-9027
Sunfish, windsurfers, daysailers for rent.

Golf courses

East Potomac Park
Hains Point, East Potomac Park
Tel: 202-554-7660
Two 9-hole courses and driving range, and a miniature golf course.

Langston Golf Course
26th Street and Benning Road, NE
Tel: 202-397-8638
18 holes
Rock Creek Park Golf Course
16th and Rittenhouse streets, NW
Tel: 202-882-7332
18 holes

Horseback riding

Rock Creek Horse Center
Military and Glover roads, NW
Tel: 202-362-0117

Ice Skating

National Gallery Sculpture Garden
Constitution Avenue
Tel: 202-737-4215
Pershing Park
Pennsylvania Avenue, near 14th Street, NW
Tel: 202-737-6938

Running

There are several popular routes for runners including the C&O Canal towpath, the Mall between the US Capitol and the Washington Monument, Rock Creek Park, and in Virginia the Mt. Vernon Trail, which stretches between Roosevelt Island and the Mt. Vernon Estate. For more details and information about group runs, contact **Road Runners Club of America** (tel: 703-836-0558).

Tennis

East Potomac Park
Hains Point, East Potomac Park
Tel: 202-554-5962
Rock Creek Tennis Center
16th and Kennedy streets, NW
Tel: 202-722-5949

BELOW: rowing at dusk on the Potomac River.

A–Z

A HANDY SUMMARY OF PRACTICAL INFORMATION, ARRANGED ALPHABETICALLY

A dmission Charges

Almost every attraction worth seeing in Washington is free of charge, courtesy of the US taxpayers, which makes DC one of the world's best travel bargains. None of the major museums charge admission. Memorial sites, such as Arlington Cemetery and the Lincoln Memorial, are also free, though some, such as the Washington Monument, require timed tickets. Smaller museums and historic houses, such as the Phillips Collection and the Decatur House, do charge a fee but it's usually nominal and well worth it. There are a few excep-

tions, however, namely the International Spy Museum, one of the newer attractions which charges a hefty admission, at least by DC standards. Ticket prices for Kennedy Center performances can range anywhere from free (the Millennium Stage, in the lobby, has free concerts) to $100 or more, depending on seat and on performance (opera is probably the most expensive). Tickets for other theaters in town, such as Arena Stage and Ford's Theater are more affordable. You can also try Ticket Place at 407 7th Street, NW *(see page 228 for more details)* on the day of the performance for half-price tickets.

B udgeting for a Visit

What you gain in free admission to many of the attractions you'll unfortunately lose in hotel and meal costs, which can be expensive. Washington is among the country's priciest cities in which to both live and to visit, fueled in part by an underlying private economy that depends upon the unlimited expense accounts of legions of business executives and lobbyists, all here to either schmooze government officials for those lucrative government contracts or to wrangle members of Congress into seeing things their way. For them, money is usually no object but for the average tourist the tariff can get out of hand. A decent hotel can easily cost $200 a night, but if you're willing to travel in the off-season (winter and late summer) and if you look for deals, whether negotiated through the hotel directly or through a website. As for restaurant meals, much of Washington's business is conducted over them which, unfortunately, jacks up the price for the average visitor. A decent dinner can easily set you back $50 or more per person, though a good alternative, especially if you're on a budget, is to make lunch your main meal, then go for an occasional splurge at dinner.

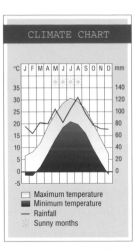

CLIMATE CHART

☐ Maximum temperature
■ Minimum temperature
— Rainfall
☀ Sunny months

Business Hours

Museums are generally open daily 10am to 5.30pm. Smaller museums may have varying hours and usually close one day a week, often on Monday. Business and offices are open 9am to 5pm, though some government offices open and close earlier. Stores and shopping malls are usually open between 9.30am and 9pm and many are open on Sundays. Large supermarkets and some pharmacies, or drug stores as they're also known, are open 24 hours. Banks are open at least between 9am and 2pm weekdays, some with hours beyond that, and on Saturdays until noon.

C hildren

For some ideas of what your children might like to see, turn to the "Washington for Families" list on page 6. If you're visiting in summer, the peak season for families, keep in mind that lines can be long for many attractions, the weather is usually quite warm, and that there's lots of walking. Outfit your kids with comfortable shoes, and be sure to bring along bottled water. As for strollers, leave them at home. Many sites don't permit

them, and while they're allowed on the Metro, they can be a serious hazard in crowds, especially in packed cars and station platforms. Harried commuters, rushing to catch trains, object to hurdling an obstacle course of tourists' strollers, a situation that also imperils your child. Immobilized in his chair, your child is defenseless against an unintended briefcase blow to the head. If you must bring a stroller, make it collapsible, or opt for a backpack.

It's a good idea to equip your child with some form of identification and a few dollars, just in case you're separated. Decide on a central meeting place, such

as the information desk at any of the museums, and instruct your child to wait for you there. Make sure your child also understands not to panic if you lose each other while riding the Metro. Your child should simply get off at the next station and go to the stationmaster's booth near the exit and Metro authorities will page you.

Most hotels do accept children, but be sure to ask when you book and also ask if the hotel offers a reduced rate. Most restaurants accept well-behaved children, but don't expect to find a children's menu. Restaurants in Washington are intended mostly for grown-ups and as for lounges and bars, no child is permitted.*(see Liquor Laws, page 238).* There are, however, good meal choices for children at the food courts at Union Station, the Old Post Office Pavilion, and the Ronald Reagan Building as well as many of the cafes in the Smithsonian museums.

Climate

Washington's summers are long and notoriously hot with lots of humidity. They extend generally from May into October, and peak in June, July and August. Summer rains often come with violent thunderstorms. In winter, snowfall can be significant, which makes getting around almost impossible, though most

BELOW: science for kids at the National Museum of American History.

winters see little or no accumulation. The best seasons for visiting are fall (mid-October through November) and the brief spring (April) when temperatures are most comfortable and Washington is in bloom.

Monthly Temperature Range:

January	34°–47°F (–1°–8°C)
February	31°–47°F (–1°–8°C)
March	38°–56°F (3°–13°C)
April	47°–67°F (8°–19°C)
May	58°–76°F (14°–24°C)
June	65°–85°F (18°–29°C)
July	70°–88°F (21°–31°C)
August	68°–86°F (20°–30°C)
September	61°–79°F (16°–26°C)
October	52°–70°F ((11°–21°C)
November	41°–56°F (5°–13°C)
December	32°–47°F (0°–8°C)

Clothing

Washington's long, hot and humid summers demand light clothing, but not so light as to be indecorous. This is still a capital city and while casual is perfectly acceptable, sloppy or skimpy is not. Crossing the lobby of some of the city's better hotels in your swimsuit will likely earn you a word from the manager. Better restaurants require coats and ties for men and suitable outfits for women.

That said, dress sensibly for seeing the sights. On a hot, steamy day, tailored shorts and tidy-looking t- or polo-shirts are perfectly fine. Comfortable, sturdy shoes are a must in all weather, as are sunglasses and sunscreen in summer and a coat in winter, one with a zip-out lining will usually do.

Everything is air conditioned, often to excess, so bring a sweater – and an umbrella.

Crime

Washington has one of the highest murder rates of any US city, though homicides are confined mostly to the depressed areas. Travelers here to see the major attractions are reasonably safe from most crimes, such as assault and robbery usually associated with a large urban area, because the sites are located in the city's better sections and because police presence has increased to combat potential terrorist attacks.

Besides the DC police force, Washington is also patrolled by the Capitol Hill Police, the National Park Police and the Metro Police, not to mention the FBI and the Secret Service. If you're going to be safe anywhere, it's probably in DC. Even so, don't tempt fate. Avoid carrying large sums of cash and leave your expensive jewelry at home. If your hotel has a safe, use it. Hang on to your purse, and keep your wallet in your front pocket.

Most crimes are crimes of opportunity, and if you aren't easy prey you'll more than likely avoid being a victim. Avoid strange or deserted areas at night and always know where you're going and how you'll get back. Serious crime on the Metro is rare, thanks to those vigilant Metro police, but it's best at night to ride in the front car along with the conductor.

As for any potential threat that you yourself may pose to public safety, be prepared to pass through a metal detector and have your bags inspected whenever you enter a public building. Security is a major concern and ensuring it is taken very seriously. Don't even think about making a wisecrack to a security officer, who can and will arrest you. Leave your aerosol cans, Swiss Army knives, mace spray and anything else that might be thought of as suspect at home. Otherwise, it will be confiscated.

Customs Regulations

Meat or meat products, illegal drugs, firearms, seeds, plants, and fruits are among prohibited goods. Also, do not bring in any duty-free goods worth more than $400 (US citizens) or $100 (foreign travelers). Visitors over 21 may import 200 cigarettes, 3 lb (1.3 kg) of tobacco or 50 cigars, and 34 fl oz (1 liter) of alcohol.

Non-residents may import, free of duty and internal revenue tax, articles worth up to $100 for use as gifts for other persons, as long as they remain in the US for at least 72 hours and keep the gifts with them. This $100 gift exemption or any part of it can be claimed only once every six months. It can include 100 cigars, but no alcohol. Do not have the articles gift wrapped, as they must be available for customs inspection.

If you are not entitled to the $100 gift exemption, you may bring in articles worth up to $25 free of duty for your personal or household use. You may include any of the following: 50 cigarettes, 10 cigars, 150 ml of alcohol, or 5 fl oz (150ml) of alcoholic perfume or proportionate amounts. Articles bought in duty-free shops in foreign countries are subject to US customs duty and restrictions but may be included in your exemption. However, if you stop off in Vegas for a couple of days "in-transit," these may be confiscated.

For details regarding customs allowances, contact the United States Customs Service through its website, www.customs.ustreas.gov

D isabled Access

Thanks to the Americans with Disabilities Act, federal law mandates that all public places, including museums and other sites of interest to visitors, be outfitted to accommodate anyone who's wheelchair-bound or otherwise disabled. Most buildings have ramps, elevators, widened doorways and specially marked entrances. Sidewalk curbs all have cuts in them to make it easier to wheel not only chairs but strollers and bicycles across the city streets. Public restrooms, including those in restaurants, all have stalls specifically designed for the disabled. Most office buildings, retail stores, and even tour buses and the Metro system can and willingly do accommodate disabled travelers wherever possible.

The best source of information for disabled travelers visiting Washington is Disability Guide, an organization founded by a Washingtonian who is himself disabled. Contact them at 301-528-8664, or visit their website at www.disabilityguide.org

E lectricity

Standard is 110 volts; if you plan to use European-made appliances, lower the voltage with a transformer and bring a plug adaptor.

Embassies

Australia 1601 Massachusetts Avenue, NW. Tel: 202-797-3000
Canada 501 Pennsylvania Avenue, NW. Tel: 202-682-1740
Ireland 2234 Massachusetts Avenue, NW. Tel: 202-462-3939
Italy 1601 Fuller Street, NW. Tel: 202-328-5500
Singapore 3501 International Place. Tel: 202-537-3100
United Kingdom 3100 Massachusetts Avenue. Tel: 202-588-6500

Emergencies

For any police or medical emergency, pick up any phone and dial **911**. You'll be connected to a dispatcher who'll send help. Your cell phone will also work.
Non-emergency calls:
District of Columbia Police: 202-727-1010
US Capitol Police: 202-228-2800.
If you're stranded or have any other travel-related difficulty, contact **Travelers' Aid**, Union Station. Tel: 202-371-1937. Open daily, 9:30am–5pm.

Entry Requirements

Since 2001's terrorist attacks, requirements for entry into the US have tightened considerably. Generally, you'll need a visa, a passport, and evidence of intent to leave the US, though citizens of certain countries, such as the UK, Australia, Canada and Ireland, can visit under the guidelines of the Visa Waiver Program. An international vaccination certificate may also be required, depending on your country of origin. You will be finger-printed and an eye scan will be taken.

At customs your bags will be inspected either by hand or machine. You may bring up to $10,000 into the US, as many as 200 cigarettes, gifts valued at less than $400, and only such prescription drugs as you'll need during your stay.

Requirements can change, so it's worth checking www.united-statesvisas.gov, or www.customs .ustreas.gov. You may also phone for information, toll free: 1-877-287-8667 or 202-354-1000, but the lines are often busy.

G ays and Lesbians

Dupont Circle is ground zero for the gay and lesbian scene. For details, stop in at Lambda Rising, a bookstore at 1625 Connecticut Avenue, NW (tel:

BELOW: drinkers must be over 21.

202-462-6969) and pick up a copy of *The Washington Blade* for men, or *Woman's Monthly*, where you can find the latest on clubs and more. Two of the more popular night spots are:
Club Chaos. 1603 17th Street, NW. Tel: 202-232-4141
JR's. 1519 17th Street, NW. Tel: 202-328-0090

Genealogy

The National Archives, best known for their original copies of the Declaration of Independence and the Constitution, also allow Americans to trace their family history here, sifting through more than 3 billion documents for priceless ancestral footprints. Passenger lists for immigrant ships, the national census back to 1790, military and naturalization records, passport applications, pensions and land grants – the Archives contain the country's principal database for family histories and other uses.

A free booklet provides a basic guide to the collection; but a serious search requires an investment in the National Archives' paperback book *Guide to Genealogical Research*, which offers a step-by-step procedure on how to go about research on the flimsiest of details, like "great-great grandfather Abner Smith who moved to Indiana sometime after the Civil War." Ironically, since they lost their land to the white immigrants, some of the most reliable data concerns Native Americans.
National Archives. Pennsylvania Ave. between 7th and 9th streets, NW. Tel: 202-501-5000. www.nara .gov/genealogy/

L iquor Laws

You must be 21 in DC and in the surrounding Virginia and Maryland suburbs to purchase and consume alcohol and you will be "carded" – that is, asked to show picture identification, such as a driver's license, to verify your age. Wine, beer and mixed drinks are generally available by the glass or drink at most restaurants. Nightclubs also serve drinks, though they're usually very strict about following the law since they could be closed down if caught serving minors. You can buy wine, beer and spirits in several stores in the city. Here are a few shops: **Cairo Wine and Liquor**. 1618 17th Street, NW. Tel: 202-387-1500

Press Liquors. 527 14th Street NW. Tel: 202-638-2080

Schneider's of Capitol Hill. 300 Massachusetts Ave., NE. Tel: 202-543-9300

M aps

Insight Guides' *FlexiMap Washington DC* is laminated for durability and easy folding. Two companion FlexiMaps are *Museums and Galleries of Washington DC* and *Washington DC for Kids*.

Medical Services

For any medical emergency, dial 911 from any phone, including your cell phone, for an ambulance, or go directly to the nearest hospital emergency room. There are several excellent hospitals in the city, including: **Children's National Medical Center**. 111 Michigan Avenue, NW. Tel: 202-884-5000 **The George Washington University Hospital**. 901 23rd Street, NW. Tel: 202-715-4000 **Georgetown University Hospital**. 3800 Reservoir Road, NW. Tel: 202-784-2000 **Howard University Hospital**. 2041 Georgia Avenue, NW. Tel: 202-865-6100 **Washington Hospital Center**. 110 Irving Street, NW. Tel: 202-877-7000. Also operates a doctor referral service to guarantee a medical appointment within 48 hours.

Although the US delivers some of the world's best health care, it is prohibitively expensive

unless you carry health insurance, which you should have before you leave home.

Money

The basic unit of money is the dollar ($), which is made up of 100 cents. Dollars come in denominations of: $1, $5, $10, $20, $50 and $100. Each bill is the same color (green), size and shape, so check the dollar amount on the face of the bill. The dollar itself is broken down into the penny (1 cent), the nickel (5 cents), the dime (10 cents), and the quarter (25 cents). You can change money at:
Reagan National Airport. Business Service Centers in terminals B and C.
Dulles International Airport. Business Service Centers at the east and west ends of the ticketing level in the main terminal and in concourses B, C, and D. There are also three Thomas Cook Foreign Exchanges here.
Baltimore-Washington International Airport. International Arrivals, adjacent to the baggage claim.
Union Station. Thomas Cook office.
Thomas Cook Foreign Exchange. Downtown office, 1800 K Street. Tel: 1-800-287-7362
American Express Travel Services. 1150 Connecticut Avenue, NW. Tel: 202-467-1300

Many banks, open generally between 9am and 2pm, will also exchange money. It's a good idea to arrive with at least $100 in cash, in small bills, to pay for ground transportation and incidentals. Travelers' checks are another good idea. While cash certainly works, all major credit cards are widely accepted. You can use them in ATMs, or automatic teller machines, located in many stores, hotel lobbies, and outdoor kiosks to withdraw cash, though usually at a hefty service fee. If you rent a car, you'll need a credit card.

N ewspapers

The *Washington Post* began publishing in 1877 and is the capital's oldest daily and enjoys a respected and international reputation. It's Friday "Weekend" section is the best up-to-date source of information about museum exhibits, shows, gallery openings and other activities.

The city's lesser known daily, the *Washington Times*, was established in 1982 and has looser standards for accuracy. Decidedly conservative in outlook, it is published by the head of a religious cult who is also an occasional source of embarrassment to several prominent Republicans.

The *City Paper* is a free weekly news, arts and information sheet, available from street corner machines and some outlets, such as book stores, restaurants and cafés.

The *Washingtonian* is a glossy monthly magazine, covering local news, politics and gossip, with reviews of new art and culture presentations, restaurants and specialty shops. Check its website, www.washingtonian.com, for the latest in activities and restaurant features and reviews.

Foreign newspapers are available at many bookstores, including Barnes and Noble and some Olsson's stores. The newsstand at the National Press Building, 14th and F streets, NW, carries a wide range of foreign and US regional dailies.

P harmacies

Pharmacies – or drug stores, as they're also known – sell all manner of over-the-counter remedies without prior approval from the doctor. Any controlled substance, however, such as antibiotics and narcotics, will require the doctor's prescription. The biggest pharmacy chain, operated by CVS, has 24-hour branches at 1199 Vermont Avenue,

NW. Tel: 202-628-0720 and 4555 Wisconsin Avenue, NW. Tel: 202-537-1587.

Population and Size

Washington, DC is the capital of the US, seat of its federal government and a federal enclave situated between the states of Maryland and Virginia. Its diamond-shaped area occupies 61 sq. miles (158 sq. km) along the banks of the Anacostia and Potomac rivers. The city itself has a permanent population of about 600,000, but add the surrounding suburbs and the number increases to close 6 million. Three-quarters of the city's population is African-American and resides in the Northeast, Southeast and Southwest quadrants. About 10 percent of the population is comprised of Hispanic immigrants residing mainly in the Adams-Morgan section and in some neighborhoods of close-in northern Virginia. The rest of the population lives in the city's northwest quadrant, the city's largest and most affluent area.

Postal Service

Purchase stamps at any post office between 9am and 5pm, Monday through Friday, and 9am to noon on Saturday. You can also buy stamps from vending machines in airports and many hotels and stores. The headquarters for the entire US Postal System is at 475 L'Enfant Plaza, SW. Tel: 202-268-2000. Other post offices in the city include:
Ben Franklin. 1200 Pennsylvania Avenue, NW. Tel: 202-523-2386
Farragut. 1800 M Street, NW. Tel: 202-523-2506
Georgetown. 3050 K Street, NW. Tel: 202-523-2405
Pavilion Postique. 1100 Pennsylvania Avenue, NW. Tel: 202-523-2571
Union Station. 50 Massachusetts Avenue, NE. Tel: 202-523-2057.

ABOVE: St Matthew's Cathedral.

Public Holidays

All government offices, bank and post offices are closed on public holidays, many of which are observed on the closest Monday, creating several three-day weekends. Public transportation doesn't run as often on these days, but most retail stores, museums, and other attractions are open.
● **January** New Year's Day; Martin Luther King Day (third Monday)
● **February** President's Day (third Monday)
● **March/April** Easter Sunday
● **May** Memorial Day (last Monday)
● **July** Independence Day (4th)
● **September** Labor Day (first Monday)
● **October** Columbus Day
● **November** Thanksgiving Day (last Thursday) and following day
● **December** Christmas Day (25).

R adio Stations

Several AM and FM radio stations serve DC including:
88.5FM WAMU: news and public affairs; National Public Radio
90.9FM WETA: classical music and news; National Public Radio
97.1FM WASH: soft rock
103.5FM WGMS: classical
105.9FM WJAZ: contemporary jazz
107.7FM WTOP: all news, weather and traffic; also 1500 AM

Religious Services

Virtually every religion is represented in Washington with places of worship spread across the city. Check the Yellow Pages of the phone directory or see the concierge in your hotel. The following are some of the largest and oldest congregations.
Christian
Basilica of the National Shrine of the Immaculate Conception. Michigan Avenue and 4th Street, NE. Tel: 202-526-8300. www.nationalshrine.com
The Church of the Epiphany. 1317 G Street, NW. Tel: 202-347-2635. www.epiphanydc.org
St. John's Episcopal Church. Lafayette Square, 16th and H Streets, NW. Tel: 202-347-8766
St. Matthew's Cathedral. 1725 Rhode Island Avenue, NW. Tel: 202-347-3215. www.stmatthews-cathedral.org
Washington National Cathedral. 3001 Wisconsin Avenue, NW. Tel: 202-664-6616
Jewish
Adas Isreal Congregation. Connecticut and Porter streets, NW. Tel: 202-362-4433
Temple Sinai. 3100 Military Road, NW. Tel: 202-363-6394
Tifereth Isreal Congregation. 7701 16th Street, NW. Tel: 202-882-1605
Islamic
Islamic Center. 2551 Massachusetts Avenue, NW. Tel: 202-332-8343

S moking

Avoid if possible. If you must, be prepared to either step outside or, in a restaurant, accept a table in one of the smoking sections. Most bars still permit smoking, but overall it's frowned upon. Hotels often have a separate bank of rooms for smokers. To demonstrate just how much smoking is discouraged these days, a pack of cigarettes will cost you several dollars, much of that in taxes which go to fund anti-smoking campaigns.

Taxes

Whenever you make a purchase, buy a meal, or pay for a hotel room, be prepared to pay an additional charge, which comes in the form of a sales tax and is not part of the price quoted. Museum shops are usually exempt, but little else is. In DC, the sales tax on goods is 5.75 percent, on restaurant meals it is 10 percent, and for a hotel room, the tax is 14.5 percent. Virginia and Maryland have similar sales taxes. In Virginia, the sales tax on goods is 4.5 percent, and on a restaurant meal anywhere from 2 percent to 9 percent, depending on the type of meal and the jurisdiction. In Maryland, the sales tax on goods and on restaurant meals is 5 percent.

Telephones

All telephone numbers in DC and surrounding Virginia and Maryland are 10-digit, beginning with the prefix, or area code. These are: DC **202**; Virginia **703**; Maryland **301**. Dial the area code first, then the number. All calls within these three area codes are local. To make a long-distance call, first dial 1, then the ten-digit number. For directory information, dial the area code and 555-1212, or simply 411. Take advantage of toll-free 1-800 numbers whenever possible. Some toll-free numbers have the prefix, or area code, 877 or 888. You can use your cell phone, but consider that your provider at home may charge a local call here as long-distance. There are pay phones everywhere and for 35 cents you can be connected to a local number. You can also use your dialing card from a pay phone. For emergencies, dial **911**.
Phoning abroad: You can telephone abroad directly from any phone. Dial 00 followed by the international code for the country you want, and then the number.

Some country codes:
Australia (61); **Hong Kong** (852); **Ireland** (353); **New Zealand** (64); **Singapore** (65); **South Africa** (27); **US and Canada** (1).

Television Stations

Washington, DC's television stations include three local commercial networks — **NBC (WRC-TV)**, **ABC (WJLA-TV)**, and **CBS (WUSA-TV)** — plus many other stations such as **CNN** and **Fox News** available with cable. There are also three commercial-free public broadcasting stations, **WETA** the most prominent.

Time Zones

Eastern time zone. GMT minus 5 hours in eastern standard time (last Sunday in October to first Sunday in April); GMT minus 4 hours in daylight savings time (April to October).

Tipping

Service personnel in Washington, as in most cities, depend on tips for a large part of their income. With few exceptions, tipping is left to your discretion; gratuities are not automatically added to the bill. In most cases, 20 percent is the going rate for waiters, taxi drivers, bartenders, barbers and hairdressers. Porters and bellmen usually get

BELOW: a 20 percent tip is usual.

$1 per bag, but never less then $1 total.

Toilets

They're plentiful here, usually available off the lobbies of the larger hotels, located in shopping malls and larger department stores, and within every museum, though non-existent at some of the memorials and outdoor sites. Every museum on the Mall has them, spacious, convenient and clean facilities.

Tourist Offices

Contact the following organizations for maps, travel brochures, information about travel sites and attractions, and special seasonal events.
Washington DC Convention and Tourism Corporation. 1212 New York Ave., NW. Washington, DC 2005. Tel: 202-789-7000.
www.washington.org
Washington DC Visitors Information Center. Ronald Reagan International Trade Center Building, 1300 Pennsylvania Ave., NW. Washington, DC 20004. Tel: 202-328-4748. www.dcvisit.com
Alexandria Convention and Visitors Association. 421 King St., Alexandria, Virginia 22314. Tel: 703-838-4200.
www.funside.com
Arlington Visitors Center. 735 South 18th St., Arlington, Virginia 22202. Tel: 800-677-6267. www.stayarlington.com

Websites

www.dcvisit.com offers good all-round information.
www.washington.org provides lots of information from the Washington DC Convention and Tourism Corporation.
www.washingtonpost.com has eating and shopping tips.
www.si.edu covers all the Smithsonian's museums.
www.nga.gov shows what's on at the National Gallery of Art.

TRANSPORT

ACCOMMODATION

ACTIVITIES

A – Z

FURTHER READING

History & Architecture

AIA Guide to the Architecture of Washington DC, by Christopher Weeks, Johns Hopkins University Press (1994). Catalogues notable buildings and provides fascinating historical details.

On This Spot: Pinpointing the Past in Washington, DC, by Douglas E. Evelyn and Paul Dickson, National Geographic Press (2002). Lively "It happened here" account of the nation's capital with period photos, in paper, affordable, usually available at Olsson's Books.

Washington's Monuments: A Guide to the Monuments and Memorials of the Nation's Capital, by Alex Padro, Monument Books (2000). Exhaustive, fascinating inventory covers historical details of the city's 750-plus monuments.

Biographies

American Heritage: The Presidents, by Michael Beschloss, I Books (2003). Pre-eminent historian explains all; look for other titles by this erudite, accessible historian.

American Sphinx: The Character of Thomas Jefferson, by Joseph J. Ellis, Alfred A. Knopf (1997). Pulitzer winner and history professor Ellis demystifies the third and sometimes too highly revered third president.

Benjamin Franklin: An American Life, by Walter Isaacson, Simon and Schuster (2003). Top Washington journalist details the influence that one of America's more colorful founding fathers had on the nation.

Founding Brothers: The Revolutionary Generation, by Joseph J. Ellis, Alfred A. Knopf (2000) Absorbing account by respected historian of the men who made America.

The Grand Idea: George Washington's Potomac and the Race to the West, by Joel Achenbach, Simon and Schuster (2004). This veteran *Washington Post* reporter's newest re-visits GW's dreams and aspirations for his beloved country.

John Adams, by David McCullogh, Simon and Schuster (1991). Pulitzer Prize-winning author on the often overlooked, brilliant, and visionary second president.

My Life, by Bill Clinton, Alfred A. Knopf (2004). Long-awaited, tome of charismatic but distracted popular president.

Theodore Rex, by Edmund Morris, Random House (2001). Roosevelt's bully years in the White House by respected historian and presidential biographer (see *Dutch*, Morris's controversial account of the life of Ronald Reagan).

Washington: The Indispensable Man, by James Thomas Flexner, Back Bay Books (1994). The essential recounting of the Founding Father's life and times.

The Stranger and the Statesman: James Smithson, John Quincy Adams, and the Making of America's Greatest Museum: The Smithsonian, by Nina Burleigh, Smithsonian Institution Press (2003). Englishman Smithson's mysterious life and influence on one of the world's greatest museums.

Washington Insiders

Front Row at the White House, by Helen Thomas, Scribner (2000). Veteran DC journalist (since FDR in the '40s) tells her side of the story.

Katharine Graham's Washington, Katharine Graham, ed., Alfred A. Knopf (2002). Anthology of 100-plus articles, essays, humor pieces assembled by the *Post's* late publisher.

Personal History, by Katharine Graham, Vintage (1998). Former *Washington Post* publisher tells of her rise to the top after having been an uninformed widow.

Washington, by Meg Greenfield, Katharine Graham, Michael R. Beschloss. Public Affairs Press (2002). Sharp observations about the city and its people by prize-winning *Post* editorial team.

The Natural World

Beautiful Swimmers, by William W. Warner, Penguin (1976). Absorbing Pulitzer Prize-classic focuses on nearby Chesapeake Bay and its famous blue crabs.

Other Insight Guides

Insight Pocket Guide: Washington, DC contains personal recommendations from a local host on how to make the most of a short visit, and contains a fold-out map. *Insight Compact Guide: Washington, DC* is the perfect book to carry with you as you explore – text, pictures and maps are all cross-referenced for ease of use. Three easy-fold Insight FlexiMaps, laminated to make them durable and waterproof, and containing useful travel details, cover *Washington, DC* in general, *Washington, DC for Kids*, and *Museums & Galleries of Washington, DC*.

WASHINGTON DC STREET ATLAS

The key map shows the area of the city covered by the atlas
section. An index of street names and places of interest
shown on the maps can be found on the following pages.
For each entry there is a page number and grid reference.

Map Legend

▬▬▭▬	Freeway with Exit	
▭▭▭	Freeway (under construction)	
▭▭▭	Divided Highway	
▬▬▬	Main Road	
▬▬▬	Secondary Road	
▬▬▬	Minor road	
▬▬▬	Track	
▬▬▬	International Boundary	
▭▭▭	State Boundary	
▬▬▬	National Park/Reserve	
▭▭▭	Ferry Route	

✈ ✈	Airport
✝ ✝	Church (ruins)
✝	Monastery
🏰🏛	Castle (ruins)
⁂	Archaeological Site
∩	Cave
★	Place of Interest
🏠	Mansion/Stately Home
※	Viewpoint
⚑	Beach

	Freeway
	Divided Highway
	Main Roads
	Minor Roads
	Footpath
	Railroad
	Pedestrian Area
	Important Building
	Park

Ⓜ	Metro
🚌	Bus Station
❶	Tourist Information
✉	Post Office
✝	Cathedral/Church
☾	Mosque
✡	Synagogue
🗼	Statue/Monument
▯	Tower
⚓	Lighthouse

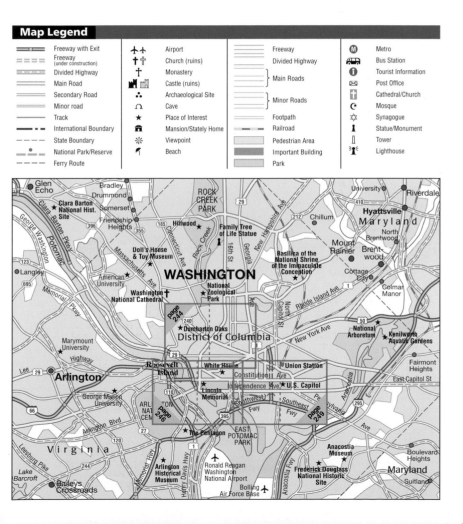

WOODLEY PARK

Vice President's House

U.S. Naval Observatory

Observatory Ln.

NORMAN-STONE PARK

Normanstone Ter.

Calvert St

McGill Ter.

Shoreham Dr.

D. Ellington Mem. Bridge

Cal

Observatory Cir.

Massachusetts Avenue

Benton Pl.

Rock Creek Dr.

Rock Creek and Potomac Parkway

Connecticut Avenue

Beach Dr.

Allen Pl.

ADAM

Whitehaven St

DUMBARTON OAKS PARK

Walk

ROCK CREEK PARK

Waterside Dr.

Belmont

Islamic Center

Kalorama Cir.

Kalorama Rd

Windsor Lodge

Connecticut Avenue

Wisconsin Avenue

34th St

Georgetown Library

Dumbarton Oaks

MONTROSE PARK

Lovers Lane Ped.

"Embassy Row"

Waterside Dr.

Wyoming Ave

Kalorama Pl.

California St

Wyoming

Bancroft Pl.

24th St

23rd St

Woodrow Wilson House

Textile Museum

Florida Ave

Le Roy Pl.

Phelps Pl.

Decatur Pl.

Fond Sol

Phillip Collec

Reservoir Rd

Cal'ot Scott Pl.

31st St

S St

R St

Avon Pl.

OAK HILL CEMETERY

St

Hauge Mansion

Barney Studio House

Sheridan Circle

Massachusetts A

Dent Pl.

Tudor Place

Avon Ln.

Dent Pl.

Cambridge Pl.

Dumbarton House

Dumbarton Br.

Anderson House

Shevchenko Memorial

Walsh McClean House

Cooke's Row

Ln. Key

West

Dum-barton

Rock Ct.

East Pl.

27th St

26th St

29th St

Poplar St

Street

22nd Street

Newport Pl.

Ward Pl.

21st St

Twining

Volta Pl.

33rd St

Q St

P St

O St

GEORGETOWN

United Methodist Church

Dumbarton Baker House

30th St

28th St

Rock Creek and Potomac Parkway

Rock Creek

N St

Street

Bodisco House

St John's

Cox's Row

Smith Row

N St

34th St

Gerry Hill Ln.

Olive St

Old Stone House

M

25th St

M Street

Bank Al.

Prospect St

Congress Ct.

Georgetown Park Shopping Mall

M Street

Marbury House

Canal Visitor Center

Pennsylvania Avenue

26th St

23rd Street

Hampshire

Washington Circle

K

Creighton Davis Gallery

Ware-house Pl.

ALT 29

Cecil Pl.

Grace St

South St

Cooperwaithe Ln.

Thomas Jefferson St

31st St

30th St

29th St

George Washington University Hospital

FOGGY BOTTOM

GWU

George

Whitehurst Freeway

West Al

Washington Harbour

K Street

New

Washington

Potomac

Thompson Boat Center

Virginia Ave

25th St

24th St

H St

23rd Street

22nd St

Washingto

University

Benito P. Juarez

St Mary's

M

0 500 yards

0 500 m

WOODLEY PARK

205

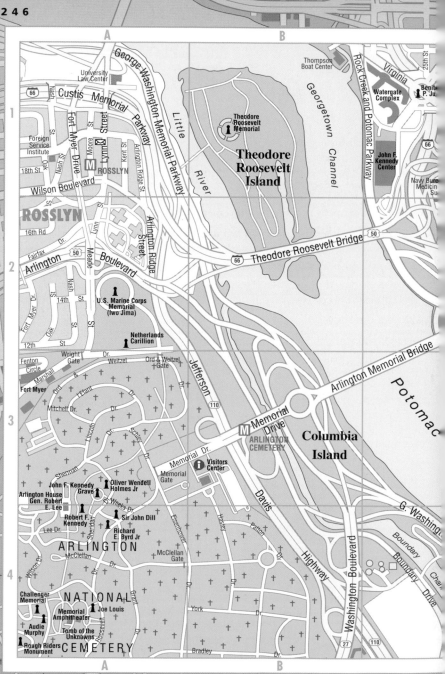

University
Law Center

George Washington Memorial Parkway

Thompson
Boat Center

25th St

Virginia

66

Nash

Custis Memorial Highway

Watergate
Complex

Benit
P. Ju

Fort Myer Drive

Lynn Street

Moore St

Kent St

Arlington Ridge St

Little

River

Georgetown Channel

John F.
Kennedy
Center

66

Foreign
Service
Institute

Oak

Nash

18th St

ROSSLYN

Theodore
Roosevelt
Memorial

**Theodore
Roosevelt
Island**

Wilson Boulevard

Navy Bure
Medicin
Su

ROSSLYN

St

Lynn St

16th Rd

Dr

Fairfax

Arlington Ridge Street

Meade

Boulevard

50

Theodore Roosevelt Bridge

50

Arlington

66

Fort Myer Dr.

Oak St

Nash St

14th St

U.S. Marine Corps
Memorial
(Iwo Jima)

Arlington Memorial Bridge

Potomac

12th St

Netherlands
Carillion

Jefferson

Wright Gate

Dr.

Weitzel

Ord & Weitzel
Gate

Fenton
Circle

Marshall

Ord

&

Grant

Dr.

110

Fort Myer

Mitchell Dr.

Lincoln

Dr.

Schley

Dr.

Memorial Drive

**Columbia
Island**

G. Washing

Sherman

Memorial Dr.

Memorial
Gate

**ARLINGTON
CEMETERY**

Davis

John F. Kennedy
Grave

Oliver Wendell
Holmes Jr

Visitors
Center

Boundary

Arlington House
Gen. Robert
E. Lee

D. Weeks Dr.

Eisenhower

Hatley

Patton

Boundary

Boundary

Robert F.
Kennedy

Sherman

Sir John Dill

Lee Dr.

Richard
E. Byrd Jr

Highway

Cham
Drive

ARLINGTON

McClellan

McClellan
Gate

Washington Boulevard

Wilson Dr.

Grant

Roosevelt

Dr.

Dr.

Challenger
Memorial

NATIONAL

Joe Louis

York

Dr.

27

110

Memorial
Amphitheater

Audie
Murphy

Tomb of the
Unknowns

Rough Riders
Monument

CEMETERY

Bradley

Dr.

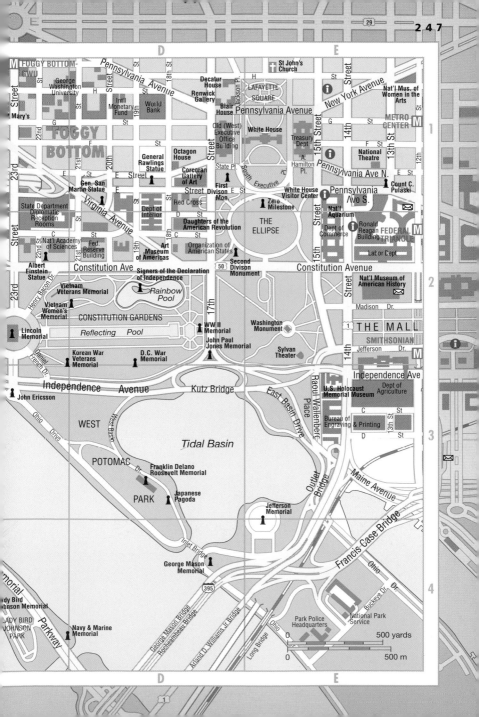

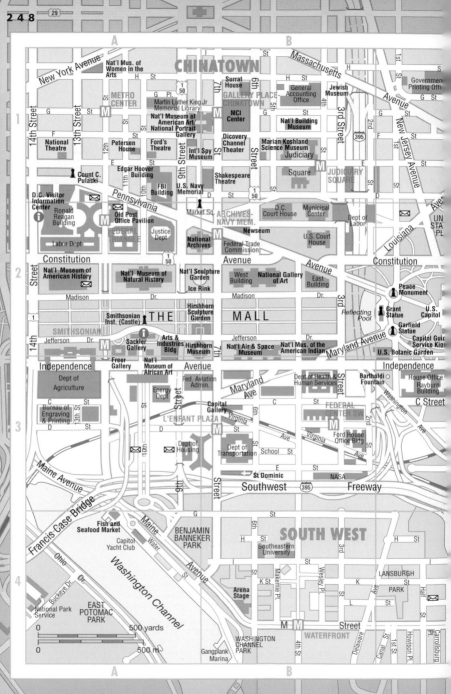

Capital
Children's Museum

Wylie St

Union Station

Union
Station

Columbus

Thurgood
Marshall
Judical Building

Morris Pl.

Groff Ct

Acker Pl.

Lexington Pl.

Maryland

Corbin Pl.

STANTON

Greene
Statue

PARK

Capitol Hill
Hospital

Constitution

Constitution Avenue

Avenue

Street

North Carolina Ave

CAPITOL HILL

Supreme
Court

Folger
Shakespeare
Library

Capitol

Street

LINCOLN PARK

East Capitol St

Emancipation
Monument

East

Library of
Congress

Library of
Congress
Adams Building

Jefferson
Building

Independence

Avenue

Library of
Congress
Madison Building

Seward

Carolina

Eastern
Market

Walter St

St Peter

Square

CAPITOL
SOUTH

FOLGER
PARK

EASTERN MARKET

POTOMAC
AVENUE

MARION PARK

GARFIELD PARK

SOUTH EAST

Southeast

Freeway

Marine
Barracks

11th Street

Washington Navy Yard

Main Gate

Warrington Ave

Marine Corps
Museum

Massachusetts

Maryland Ave

Avenue

Pennsylvania

STREET INDEX

ART & PHOTO CREDITS

Agence France-Presse 27, 39, 59
AKG-images 58, 103
Art Archive 60
Bettmann/Corbis 74
Getty Images 46/47, 233
Hulton Getty 29, 173
C.M. Glover 208
Catherine Karnow 1, 10/11, 12/13, 14, 16, 26, 32/33, 42, 44, 45, 50/51, 52/53, 73, 80, 86, 87, 105, 108, 114, 115, 128, 133L, 136R, 146, 150, 152, 162, 165, 166, 167T, 168T, 171T, 172, 174T, 175T, 175, 181, 188, 213, 227
Department of Tourism 116T, 122T, 148T, 156, 190/191, 192, 193, 195T, 195, 197T, 198T, 198, 199T, 200T, 201, 202T, 204, 206T, 209T, 210T, 211T
Lyle Lawson 206
Robert Llewellyn 263
Peter Newark's American Pictures 19
Richard T. Nowitz all cover pictures, 2, 3, 4, 5, 6/7 (all pictures), 8/9 (all pictures), 20, 30/31 (all pictures), 34, 35, 37, 38, 40, 41, 49, 54, 64, 68, 69, 70, 72T, 72, 75, 76T, 76L, 76R, 77T, 77, 78, 79T, 79, 80T, 81, 82T, 82, 84/85 (all pictures), 88, 89, 90, 91T, 91, 95, 96T, 96, 97, 98/99 (all modern pictures), 100, 101, 103T, 104T, 105T, 106, 107, 108T, 109T, 109, 110, 111T, 111, 112T, 112, 117T, 117, 118T, 118, 119, 120, 121T, 121, 122, 123, 124T, 124, 125, 127, 129, 131, 132, 133R, 134T, 134, 135, 136L, 137, 138, 139, 140T, 140, 141T, 141L, 141R, 142T, 142/ 143, 143T, 143R, 144, 145, 147, 149, 151T, 151, 153T, 153, 154L, 154R, 155T, 155, 158, 159T, 159, 164, 167, 169, 170, 178, 179, 180T, 182T, 183T, 183, 184T, 184, 185T, 185, 186, 187T, 187, 189, 196, 197, 200, 202, 207, 210, 211, 215, 216, 218, 223, 226, 229, 234, 236, 238, 240, 241
Office of the Vice President 161
Topham/Asociated Press 25
Topham/ImageWorks 36, 43, 65, 92, 93, 94, 95T, 104, 177, 199
Topham/PA 48
Topham/Photri 66, 67
Topham Picturepoint 24, 28, 61T
Ulanowsky, Philip/Apa 163T, 163R, 231, 232, 242

Map Production: James Macdonald, Maria Randell, Laura Morris and Stephen Ramsay
©2005 Apa Publications GmbH & Co. Verlag KG, Singapore Branch

GENERAL INDEX

USING METRORAIL

The Metrorail system is made up of five color-coded lines that wind through the city and extend into the suburbs. There's a Metrorail station at or near every DC attraction, and the system is easy to master. Transit fees are collected by magnetic card, which you buy from the fare-card machines in each station. Run your card through the faregate when you enter the station, then again when you exit at your destination, and your fare will be automatically subtracted.

The only trick is to make sure you don't lose your card. If you do, you'll have to pay the maximum fare. Fares differ between stations, and at various times of day – higher fees apply during rush hour, for example. You can buy several trips' worth of fares with one stop at the fare-card machine, which will save time. Farecard machines will take paper money, including $20 bills, but be forewarned that they make change only in coins.

Washington Metro

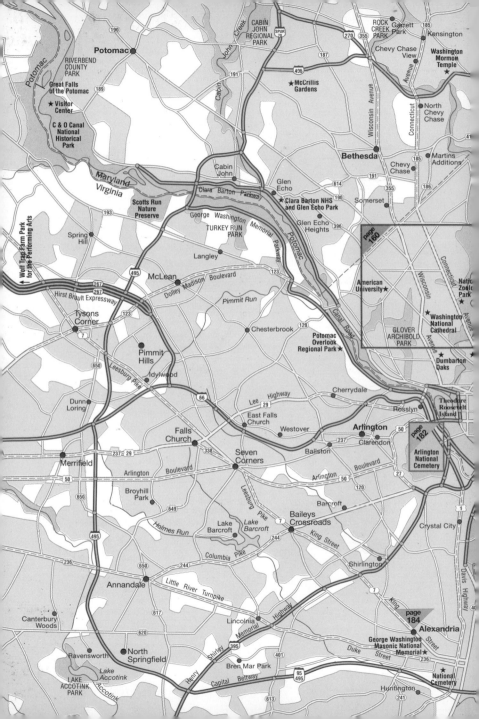